11518171

T5-AGV-194

WORDSWORTH'S
HEROES

WORDSWORTH'S HEROES

WILLARD SPIEGELMAN

University of California Press
Berkeley
Los Angeles
London

University of California Press
Berkeley and Los Angeles, California

University of California Press, Ltd.
London, England

© 1985 by
The Regents of the University of California

Printed in the United States of America
1 2 3 4 5 6 7 8 9

Library of Congress Cataloging in Publication Data

Spiegelman, Willard.
  Wordsworth's heroes.

  Includes index.
    1. Wordsworth, William, 1770–1850—Characters—
Heroes.   2. Heroes in literature.   I. Title.
PR5889.S64   1985   821'.7   84-28015
ISBN 0-520-05365-6

PR
5889
S64
1985

For My Parents

Contents

Acknowledgments

For his financial generosity, and even more for his personal encouragement, I wish to thank Dean R. Hal Williams of Dedman College at Southern Methodist University. The cheerful, professional attentions of Peggy Lynn Smith and Kathleen Triplett opened my eyes to the wonders of word processing even as they made it, as yet, unnecessary for me to master the process myself. Gordon Birrell and Jutta Van Selm offered last-minute assistance in locating and translating some German excerpts. A timely utterance from Stephen Orgel gave relief to several untoward thoughts. Charles Beye and John Paul Riquelme read the manuscript with scrupulous attention to stylistic infelicities and saved me from perishing beneath the weight of my own subordinations. Kenneth Bleeth provided intellectual companionship, and more, during the overlong gestation of the entire project.

Reading the manuscript for the University of California Press, Professors Frederick Crews, Frances Ferguson, and Kenneth Johnston made valuable suggestions for its improvement. I regret having finished my book before the publication of Professor Johnston's *Wordsworth and The Recluse*, a work from which I subsequently have learned a great deal, and which also supports some of my own hunches about Wordsworth with depth of scholarship and strength of argument. The eagle eye of Amy Einsohn scanned the manuscript and made me fully aware of the complexity and necessity of the copy editor's job. Mary Renaud oversaw the entire project with efficiency, and Jeanne

Sugiyama acted as both a helpful liaison and a friendly comforter.

To Jonathan and Richard Wordsworth I shall be indebted in ways that only afteryears will fully clarify for their invitation to attend the 1983 Wordsworth Summer Conference at Grasmere. In the charmed setting of the Dove Cottage Library I delivered a shortened version of Chapter 6 to an audience of amateur as well as professional Wordsworthians who received it with equal measures of tolerance and severity. An exhilarating two weeks in the company of such people as Beverly Fields, Barbara Hardy, Peter Larkin, Peter Manning, and Sue Schopf provided both a literary education and a reminder that our deepest identity is shared, embedded in a community. It is also appropriate to record my pleasure in having briefly known the late Peter Laver, librarian of Dove Cottage, whose untimely death on Scafell one week after the conference darkened the memory of those golden weeks with a tragic intrusion into the midst of fellowship.

Of all the English poets, Wordsworth most demands an acknowledgment of one's teachers, since it was *his* highest wish to teach others how to love what he had loved. To my earliest instructors I have dedicated this book with appreciation and gratitude. And to four men, none of them a Wordsworthian, whose intellectual energies, stringent standards, and nuanced perceptions convinced me that a life devoted to literature could be accounted heroic, I offer the humble thanks of one coming after: Lawrence Graver, Alan Wilde, and the late Clay Hunt and Charles Samuels. I conned my part, and chose my vocation, in imitation of their examples.

A Note on Editions

The following editions of Wordsworth's works are referred to, and abbreviated as follows, in the text of this book:

Poetical Works (hereafter *PW*), ed. Ernest de Selincourt and Helen Darbishire (5 vols., Oxford: Clarendon Press, 1940–49).

The Prelude, ed. Ernest de Selincourt, rev. Helen Darbishire (Oxford: Clarendon Press, 1959; I have used the 1805 version unless otherwise indicated).

Prose Works (hereafter *PrW*), ed. W. J. B. Owen and Jane Worthington Smyser (3 vols., Oxford: Clarendon Press, 1974).

Letters of William and Dorothy Wordsworth, ed. Ernest de Selincourt, *The Early Years, 1787–1805* (hereafter *EY*), rev. Chester L. Shaver (Oxford: Clarendon Press, 1967); *The Middle Years* (hereafter *MY*), Part I, *1806–11*, rev. Mary Moorman (Oxford: Clarendon Press, 1969) and Part II, *1812–20*, rev. Mary Moorman and Alan Hill (Oxford: Clarendon Press, 1970); *The Later Years, 1821–50* (3 vols., Oxford: Clarendon Press, 1939), hereafter *LY*.

Introduction:
"Character of the Happy Warrior"

This is a book about people in Wordsworth's poetry, some of whom are recognizable versions of himself, and of his friends and family, and others of whom are conventionally "fictional" characters. It is also about the problems of growth, feeling, and learning that we all share rather than those that belong exclusively to the artist. For almost two hundred years, one critical tradition has seen Wordsworth as the prototype of the eccentric or egocentric poet, and now more than ever it seems to me important to move him back toward the center of the ordinary human sphere.

To this end, the following study isolates certain types of characters as Wordsworth's representative men and women. Some are named, others anonymous, some merely glances in the direction of human life. I do not deal specifically with Wordsworth's political heroes, nor do I discuss the characters in *The Borderers*, types that he handles more forcefully in genres other than drama. After an introductory chapter that defines the scope and presentation of Wordworth's heroism, three chapters deal with certain kinds of people—readers, children, and old men—and then three with individual works. These are *The Prelude*, where the growth of the heroic self is played off against other human figures who make rival claims on the narrator's and the audience's attention; *The White Doe of Rylstone*, finished in 1808 but not published until 1815, the central crystallization of Wordsworth's ideas about action and suffering; and, finally, *The Excursion*, where what

might be labeled the poet's "divisionary" imagination reduces characterization to a series of exempla, related by localized but anonymous men in a debate that always fails to
resolve itself. The most populated of Wordsworth's poems,
The Excursion shows us the great society of the noble living
and the noble dead, and of the disembodied, the theoretical, and the unnamed.

Although critical clichés memorialize Wordsworth's egocentrism, even when he seems to stand most sublimely
alone and unattended he refuses ever to remove other people entirely from his poetry. His central conception of the
self, even in *The Prelude*, always involves the presence—actual, invoked, or subsumed—of others. The three "roles" I
have chosen to stress—readers, children, and old men—
are but several among the many that Wordsworth investigates throughout his poetry. The seventh stanza of the Intimations Ode reminds us of Wordsworth's sensitivity to
the stages of life, whether we wish to define these stages
by theatrical, Renaissance formulas or in the modern language of psychology, as Helen Vendler does in describing
the stanza as the behaviorist's view of the child. Our human "vocation" is based on imitation of others, and we
"con" one part after another during our lives. Child,
Reader, Old Man: to those one could add Brother, Lover,
Parent, or any other element from the spectrum of familial,
social, and natural relationships that everywhere provoke
Wordsworth's attention.

By mingling an overview of Wordsworthian themes or
figures with a closer look at certain poetic habits, I hope to
show the relationship between Wordsworth's characteristic
styles and the habits of his characters. *Characteristic* here
means not only that *"le style c'est l'homme"* but also that
moral character depends literally upon habits of speech.
That representative poem of 1807, "Character of the Happy
Warrior" (written in the winter of 1805–06), demonstrates
this dependency. Although too uplifting, Roman, or didactic for modern taste, both the language and the procedure
of this poem indicate the Wordsworth I am proposing as an

alternative to the egocentric prophet we are more accustomed to. It is a poem about a "type," which puts us in mind of the classical and Renaissance moral and political principles Wordsworth inherited. This figure may also recall those dramatic character types announced as early as Theophrastus and used by Menander, reaffirmed by La Bruyère and Molière in the neoclassical period, and finally denounced by Goethe, who claimed in his essay "Dramatische Preisaufgabe" that the character play was finished. The year of that essay (1800) ironically saw as well the publication of the second edition of *Lyrical Ballads*, in which Wordsworth most clearly introduces those characters whom he continues to plumb for the rest of his career. Wordsworth uses *character* itself, as I shall show in Chapter 5, with a full awareness of its Greek original, "to scratch" or "etch." A character is indelible, engraved; it is, in Latin, a brand, a letter, and, by extension, a writer's hallmark. It comes, of course, after Theophrastus, to refer to inner nature as well as exterior marks.

In "Character of the Happy Warrior" (the omission of an initial article calls even greater attention to the Latinate first word), Wordsworth's procedure is as interesting as the substance of his nominal subject. Although the poem was inspired by the death of Lord Nelson—with hints as well of John Wordsworth, recently drowned, and Michel Beaupuy, dead for more than a decade but still present in Wordsworth's mind as a result of his recent completion of *The Prelude*—the anonymous Happy Warrior himself exists at a level of pure abstraction to which we all may aspire. "Happy," a word the poet uses sparingly, here primarily reflects Wordsworth's absorption of the *beatus ille* of Augustan poetry, which he repeats in *The Excursion* (IV, 332; VIII, 82). But in general, happiness in Wordsworth rarely belongs to active, living adults. He makes it remote, by virtue either of time (a condition of bygone childhood), space ("happy fields"), agent ("happy creatures" rather than happy people predominate), or ironic commentary (the poet in "Resolution and Independence" mistakenly thinks of himself "as happy as a boy," or as "a happy Child of earth"). Wordsworth distances happiness, conferring it upon the very simple ("Oh happy, happy, happy, John," in "The Idiot Boy"), or the very abstract ("the happy man"). The memory of a previous condition may depress as well as sustain. Thus, "The Brothers" ends with Leonard's realization that he must leave his native valley: "This vale, where he had been so happy, seemed / A place in which he could not bear to live," and in "The Fountain" Matthew, himself "a gray-haired man of glee," distinguishes the birds who "see / A happy youth" and a beautiful old age, from the humans who feel the weight of the past in what it has taken away and what continued. It comes as some surprise, then, to see the word featured so prominently in the title, and opening and concluding couplets, of a poem that uses the epithet only once otherwise, in a cliché phrase in the middle, "happy as a Lover," which significantly allies one characteristic *role* with another.

This poem looks like a catechism: an initial question ("Who is the happy Warrior? Who is he / That every man in arms should wish to be?") precedes a lengthy discursive answer, which settles into a complacent summation ("This is the happy Warrior; this is He / That every Man in arms should wish to be"). Its form, however, is also that of the Romantic nature lyric, as defined by M. H. Abrams, which rounds in its conclusion to the very place it began, and the body of which meanders freely, speculating and working out the initial poetic question or dilemma. For what seem like pat echoings of all the classical moralists whom its author had by heart, from Aristotle and Cicero down to Erasmus and More, this poem also sounds like a typically Wordsworthian meditation on the relationship of heroism to ordinary life. The title's warrior is not necessarily a military man. The poem's connections to other poems of Wordsworth, as well as its deliberate mingling of the mundane and the extraordinary in the portrait it limns, clearly restore it to a central place in Wordsworth's oeuvre, just as it restores him to a central place in classical ethics. He echoes the rhyme of lines 15–16 ("In face of these doth exercise a power/ Which is our human nature's highest dower"), two years later in *The White Doe* (lines 1832–33). "The plan that pleased his boyish thought" (line 5) returns us to the Intimations Ode. Even though the organization of the poem in couplets, thirty-five of them, interspersed with five triplets, may look unWordsworthian, we must remember that he chose the couplet for his earliest work (e.g., "An Evening Walk") as well as for the incomplete translation of *The Aeneid* of 1822.

One of these echoes attests to Wordsworth's constant effort to elevate the ordinary and press it into the heroic, or to embed the latter tightly within the former. The Happy Warrior is closer, poetically, to the leech-gatherer of "Resolution and Independence"—written in 1802, well before the crises that precipitated what critics traditionally label the middle years of Wordsworth's decline into stoicism and orthodoxy—than to Nelson, John Wordsworth, or any other heroic antecedent, real or imagined. It is for this reason that the poem remains resolutely abstract, going so far as to settle the reader with a shock into the initially distressing, unhumanizing pronoun of line 3: "*It* is the generous Spirit" (emphasis mine). Such dehumanization is part of Wordsworth's standard technique of distancing and then redeeming patterns of human behavior. The leech-gatherer is also made human only gradually. When we reach the center of "Character of the Happy Warrior," the connection between the abstract "warrior" and the grim old man becomes unmistakable: "Whose powers shed round him in the common strife,/ Or mild concerns of ordinary life,/ A constant influence, a peculiar grace" (lines 45–47). The meeting with the leech-gatherer began with the realization: "Now, whether it were by peculiar grace,/ A leading from above, a something given" (lines 50–51). A verbal echo in a different context makes the same connection:

—He who, though thus *endued* as with a *sense*
And faculty for storm and turbulence,
Is yet a Soul whose master-bias leans
To homefelt pleasures and to gentle scenes
(lines 57–60, emphasis mine)

This refers us to the famous description of the leech-gatherer, which Wordsworth isolated in his 1815 preface as an example of the modifying powers of the Imagination:

As a huge stone is sometimes seen to lie
Couched on the bald top of an eminence;
Wonder to all who do the same espy,
By what means it could thither come, and whence;
So that it seems a thing *endued* with *sense*:
Like a sea-beast crawled forth, that on a shelf
Of rock or sand reposeth, there to sun itself
(lines 57–63, emphasis mine)

My comparison of the Happy Warrior to the leech-gatherer merely amplifies a suggestion of Wordsworth's in the earlier poem: the very rhyme of "sense" with "eminence" unites an intimation of loftiness with the fact of ordinariness. This is the conjunction we find at all levels—thematic, stylistic, and self-referential—within his poetry, and this alliance first encouraged me to examine Wordsworth's "heroes." I use that word to evoke a whole tradition, or several of them, of effort, expectation, and desire, as well as ordinary achievement and knowledge. We find Wordsworth's heroes in the very world where we find our happiness or we find them not at all. Throughout, I work from the conviction that for Wordsworth, as for Wallace Stevens, the hero is assuredly not "the exceptional monster," but an ever-present reality. To appropriate Stevens once more, we might say that Wordsworth's ideas about "natural heroism" infuse his poetry "from that ever-early candor to its late plural" with "a pure power," the power of the heroic commonal (*Notes Toward a Supreme Fiction*: "It Must Be Abstract"). Wordsworth's heroes are, paradoxically, ourselves.

1

Some Versions of Heroism

Ours is the age of the common man and of the superman, but the roots of contemporary anonymity and hero worship reach well back into the nineteenth century. Our humanism and its violations alike can be traced to the very consciousness that in both Europe and America riveted attention on the spectacular energies of the heroic achiever, the realistic compass of ordinary life, and most important, on the connections between them. In 1845, well after the bard of Grasmere had proclaimed that his theme, in a neoclassical generality one might not expect from so ardent a romantic individualist, would be "no other than the very heart of man," the sage of Concord introduced a series of lectures with some thoughts on the "uses of great men."

The primary function of great men, says Emerson, is only peripherally to lead, to govern, or to control; they educate us but, ironically, by improving the species, they will eradicate themselves. Others will be promoted, and the race of heroes will wither away: "I applaud a sufficient man. . . . But I find him greater when he can abolish himself and all heroes."[1] Greatness commands imitation as well as respect, and the contagion of wisdom spreads rapidly through the land. One superior apple improves the bunch: "within the limits of human education and agency, we may say great men exist that there may be greater men. The destiny of organized nature is ameliorization, and who can tell its limits?" (p. 35).

Who is man that the poets are mindful of him? And who is the hero who will improve or save "organized nature," and fulfill both a single and a collective destiny? In Emerson, the relationship between the general and the particular, the common plural and the heroic singular, provokes divergent responses. The hero is both leader and mirror since man is all that we can see or know: "Other men are lenses through which we read our own minds" (p. 5). But we must eschew merely passive reception of material stimulus or inspiration in favor of forceful action: "We must not be sacks and stomachs. . . . Activity is contagious" (p. 13). Yet the drive to ensure personal greatness gradually sputters out; its finest achievement is its evaporation: "The genius of our life is jealous of individuals, and will not have any individual great, except through the general" (p. 189). This jealousy, which refuses to personal identity a rightful elevation, extends even to artistic efforts. From the "activity" of greatness, Emerson turns quite comfortably to the complete passivity that equally condemns it to extinction: "Great genial power, one would almost say [he is writing of Shakespeare], consists in not being original at all, in being altogether receptive; in letting the world do all, and suffering the spirit of the hour to pass unobstructed through the mind" (p. 191).

In retrospect, Emerson and his gnomic ambivalences seem much more sensible than Carlyle, with his puffing up of courage as more valuable than love and his preference for the nobleman to the saint; strangely passed over by Eric Bentley, Emerson might have suggested a sane middle path between the two extremes that Bentley saw engulfing the world when he published *A Century of Hero-Worship* in our darkest time. In his afterword, he says he wishes to propose "a position between blind hero-worship and the opposite extreme—impersonal determinism, the denial of individuality. Yet blind hero-worship, as Hitlerism has shown, is actually accompanied by denial of individuality. Conversely, to accept individuality, to glory in it, is to accept the hero, the superior man, and to glory in him."[2] By tracing back through Shaw, Wagner, Nietzsche, and Carlyle the roots of contemporary disaster, Bentley, however understandably, limits himself to one tradition of Romanticism. In his introduction, he states, "the word *heroism* does not mean just any sort of human goodness" (p. 8) but rather, for his purposes, the new philosophy of the nineteenth century. By seeing only a century of overreachers, outcasts, and *Übermenschen*, he blinded himself to the other, gentler race that Romanticism itself also sired.

The other tradition was Emerson's and, more humanely, Wordsworth's. "We have all of us one human heart," proclaims the poet of the egotistical sublime, who, according to his earliest critics, was a spectator *ab extra*, writing a poetry with only himself confronting the universe. But the line from "The Old Cumberland Beggar" commends itself to our attention because it is the crucial starting place for Wordsworth's life's work. Not only, to paraphrase the Preface to *Lyrical Ballads*, is the poet a man speaking *to* men, but he is also speaking *of* and *for* them, in their characteristic roles, positions, and ages, and with the assurance that the species is more united than disparate. Wordsworth preaches our sameness (all human hearts are alike) and also divides The One Human Heart, his major abstraction, into its individual constituents and particles. It is Wordsworth, not Byron or Carlyle, who is behind the other myth of the major man in our century, the one offered in time of war by Wallace Stevens:

> Yet look not at his colored eyes. Give him
> No names. Dismiss him from your images.
> The hot of him is purest in the heart.
>
> The major abstraction is the idea of man
> And major man is its exponent, abler
> In the abstract than in his singular,
>
> More fecund as principle than particle,
> Happy fecundity, flor-abundant force,
> In being more than an exception, part,
>
> Though an heroic part, of the commonal.
> The major abstraction is the commonal,
> The inanimate, difficult visage. Who is it?[3]

Stevens's major man combines gestures from Yeats and Charlie Chaplin; he is a man in an old coat, partly pathetic and partly comic as such figures tend to be. The paradox of the heroic commonal is one that Wordsworth would have understood entirely, because he invented it, as he would have appreciated Stevens's appropriation of the old man, the severest challenge to our faith, as an example of human heroism. For Wordsworth, as for Stevens, the arduous fact of survival deserves the hero's label, formerly reserved for doers of great deeds, or winners of abundant grace. Wordsworth would applaud Stevens's succinct, but not new, formulation, "merely going round is a final good . . . / The man-hero is not the exceptional monster, / But he that of repetition is most master" (*Notes Toward a Supreme Fiction*: "It Must Give Pleasure").

Can there exist the unexceptional hero? the anonymous hero? the marginal hero? The question is not original nor does Wordsworth propound definitive answers; rather, the very asking of the questions may allow us to see Wordsworth's poetry in a clearer light. For our vision has been obscured by the commonplace "separatist" view of the Romantic hero. Walter L. Reed, for example, comments, "The Romantic hero is set apart from the rest of the society," and Bentley affirms, "One of the few beliefs which the romanticists had in common was that the artist is both solitary and superior, a hero apart from the herd."[4] But it was Wordsworth's deepest belief that the eccentric, the tangential, or the most tentative human figures themselves participate in the common experiences and consequently merit our steady attention. Emerson's conjectures provide the countermyth to Romantic alienation: "There is no outside, no inclosing wall, no circumference to us. . . . The only sin is limitation."[5] Where a circle is boundless, there can be no eccentricity.

Poets and critics alike have been uncertain about locating their heroes with respect to the crowd from whom they derive, whose values they may embody or reject. For Jungians and other mythographers, all heroes are one, the single individual with the myriad appearances, the one who "should always be interpreted as a collective ego, which is equipped with all the excellences."[6] Individuality is illusory; the surface may deceive us into honoring what is little more than the latest model. Even recent discussions of classical Greek literature have tended to blot out the individual and to see the tribe as the central figure.[7] The values and solidarity of the group reduce Olympian strivings to quotidian play; the winners of the games are interchangeable. Not only are the generations of men as leaves to the trees, but so, too, are their kings.

The standard image of heroism, whether classical, Christian, or modern, demands individual identity, action, and above all, naming. As we may recall from Book 9 of *The Odyssey*, Odysseus's refusal to escape from Polyphemus beneath a cloak of pseudonymity prolongs his adventures by incurring the wrath of Poseidon. But without the proper credit for his deed, without proper signature as it were, the deed would be as good as undone. Naming puts a cap upon action. It confers heroic status upon the doer of heroic deeds. Even when he is part of some anthropologist's composite figure, the hero is, within his life and within the pages of his book, requited by patronymics and epithets to assure proper remembrance.[8]

The will is all: "To be a hero means to be one out of many, to be oneself. . . . This will to be oneself is heroism." Thus, a new twist on the classical definition by José Ortega y Gasset.[9] The will may move toward deeds, as the opening of C. M. Bowra's *Heroic Poetry* reminds us: "In their attempts to classify mankind in different types the early Greek philosophers gave a special place to those men who live for action and for the honour which comes from it."[10] Or the will may be that of the absolute spirit to manifest itself in history through the vessel of the hero; thus, Hegel: "they have derived their purposes and their vocation, not from the calm, regular course of things, sanctioned by the existing order, but from a concealed fount . . . from that inner spirit, still hidden beneath the surface, which, impinging on the outer world as on a shell, bursts it in pieces."[11]

Wordsworth was not insensitive to the attractions of the ancient models, nor was he uninterested in the concealed fount from which the exceptional man-heroes derived, nor was he deaf to the claims of Christian heroism which Milton so persuasively argued as antidotes to the wrath of stern Achilles. But it was the "calm, regular course of things," a phrase whose stylistic simplicity hits the true Wordsworthian note, that was Wordsworth's center, his fountain, subject, and capital. He could share Emerson's enthusiasm: "All these great and transcendent properties are ours. . . . Where the heart is, there the muses, there the gods sojourn, and not in any geography of fame."[12] Wordsworth's heroes perform no actions beyond the ability of most men; they neither derive from nor occupy a divine space, although it is one of Wordsworth's distinct achievements to have made famous the geography of his main regions and to have granted fame to those who inhabit that geography.[13] Indeed, most of Wordsworth's characters resist even naming: the typed speakers in *The Excursion*, as well as the tales they relate, populated by largely anonymous persons, represent the last major flowering of Wordsworth's heroic aspirations. But even these are not his strongest anonymous heroes: in *The Prelude*, the hero never names himself. He compounds his egoism with the most self-effacing and self-denying of gestures.

However disturbing we may find the paradox, the most individuated of poets gives us poems about persons largely anonymous. And these poems contain a populous commonwealth of persons unnamed, intimated, generalized, and localized. Never has there been a poetry in which human identity—not just the poet's—figures so prominently, and in which human individuality is so strikingly absent. The Central Man in Wordsworth is only partly himself; he reads others as models of what he will become as readily as he projects from the example of his own life a model for others. Wordsworth's lives are bright and many, a Shelleyan dome of many-colored glass. Like a medieval cathedral, his own image for his work, the poetry is studded with human figures, who help us to find in Wordsworth a prophet of shared humanity rather than a voice crying to itself in a wilderness of sublime solitude. The poet is speaking of men, and of women and children as well.

The twentieth-century Wordsworth looks like Coleridge's and Hazlitt's: the solitary mind observing the world, a Lucretian philosopher removed *hors de combat*, or the voice conducting its relentless monologue against a chorus of nothing less than the universe itself.[14] More recently, this composite figure has acquired new touches, most notably from Lionel Trilling (the untragic poet among the rabbis) and Geoffrey Hartman (the fearful shunner of apocalypse).[15] The figure of Wordsworth everywhere confronting his own daemon and his ghostly forebears needs reappraisal. Harold Bloom's agonistic poet who "had no true subject except his own subjective nature" is a critical myth to be exorcised.[16] Wordsworth's inward turnings are everywhere balanced by his return to outward things and to other persons. By attending to the variety of subjects, human and topical, within the poetry, we move Wordsworth back to the center of common concerns.

In spite of his claim that "to freeze the blood I have no ready arts" ("Hart-Leap Well"), the public life, warfare, and the traditional arenas of masculine achievement are never far from Wordsworth's mind. Even in rejecting them, he must first consciously consider them, as he does when he rehearses his possible themes for an epic (*The Prelude* I, 157–228), the "glorious work" for which he finds himself more ready in the contemplating than in the doing. Or when in the Highlands, he hears the Solitary Reaper singing, he instinctively outlines a range of possible themes for her incomprehensible song:

> Perhaps the plaintive numbers flow
> For old, unhappy, far-off things,

And battles long ago:
Or is it some more humble lay,
Familiar matter of today?
Some natural sorrow, loss, or pain,
That has been, and may be again?

"Natural sorrow" implies that unhappy, far-off things are unnatural in their remoteness or, more probably, in their battle origin. Repetition—here the renovation of distress—is for Wordsworth as for Stevens the very proof of nature and man's place in it, just as "natural piety," in "My Heart Leaps Up," provides the chain to bind past, present, and future days. The fullness of Wordsworth's ambivalence toward the traditional heroic life surfaces in *The Prelude* as he mulls over possible subjects, among them the Roman general Sertorius, whose followers, after his assassination in 72 B.C., fled to the Canary Islands, there to found a race that lasted until the end of the fifteenth century; they

Flying, found shelter in the Fortunate Isles;
And left their usages, their arts, and laws,
To disappear by a slow gradual death;
To dwindle and to perish one by one
Starved in those narrow bounds: but not the Soul
Of Liberty, which fifteen hundred years
Surviv'd, and, when the European came
With skill and power that could not be withstood,
Did, like a pestilence, maintain its hold,
And wasted down by glorious death that Race
Of natural Heroes.
                    (*The Prelude* I, 191–201)

The strange paradoxes here attest to Wordsworth's uncertainty, and his verse has it two ways at once. First, Is it the men or "their arts and laws" that are disappearing? The infinitives of lines 192 and 193, which may be of purpose or result, may refer to either. The men die and their spirit survives ("but not the Soul / Of Liberty"), although it controls their descendants perversely, sustaining by killing them, holding them like the plague in its grip. Liberty perpetuates itself by strangling its defenders. Even death is subject to diverse interpretations: "glorious" may suggest the clichés of military achievement or the tragic consequences of loss, but "wasted," especially in conjunction with "pestilence," and the favorite epithet "natural," makes us, as it evidently made the poet, less than definite about the relationship between nature and the claims of heroism.

A later Wordsworthian poet has also invoked, in a completely different context, the paradoxical notion of "natural heroism"; in her genial invitation to Marianne Moore to "come flying" into Manhattan for a day's spree, Elizabeth Bishop conjures up an image of Miss Moore as a good witch of Oz, her shoes "trailing a sapphire highlight" as a kind of neo-Wordsworthian glory, her cape full of butterflies, her broad black hat conveying "heaven knows how many angels," rising into the daylight: "Mounting the sky with natural heroism, / above the accidents, above the malignant movies."[17] The "moving accident," which Wordsworth claims is not his trade in "Hart-Leap Well," is here disowned by Bishop, too, whose oxymoron, "natural heroism," we may trace back to her English predecessor. Nature and heroism are not steady mates: although the hero is rooted in some geographical, historical, or cultural reality, he usually stands apart by virtue of his superiority, or else his very excesses make him a cynosure, the object of all sight at a distant point away from the center. But for Bishop as for Wordsworth, the great challenge is to locate heroes within the very nature, human as well as local, that we all share.

A better-known passage from *The Prelude*, in the Simplon Pass episode, may attest to Wordsworth's ambivalence on the matter of heroism. The imagery, rhetoric, and syntax of the lines on the origin and destiny of the imagination have been discussed many times, but one important discord seems to have gone unremarked:

> our being's heart and home,
> Is with infinitude, and only there;
> With hope it is, hope that can never die,
> Effort, and expectation, and desire,

And something evermore about to be.
Under such banners militant, the soul
Seeks for no trophies, struggles for no spoils
That may attest her prowess, blest in thoughts
That are their own perfection and reward,
Strong in herself and in beatitude
That hides her, like the mighty flood of Nile
Poured from his fount of Abyssinian clouds
To fertilise the whole Egyptian plain.

(1850 version, VI, 604–16)

As striking as the dilemma of origins and destinations upon which the whole passage turns is the simultaneous attraction to and flight from the language of heroic ardor. The soul need neither seek nor struggle, even though, or perhaps *because*, it is marching proudly beneath its own militant banners. Only in the presence—rhetorical as well as spiritual—of heroic apparatus can the self ignore the conventional goals of heroic aspiration. The Wordsworthian soldier marches, with the banner of his expectations before his eyes, into no battle.[18]

While refocusing critical attention upon an "other-directed" Wordsworth in the chapters to follow, I do not wish to ignore the heroic status everywhere accorded to the first-person self in his poetry. The lines from *The Prelude* cited above intimate the range of Wordsworth's concern with heroism, whether externally or internally considered. While recognizing that heroism, I want to emphasize the place of certain kinds of human figures. Additionally, I shall examine the continuing interest, throughout his career, in the relationship between the active and contemplative lives. Drawn temperamentally to the latter, Wordsworth always gives the former its due, and often blurs the line between them as he strangely does between the claims of nature and those of heroic human activity in the excerpts preceding. Even the act of reading, as I shall show in more detail in the next chapter, encourages the mingling of intellectual receptivity and imaginative action:

Yea to this hour I cannot read a tale
Of two brave Vessels matched in deadly fight,
And fighting to the death, but I am pleased
More than a wise man ought to be. I wish,
Fret, burn, and struggle, and in soul am there.
("Home at Grasmere," lines 721–25)

Of the old tropes, *agere et pati*,[19] Wordsworth makes new configurations, constantly entertaining their rival claims and aligning them in various rhetorical patterns.

Wordsworth promotes "suffering" and contemplation to a heroic level just as he often dismisses "mere" action as a passive obedience to instinct. His most powerful verse confronts these problems with a dialectical fervor that almost undermines the positive assurance of his bardic voice. For example, just before he launches into the miniature autobiography, of which the lines above are a part, he turns from celebrating the communal "happy Band" of friends and relatives with whom he plans to share the paradisal seclusion of Grasmere, to consider his life's prospective work:

Yet 'tis not to enjoy that we exist,
For that end only; something must be done.
(lines 664–65)[20]

The passive voice enforces a sense of doubt even in the process of Wordsworth's proclaiming new and independent authority for himself. Goading himself toward the realization of personal achievement, he simultaneously backs away from what he calls "ill-advised Ambition and . . . Pride" (line 673) but resolves his ambition and his doubts with an assurance

That an internal brightness is vouchsafed
That must not die, that must not pass away.
(lines 675–76)

This brightness, which he desperately reiterates as eternal ("It must be possible," as Stevens would say) is the power of speech. That power originated in the sublimation of boy-

hood's motions of savage instinct, its readings of natural
scenes, its innate and deviant patterns of disobedience,
into the settled calm authority of adult wisdom. Heroic
zeal does not vanish. Reason preempts and internalizes it,
thereby assuring its immortality:

> "Be mild [Reason enjoins him] and cleave to gentle things,
> Thy glory and thy happiness be there.
> Nor fear, though thou confide in me, a want
> Of aspirations that *have* been, of foes
> To wrestle with, and victory to complete,
> Bounds to be leapt, darkness to be explored,
> All that inflamed thy infant heart, the love,
> The longing, the contempt, the undaunted quest,
> All shall survive—though changed their office, all
> Shall live,—it is not in their power to die."
>
> (lines 735–44)

From the earlier, worried "That must not die," Wordsworth has glided, on the strength of his own rhetoric, to
the simple assurance that "all shall live." From paradox to
tautology, from tension to simplicity, is always the dialectic
pattern in his verse. He now turns, with a bold allusion, to
an earlier hero whose deeds and whose farewell to them
alike he now surpasses:

> Then farewell to the Warrior's schemes, farewell
> The forwardness of Soul
>
> (lines 745–46)

Othello's greatness, like all classic military heroics, is dis-
placed or absorbed by the new heroic ventures that Wordsworth cites in the concluding lines, those affixed to the beginning of *The Excursion* to mark his plans for his life's
work. "On Man, on Nature, on Human Life": his major
themes will incorporate the new configurations of doing
and suffering, *agere et pati*, active and passive forms of life
and language.

One additional poem stands out as exemplary of Wordsworth's sometimes baffling attempts to accommodate action and repose, heroic achievement and meditative calm,

singleness and commonalty, and significantly, human beings and their symbolic surrogates. Even when people are nominally absent from the poetry they seem to be most at its heart. Michael Riffaterre and Geoffrey Hartman have already analyzed "Yew-Trees" with sensitive attention to grammatical and phonic details, and to the displacement of one tradition (that of the speaking monument) by another (natural description).[21] The poem keeps us moving "along a border between natural and supernatural ideas," as Hartman says, but it also keeps us aware of the line between the human and the natural, a line that Wordsworth seems almost deliberately to blur:

> There is a Yew-tree, pride of Lorton Vale,
> Which to this day stands single, in the midst
> Of its own darkness, as it stood of yore:
> Not loth to furnish weapons for the bands
> Of Umfraville or Percy ere they marched
> To Scotland's heaths; or those that crossed the sea
> And drew their sounding bows at Azincour,
> Perhaps at earlier Crecy, or Poictiers.
> Of vast circumference and gloom profound
> This solitary Tree! a living thing
> Produced too slowly ever to decay;
> Of form and aspect too magnificent
> To be destroyed. But worthier still of note
> Are those fraternal Four of Borrowdale,
> Joined in one solemn and capacious grove;
> Huge trunks! and each particular trunk a growth
> Of intertwisted fibres serpentine
> Up-coiling, and inveterately convolved;
> Nor uninformed with Phantasy, and looks
> That threaten the profane;—a pillared shade,
> Upon whose grassless floor of red-brown hue,
> By sheddings from the pining umbrage tinged
> Perennially—beneath whose sable roof
> Of boughs, as if for festal purpose decked
> With unrejoicing berries—ghostly Shapes
> May meet at noontide; Fear and trembling Hope,
> Silence and Foresight; Death the Skeleton
> And Time the Shadow;—there to celebrate,
> As in a natural temple scattered o'er

With altars undisturbed of mossy stone,
United worship; or in mute repose
To lie, and listen to the mountain flood
Murmuring from Glaramara's inmost caves.

The concluding personifications fill the poem with a ghostly half-presence; as Mary Moorman has observed, they attest to Wordsworth's recollections of *The Aeneid* (6: 276ff.).[22] But they do not constitute a new or surprising element in the poem. Rather than think of the poem's general development, as Hartman does, as one "where the initial understated figure (the impersonal construction) leads into an overstated figure (the strong personification),"[23] I propose a more harmonious whole, the sublime and simple tone of which masks a constant ambivalence about humanity in general and heroism in particular.

The poem establishes, then subverts, oppositions. Each part, the first (lines 1–13) about half as long as the second, focuses on a different scene: a single tree, a fraternity of trees. In each, Wordsworth feintingly attacks the issue of human action and its opposite. The Lorton Yew stands mysteriously alone, a monadnock of a tree, but it extends through time to a plurality of weapons and battles. Static, it gives of itself infinitely, a single source for the tools of English nationalism. It "is," it "stands"; it finally (lines 10–13) dispenses with verbs altogether, but from its pure nominalism come the actions of English heroes ("marched," "crossed," "drew"). From nature derives human heroism, as multiplicity comes from singleness and action from stillness. The Borrowdale set also appears deictically, and with no transitive verbs until the subordinate clause of line 20. Participles and passives lead to action: the ostracism of the profane from this haven of the contemplative life. As a fraternity, the trees are opposed to the single Lorton Yew, but they naturally recall the bands of Englishmen who garnered their support from that tree; even the Latinisms (lines 16–18) evoke the language of epic adventure, as did "magnificent" (line 12), whose etymology allows the tree its share of great deeds. But Wordsworth is still sparing of his verbs: only "may meet" (line 26), in a dependent clause, gives any immediacy amid participles and infinitives. The festal worshippers, emblems of the meditative life, are as distant from our view as the ancient soldiers referred to but never pictured earlier. In the "natural temple" (itself a paradox and qualified as a simile), these pious shades gather to make their united worship or to give themselves up to Wordsworthian idleness. The two possibilities, the first a qualified action and the second a passive submission, mirror the opening of the poem, which proceeds from stillness to activity.

In his refusal to picture characters in "Yew-Trees," Wordsworth has in no way subordinated a human dimension to "mere" description. Rather, the two yew scenes, each harmoniously personified, become sources for other human motifs—battle and worship, action and meditation—in which the participants are distanced by time or sheer invisibility. We have the pure essence of human choice and behavior from which all breathing human passion has been removed. This human element sits squarely as the foundation of Wordsworth's poetry: whether focused on himself or on figures in narrative encounters, through natural description or abstract speculation, it is a poetry that investigates the possibilities and qualities of natural heroes. In pride and shame, strength and weakness, accomplishment and idleness, these heroes taken together image the personal and social unity that obsesses the poet. None is ever single, even as the Lorton Yew stands poetically beside the Borrowdale fraternity. Personal integrity, when enlarged, becomes a social ideal.

Hence, Wordsworth's remark that "there is a dark / Inscrutable workmanship that reconciles / Discordant elements, makes them cling together / In one society" (*The Prelude*, 1850 version, I, 341–44) refers to the growth of individual identity through a social metaphor. (The reverse is also true: a whole society can be pictured as a quasi-human organism.) Wordsworth's diction here is typical and compelling: the strong verb ("reconciles") is relegated to the subordinate clause, depending first of all on simple identity ("is"). The polysyllabic Latinisms, "inscrutable," "reconciles," "discordant," "society," "elements," give a strong normative base to the passage and to our lives, but "cling" returns us to human frailty and to the imperiling delicacy of a society meant to be a bulwark. From human weakness, the depths of personal and social want, come the appearance and finally the fact of human strength. The unknowable Lucretian creative force builds units from warring atoms, and heroism is another word for existence.

2

Wordsworth's Readers

The supposedly unbookish Wordsworth was formed and informed by classical texts as much as any other Romantic poet.[1] The man who cavalierly invites us to quit our books, "a dull and endless strife," to come forth into the light of things, expends great psychic and poetic energy in his autobiography describing how and why books were important to his education. As a corollary, he metaphorically renders major imaginative and visionary moments as the experience of reading and interpreting the images of the world. Wordsworth may sometimes recommend an escape from the prison of the schoolroom to the wise passiveness of pastoral indolence, but more often he urges an exchange of the texts of the library for the book of nature. "Reading" is Wordsworth's synecdoche for dealing with the world.

According to Harold Bloom, "to imagine after a poet is to learn his own metaphors for his acts of reading," and "a poet attempting to make . . . language new necessarily begins with an *arbitrary act of reading* that does not differ in kind from the act that *his* readers subsequently must perform upon him."[2] As readers *of* Wordsworth, we should come to grips with reading *in* Wordsworth. If we can answer the questions What is the act of reading? and Who is capable of reading well?, we shall be well on the way to answering the more problematical How do we learn? and How does a poet differ from other men? We shall also see that, for Wordsworth, reading is a heroic act linking poet and reader. As Carlyle, a careful reader of Wordsworth, remarks: "a vein of Poetry exists in the hearts of all men; no

23

man is made altogether of Poetry. We are all poets when we read a poem well."[3]

Wordsworth often refers incidentally to books and reading even in poems not primarily concerned with them. In "Resolution and Independence," the leech-gatherer cons the water as if reading in a book, just as Peter Bell reads the pool like an enchanted book; in "To the Small Celandine," the speaker, isolated to the point of paranoia, "sighed to think I read a book / Only read, perhaps by me"; in "Love Lies Bleeding," we are taught to read the images of the flowers and "the language of the viewless air"; in "The Wishing-Gate Destroyed," the "earth is wide, and many a nook / Unheard of is, like this, a book / For modest meanings clear." One sonnet speaks of "intruders who would tear from nature's book / This precious leaf." The Old Cumberland Beggar is a "record," a history in which the community can read its past offices of charity; the blind London beggar in *The Prelude* VII, 607–22, wears his story around his neck for others to read, ironically conflating an inability to see with a failure to speak.[4]

Just as Virgil, according to Pope, found that Homer and Nature were the same, Wordsworth's discovery, in Book V of *The Prelude* and throughout his poetry generally, is that nature can be read like a book and that books uncover a nature that, like our foster-mother Earth in the Intimations Ode, is able to feed our "dumb yearnings, hidden appetites" (*The Prelude* V, 530) when we are young. Popularized by medieval pulpit eloquence, the trope of the *liber naturae* was a common one, and Wordsworth would have found ample precedent for the motif among his immediate predecessors and contemporaries.[5] The trope derives originally from the attempts in both Old and New Testaments to explain the visible universe as a manifestation of God's unseen power. The favorite Pauline speculation that God has bodied forth shapes known and visible so that we may understand, through faith, things unknown (e.g., Romans 1:20, Hebrews 11:3) distinguishes between a text or vehicle

that we read, and a subtext or tenor which we may ultimately understand. Nature is inherently metaphorical.
Variations on these and similar passages, running from the
English Reformation to the Evangelical and Methodist
movements of the eighteenth century, were obviously common coin to Wordsworth, who speaks of God as the author
of the book of nature ("The Brothers"), of the world as "the
Bible of the Universe," and of the religious man as one who
"values what he sees chiefly as an 'imperfect shadowing
forth' of what he is incapable of seeing" (*MY* 2:188; *PW*
2:412).[6]

Wordsworth sustains the motifs of Biblical "reading" in
his distinction between written and oral languages, which
sometimes are identical in their effects and sometimes at
odds with one another. Just as the Psalmist states paratacti-
cally and with the parallelism common to Hebrew verse,
"the heavens *declare* the glory of God and the firmament
showeth his handiwork" (emphasis mine), the word may be
heard, like God's primal commands, or seen, as Christ is
logos incarnate, the audible and visible evidence of the
transforming power of language.[7] What Wordsworth calls
"the speaking face of earth and heaven" (*The Prelude* V, 12)
is a text that at times can be heard, at others read. Although not usually thought of as a synaesthetic poet, like
Keats for example, Wordsworth juxtaposes reading and
hearing in dramatic ways. In the Ecclesiastical sonnet on
the translation of the Bible, he rejoices that the "sacred
book"

> Assumes the accents of our native tongue;
> And he who guides the plough, or wields the crook,
> With understanding spirit now may look
> Upon her records, listen to her song.

Or, in the well-known address to Dorothy at the end of
"Tintern Abbey," Wordsworth is pleased that

> in thy voice I catch
> The language of my former heart, and read

My former pleasures in the shooting lights
Of thy wild eyes.

Sometimes the two acts are merged, as when the ass in
"Peter Bell" hears the boy's cry and "he there can read /
Some intermingled notes that plead / With touches irre-
sistible." But Wordsworth differs from Wesley's "natural methodism" and the Protestant tradition which holds that "the
Book of Nature is written in an universal character which
every man may read."[8] Rather, he sees nature "as a sacred
language which most men have lost the power to read and
understand," and thinks of reading as an exclusive activity
of poets, natural aristocrats, or rural hierophants who have
not lost the special skill to perceive and learn.[9] Most men,
in contrast, look at nature "as doth a man / Upon a volume
whose contents he knows / Are memorable, but from him
lock'd up, / Being written in a tongue he cannot read" (*The
Prelude* X, 49–52).

Central to his hopes and fears for man is the problem of
learning to read, to develop what M. H. Abrams calls "a
prepared mind," and what Wordsworth in *The Prelude* XIII
speaks of as "higher minds" that can work and be wrought
upon. Wordsworth's major poetry grapples with the process of learning itself, a heroic preparation for living:

> In consonance with Wordsworth's two-term frame of refer-
> ence, the Scriptural Apocalypse is assimilated to an apoca-
> lypse of nature; its written characters are natural objects,
> which are read as types and symbols of permanence in
> change; and its antithetic qualities of sublimity and beauty are
> seen as simultaneous expressions on the face of heaven and
> earth, declaring an unrealized truth which the chiaroscuro of
> the scene articulates for the *prepared mind*—a truth about the
> darkness and the light, the terror and the peace, the ineluctá-
> ble contraries that make up our human existence.[10]

What kind of texts should we read? and, How shall we prepare ourselves to read them properly? These are the important questions. Harold Bloom conceives of critical reading

as a lower version of the process of poetic reading by which an ephebe is able to respond to a precursor by remaking him: for the strong poet, reading and writing are inevitably linked, not merely sequentially, like inhalation and exhalation, but simultaneously. Wordsworth, at once more commonplace and more radical than Bloom, separates the two activities. Reading is learning, conscious or unconscious, that opens one to the world and opens the world's book to the keen creative eye. It may lead to writing, but not necessarily; it is the highest state to which men may aspire who lack the final touch of divinity and luck that alone produces poets.[11]

Wordsworth's greatest testimony to reading comes at the end of *The Prelude* V, where, characteristically, the verse is so deliberately dense, almost clotted by the obscurity of antecedents and references that we cannot tell exactly what the true subject is. The youth who has been an intimate of nature

> Not only in that raw unpractised time
> Is stirred to extasy, as others are,
> By glittering verse; but further, doth receive,
> In measure only dealt out to himself,
> Knowledge and increase of enduring joy
> From the great Nature that exists in works
> Of mighty Poets. Visionary power
> Attends the motions of the viewless winds,
> Embodied in the mystery of words:
> There, darkness makes abode, and all the host
> Of shadowy things work endless changes,—there,
> As in a mansion like their proper home,
> Even forms and substances are circumfused
> By that transparent veil with light divine,
> And, through the turnings intricate of verse,
> Present themselves as objects recognized,
> In flashes, and with glory not their own.
> (1850 version, V, 589–605)

The density is functional; indeed, the importance of Book V lies in the rich synaesthesia achieved here and elsewhere rather than in the idealized version of his own education, or the theories that Wordsworth puts forward. Nature and books are literally and symbolically the same, from the start of Book V when Wordsworth sees, in a dream, a stone and a shell that stand for geometry and poetry, to his lament that the modern child, schooled by too many books, has neglected his "old Grandame Earth" and "the playthings which her love design'd for him . . . in their woodland beds the flowers / Weep, and the river-sides are all forlorn" (1805, lines 346–49).

In the long passage above, Wordsworth stresses identity, not plurality. Although the lines suggest that what others learn from books, the natural child gets firsthand (ecstasy from nature, not poetry), the subsequent grammatical haze implies equally that "great Nature" in the words of poets is not a Platonic reflection of an ideal form, but the same richness available to readers and wanderers in equal measure. Visionary power "attends upon" winds not, as we might think, in nature itself, but "in the mystery of words." Is "there" the winds themselves or the words that present them?[12] Is darkness ("viewless," "darkness," and "shadowy") inherent in nature, or reflected in books? If such darkness exists, then how does one explain the sudden illumination books seem to provide? Does a transparent veil illuminate more than it conceals? Is there not something illusory about the glory with which books clothe forms and substances?—"*as in* a mansion *like* their proper home" and "with a glory not their own" make the process curiously unreliable or tricky.

This Gordian knot of suggestiveness is a fit ending to a book on books and nature. The final mysterious illumination is the result of a visionary experience occasioned by the intricate turnings of verse but impossible without an earlier training in the ways and forms of nature. The language in this passage is virtually identical to that of the two "natural" (as opposed to literary) revelations in *The Prelude* VI and XIII. Imagination (VI, 525ff.) is an unfathered vapor surrounding and darkening like a cloud, but it is also a glory dimming the light of sense, which goes out "in flashes."[13] In crossing the Alps, Wordsworth later realizes, he experienced "a visiting of awful promise" in which "greatness make[s] abode." The following meditation (lines 556–72), first printed separately as text without context, is the literary compensation for his initial disappointment in unknowingly crossing the Alps. He sees in those "woods decaying, never to be decayed," a primal text: a combination of sights and sounds ("black drizzling crags that spake by the way-side / As if a voice were in them") followed by "Characters of the great Apocalypse, / The types and symbols of Eternity, / Of first and last, and midst, and without end." Similarly, during the moonlit ascent of Mt. Snowdon, the combination of light and sound, what is seen and heard, creates a "universal spectacle . . . through which . . . Nature lodg'd / The Soul, the Imagination of the whole" (XIII, 60–65); in retrospect, "when the scene had pass'd away," Wordsworth meditates upon the text and discovers "the perfect image of a mighty Mind / Of one that feeds upon infinity," an emblem of the mature spirit shared by poets, seers, and perfect readers.

In these major apocalyptic moments, as Geoffrey Hartman and Frank McConnell have described them,[14] a blinding light destroys the light of sense, and the scene is transformed by a lifting of the veil to uncover a hidden reality beneath what is empirically ascertainable. (Cf. Shelley, *A Defense of Poetry*: "Poetry lifts the veil from the hidden beauty of the world, and makes familiar objects be as if they were not familiar.") An aural mode mingles with, or replaces, a visual one. We are blinded not only to see better, but often to receive the word in its primal and more powerful form. We hear it. In the late poem "On the Power of Sound" the spoken word antedates and succeeds the daedal earth of visual splendor:

> A Voice to Light gave Being;
> To Time, and Man his earth-born chronicler;
> A Voice shall finish doubt and dim foreseeing,

And sweep away life's visionary stir;
        . . . though earth be dust
And vanish, though the heavens dissolve, her stay
Is in the WORD, that shall not pass away.
                                    (*PW* II, 323–30)[15]

Reading, in these moments, is initially passive. All the
readers are, in Hartman's words, "halted travellers." With
Mt. Blanc before them, the Alpine climbers are forced to
read: "With such a book / Before our eyes, we could not
chuse but read / A frequent lesson of sound tenderness"
(*The Prelude* VI, 473–75; that lesson is magnified when the
greater text—the Simplon Pass—is reached two hundred
lines later). The "we could not choose but" construction is
a favorite of Wordsworth's and is intimately connected
with acts of reading or responding to external stimuli.
"And yet we feel, we cannot chuse but feel / That [great
books] must perish" (*The Prelude* V, 20–21). The man who
communes with "the Forms / Of nature . . . cannot choose /
But seek for objects of a kindred love / In fellow-natures"
(*The Excursion* IV, 1207–16). Watching and listening to the
Mind that Nature has exhibited on Mt. Snowdon, the poet
realizes "that even the grossest minds must see and hear /
And cannot chuse but feel" (*The Prelude* XIII, 83–84). As-
tonished by daffodils, "a poet could not but be gay"; in
"Expostulation and Reply," the wise passiveness that feeds
our minds results from accepting an inevitable necessity:

> The eye—it cannot choose but see;
> We cannot bid the ear be still;
> Our bodies feel, where'er they be,
> Against or with our will.

The mind, in other words, has a mind of its own. Even
Wordsworth's dedication to poetry, at a time when his
mind was a "strange rendezvous," was not of his own
making: he tells us in *The Prelude* IV that, seeing the sunrise after a night of adolescent merry-making during summer vacation:

My heart was full; I made no vows, but vows
Were then made for me; bond unknown to me
Was given, that I should be, else sinning greatly,
A dedicated Spirit.

(lines 341–44)

All these moments, whether from the major apocalyptic ecstasies, Wordsworth's purple passages, or from the humbler matters of *Lyrical Ballads*, make education seem uncontrollable and involuntary. Learning happens, largely, against or in spite of our will to learn. It is no wonder, then, that the analogy Wordsworth uses most frequently for reading, especially in childhood, is feeding, or more specifically, being fed.[16] Nature is a foster-mother; literature is a foster-mother (e.g., *The Excursion* IV, 584–85: "for the day's consumption, books may yield / Food not unwholesome"; or *The Prelude* V, 211–12: "ballad tunes, / Food for the hungry ears of little Ones"). Both sustain the dependent child, and ready him for independence, when he will have a "prepared mind." But when does apprenticeship end and mastery itself begin? When does man feed himself?[17]

Education is a metaphor for the individual's confrontation with any literary or experiential text,[18] and we might turn to Book V ("Books") of *The Prelude* to see whether any active, instead of passive, reading is possible. The answer of this book is a tentative no. Reading, like other modes of perception, begins for Wordsworth in passivity. As Auden's aphorism has it, we don't read a good book; it reads us. Proceeding as always from primary sensory data, Wordsworth combines the assumptions inherited from Locke and Hartley with the religious implications of quietism (e.g., Joseph Allison's assertion that "it is upon the vacant and the unemployed accordingly, that the objects of taste make the strongest impression").[19]

"Majestic indolence" (*The Prelude* VIII, 389), an almost trancelike unthinking state, precedes greater imaginative lessons and pleasures, even in the case of the Boy of Winander who, only at the moment of hypnotized silence after his bafflement, receives unawares the surrounding visible scene into his mind. But for all his education by nature, the boy dies. Whether Wordsworth wishes to impress upon his readers a Virgilian sense of *lacrimae rerum*, the powerlessness of all human endeavors against unconquerable mutability, or actually to intimate some punishment exacted of the boy (which is the dramatic effect of the passage) is unknowable. In either case, Wordsworth is preoccupied with the possible dangers and threats, as well as the rewards, of reading. Book V opens with his unexplained fears that books are themselves mutable, capable of being destroyed—as if to say, *ars brevis, brevis vita*:

> Oh! why hath not the mind
> Some element to stamp her image on
> In nature somewhat nearer to her own?
> Why, gifted with such powers to send abroad
> Her spirit, must it lodge in shrines so frail?
> (lines 44–48)

Richard Onorato suggests that the fear of a literary apocalypse is distinctly related to Wordsworth's own fear of mortality, but one hardly needs a Freudian reading of *The Prelude* to reach this conclusion.[20]

Although he claims that "this Verse is dedicate to Nature's self" (line 230), Wordsworth feels compelled to memorialize books and authors:

> It seemeth, in behalf of these, the works
> And of the Men who fram'd them, whether known,
> Or sleeping nameless in their scatter'd graves,
> That I should here assert their rights, attest
> Their honours; and should, once for all, pronounce
> Their benediction; speak of them as Powers
> For ever to be hallowed; only less,
> For what we may become, and what we need,
> Than Nature's self, which is the breath of God.
> (lines 214–22)

Nominally about books and education, Book V is an extended epitaph for the works of dead men, and for dead individuals like the Boy of Winander and Wordsworth's mother. The book alternates between a focus on sustenance and growth (literature as food in line 212; nature as teacher and text; the mother hen feeding her young in lines 246ff.; newfangled education as an unnatural feeding in lines 233–45)[21] and on the stasis of the dead. Wordsworth commemorates his own past as a text when he speaks of his present sadness in rereading poems that formerly moved him and "are now / Dead in my eyes as is a theatre / Fresh emptied of spectators" (lines 573–75). Literature is powerful to idealize and commemorate, but powerless to ensure its own eternity; man is fed by books that are then often emptied of sustenance for him. Wordsworth leaves off at his adolescence—the "later influence [of books] yet remains untold"—without telling how an adult can feed himself, rather than be fed by the act of reading.

Another answer to whether active reading is possible lies not in the grand moments of *The Prelude* nor in the visionary "poems of the imagination," but in some of Wordsworth's more ordinary moments and scenes. Although the opposite of the prepared mind is the "inattentive eye" (*The White Doe of Rylstone*, line 1009), which does not observe carefully, the poems also distinguish between two kinds of texts: easy and hard, inclusive and exclusive, the ones accessible to an entire community of readers, and those available only to a select few, which often require the intervening figure of the poet as teacher of a new language or symbology.

The easiest texts are, in fact, books themselves, or written language. Despite all his claims about the universality of our responses to nature, and despite Matthew Arnold's "natural" and simple Wordsworth, he finds in the natural world not only a threat to his own imaginative integrity but also a text often so recondite as to be confusing or incomprehensible. The most public texts are epitaphs, especially those in the later books of *The Excursion*, which dramatize, insofar as that poem is capable of dramatizing, the great society of the noble dead joined to the living who read of it. Wordsworth's essays on epitaphs, written in 1810, are in some ways his strongest, bravest defense of commonalty and communication, of his earlier poetic claim that "we have all of us one human heart." Like the Preface to *Lyrical Ballads*, these essays uphold, with some variation, Wordsworth's neoclassical bias. An epitaph, he says, must be cast in a lowest common denominator to avoid fiction, peculiarity, uniqueness—anything, in short, that would complicate the image of the deceased or try the mind of the reader: "The occasion of writing an Epitaph is matter of fact in its intensity, and forbids more authoritatively than any other species of composition all modes of fiction, except those which the very strength of passion has created" (*PrW* 2:76).

Like the books destined to perish in *The Prelude* V, gravestones and their engravings are susceptible to decay: "An epitaph is not a proud writing set up for the studious . . . it is concerning all, and for all:—in the churchyard it is open to the day; the sun looks down upon the stone, and the rains of heaven beat against it" (*PrW* 2:59). Created by man, and exposed to nature, the gravestone and the epitaph are a strong symbol of the synaesthetic bond between nature and literature described at the end of *The Prelude* V. Wordsworth's definition of correct funerary diction gives the link: "Language, if it do not uphold, and feed, and leave in quiet, like the power of gravitation or the air we breathe, is a counter-spirit, unremittingly and noiselessly at work to derange, to subvert, to lay waste, to vitiate, and to dissolve" (*PrW* 2:85).[22]

Since a country churchyard, with its family plots, creates and embodies a genius loci as a force to bind a community together and keep it open to influences from the past and the dead, it is only fitting that the language of epitaphs be natural and universal, "commonplace and even trite," consoling the halted traveler. Wordsworth criticizes the antitheses of Pope's epitaphs because they anatomize rather than simplify the characters of the dead; as an example of what he prefers, he concludes his third and final essay with the history of a deaf man, an account that eventually found its way into *The Excursion* (VII, 395–481). Although he claims that "there is nothing in the detail of the poem which is not either founded upon the Epitaph or gathered from enquiries concerning the Deceased made in the neighbourhood," Wordsworth has given us not an epitaph at all but a complete biography, almost one hundred lines of a portrait that, however complete and unified it seems, is suited only in spirit—not in fact—to the form he has been discussing.

We may wonder why he chooses this particular portrait for the end of his essay, and more generally, why he should end it with a history and not a genuine epitaph. To finish these essays, which concern the way reading and writing foster a spirit of community, Wordsworth has found a way to impress upon us the figure of an exemplary reader. The man is deaf to nature, but visually astute, isolated, but surrounded by a loving family. He proves how reading, as compensation for one kind of sensory deprivation, helps to integrate and satisfy the man who cannot see *and* hear the book of nature:

> When stormy winds
> Were working the broad bosom of the lake
> Into a thousand thousand sparkling waves,
> Rocking the trees, or driving cloud on cloud
> Along the sharp edge of yon lofty crags,
> The agitated scene before his eye
> Was silent as a picture: evermore
> Were all things silent, whereso'er he moved.
> (*The Excursion* VII, 409–16)

From books, "ready comrades whom he could not tire;/ Of whose society . . . [he] was never satiate" (lines 440–42), the man receives the satisfaction that other Wordsworthian characters achieve through love, imagination, or intercourse with nature:

> Their familiar voice,
> Even to old age, with unabated charm
> Beguiled his leisure hours; refreshed his thoughts;
> Beyond its natural elevation raised
> His introverted spirit; and bestowed
> Upon his life an outward dignity
> Which all acknowledged.
>
> (lines 442–48)

Now dead, he is commemorated both by his gravestone, which "unambitiously relates . . . in what pure contentedness of mind, / The sad privation was by him endured" (lines 473–76), and by the poet's more ambitious, expanded history. In death, moreover, he achieves a wholeness (characteristic of many of Wordsworth's dead figures, especially Lucy) denied him during life. The *spirit* of unity that Wordsworth demands of an epitaph is paralleled by the paradoxical "sounds" that the dead man should now, almost, be able to hear:

> —And yon tall pine-tree, whose composing sound
> Was wasted on the good Man's living ear,
> Hath now its own peculiar sanctity;
> And, at the touch of every wandering breeze,
> Murmurs, not idly, o'er his peaceful grave.
>
> (lines 477–81)

Death bestows meaning and fulfillment. Whereas the pine tree used to murmur "idly" because unheard, the line implies, it now touches the dead man's ears. Death symbolically returns a lost faculty, or more precisely, destroys and expands the limits of our human senses. More importantly, the finality of death completes a "character" and gives the reader—of poem or epitaph—a unified text for contemplation. Completed by death, the man becomes a static perfection. The dead are unchanging, like books themselves, whereas nature, like living human beings, always changes and thereby resists our ever fully reading and knowing it.

This history stresses as well the poet's role as an exemplary reader of nature itself. An epitaph is meant to keep alive the memory of the deceased; the Boy of Winander, even more than the deaf man, is commemorated, it seems, only by the perceiving eye of the poet, who succeeds in eternalizing the boy for his readers with a poem ("There was a boy") to the same degree that external reality has failed. Wordsworth contrasts his memory with the mindlessness of the statue of the Virgin who sits

> forgetful of this Boy
> Who slumbers at her feet; forgetful, too,
> Of all her silent neighbourhood of graves,
> And listening only to the gladsome sounds
> That, from the rural School ascending, play
> Beneath her and about her.
> *(The Prelude* V, 426–31)

Nature may never betray the heart that loves her, but this stone Virgin surely prefers the living to the dead.[23]

Printed texts are easier to read than the *liber naturae* that we all take pains to understand. Although nature may often seem to be an open book for Wordsworth, his favorite nooks and valleys, like secret texts, are hidden from the eye and easy to miss or dismiss. The purpose of inscriptions, like that of epitaphs, is to protect, to solidify by naming: only "the Intellect can raise, / From airy words alone, A Pile that ne'er decays" ("For a Seat in the Groves of Coleorton," *PW* 4:197). Despite the democratic disclaimers of the Preface to *Lyrical Ballads*, the audience for many of the tales and country commemoratives is small and privileged, as Wordsworth suggests in his Advertisement to "Poems on the Naming of Places":

> By persons resident in the country and attached to rural objects, many places will be found unnamed or of unknown names, where little Incidents must have occurred, or feelings been experienced, which will have given to such places a private and peculiar interest.
>
> *(PW* 2:111)

The manuscript motto for these same poems also insists on the selectiveness of the audience:

> Some minds have room alone for pageant stories,
> Some for strong passion flesh'd in action strong;
> Others find tales and endless allegories
> By river margins, and green woods among.
>
> (*PW* 2:486)

This preference for secluded places has as its corollary the difficulty of reading natural texts correctly. Those poems describing the bowers and valleys that have special meaning for a chosen few often dramatize acts of misreading and misinterpreting, for which the act of writing the poem is a corrective. In "A Narrow Girdle" (*PW* 2:115), for example, three strollers "sauntered on [a] retired and difficult way" one September morning, playing with the time, observing natural objects in "vacant mood." Suddenly, as in "A Night-Piece" or "I Wandered Lonely as a Cloud," they perceive "through a thin veil of glittering haze" a peasant, "angling beside the margin of the lake," whom they mistake for a delinquent laborer but who turns out to be, as they approach him, sick, lean and gaunt, attempting "to gain / A pittance from the dead unfeeling lake / That knew not of his wants." Their mistake causes a moment of "serious musing and self-reproach" and, "unwilling to forget that day," they

> called the place
> By a memorial name, uncouth indeed
> As e'er by mariner was given to bay
> Or foreland, on a new-discovered coast;
> And POINT RASH-JUDGMENT is the Name it bears.

Misreading, or misseeing, although not in Bloom's sense, is the necessary cause of naming and writing.

An even more striking case of misreading corrected by later understanding is "When to the Attractions of the Busy World" (*PW* 2:118–23). The poet, retired to Grasmere vale, explores increasingly deeper and more private spaces, which culminate in a grove of firs surrounding a single beech tree. He delightedly discovers this "cloistral place of refuge" but later disappointedly abandons it because the grove is too dense and affords him no space for wandering within. A visit from his sailor brother uncovers for him possibilities he had previously missed:

> By chance retiring from the glare of noon
> To this forsaken covert, there I found
> A hoary pathway traced between the trees,
> And winding on with such an easy line
> Along a natural opening, that I stood
> Much wondering how I could have sought in vain
> For what was now so obvious.

(lines 46–52)

His brother "had surveyed it with a finer eye," had read the inner depths and discovered a walking space. Meanwhile, having returned to the sea, the sailor is a "*silent* Poet," who joins all his senses in responding to Nature: he "from the solitude / Of the vast sea didst bring a watchful heart / Still couchant, an inevitable ear, / And an eye practised like a blind man's touch" (lines 80–83). The brothers are united by this secret place, a text that provides an invisible thread of contact between them when separated (like the one between Coleridge and Lamb in "This Lime-Tree Bower My Prison"). Wordsworth can now return to the favored grove, retrace his own and his brother's steps, and think hopefully that they are pacing, although apart, together.[24]

The most meaningful and exclusive of all texts is in "Michael." The thirty-nine–line introduction has received little critical attention; indeed, Jonathan Wordsworth has called it "a clumsy address to the reader."[25] But it is crucial, like the biography of the Pedlar in Book I of *The Excursion*, to the story that follows and to an understanding of Wordsworth's ambivalent feelings about reading. The lines emphasize a move from commonalty to privacy, ignorance to knowledge, hardship to comparative ease. The would-be reader must be an explorer, turning from the "public way" (as the poet did in "When to the Attractions of the Busy World") up into the mountains, which miraculously uncover "a hidden valley of their own." Within the hidden spot is no pastoral lushness or Lake District Shangri-la, but "an utter solitude," the standard bare Wordsworthian landscape, with objects that "you might pass by, / Might see, and notice not." The unfinished sheepfold, a simple thing, in fact contains a story, worthy of report by the poet not only for its own virtues but also for the incidental relation it has to his life: the tale, "while I was yet a Boy / Careless of books, yet having felt the power / Of Nature, by the gentle agency / Of natural objects, led me on to feel / For passions that were not my own" (lines 27–31). The story in stones has the same effect as tragic art: it fosters empathy with unseen or fictitious characters. In addition, by telling Michael's story, the poet assures his own immortality and a connection with his literary heirs "who among these hills / Will be my second self when I am gone" (lines 38–39). Unlike Michael, maker of the unfinished sheepfold, Wordsworth expects to have both offspring and a completed legacy to bequeath them. His attitude is paternal, patient, and revelatory to those able to penetrate to the hidden valley in the mountains and read the text he gives them. (Cf. his remark in *Letters, MY* 1:195: "I have not written down to the level of superficial observers and unthinking minds. . . . Every great Poet is a Teacher: I wish either to be considered as a Teacher, or as nothing.")[26]

Wordsworth also shows us how there can be a middle way, between reading as a passive act by which we receive letters and words imprinted on our minds, and reading as the exclusive province of the poet-namer or pathfinder who teaches us the signs of an otherwise unknowable language. "The rhetoric of interaction," Herbert Lindenberger's phrase for the balance in Wordsworth's greatest moments,[27] defines the critical interaction between mind and nature achieved during the ascent of Mt. Snowdon, when the poet can identify the effects of "mutual domination," an eternal tension like Blake's war between contraries. A similar transaction can be seen in voluntary acts of learning. Knowledge can be purchased without loss of power.

Wordsworth is the first poet to make of the joint collaboration of writer and reader a major theme rather than a technique: hence, the more than tautological perception that "poems, however humble in their kind . . . cannot read themselves" (*PrW* 3:29). They demand an interchange with the percipient eye of the reader. The Wanderer-Pedlar, in Book I of *The Excursion*, whose biography resembles Wordsworth's own in the early books of *The Prelude*, is Wordsworth's most accomplished reader. Never attaining full creative maturity—he is no poet—the Wanderer schools the narrator of the poem, himself ironically a Poet, in a correct reading of an encompassing landscape and Margaret's cottage. If we remember that all the major characters in *The Excursion* itself are aspects of their creator, we shall see how Wordsworth has successfully externalized, among other things, a demonstration of how one teaches oneself to read. The biography of the Wanderer, far from bifurcating Book I (originally *The Ruined Cottage*) into two unconnected narratives, is an exemplum of reading, just as the tale of Margaret is an exemplum of suffering.[28] "Reading," in fact, is the thread connecting the two halves of the poem.

Like Wordsworth's brother in "When to the Attractions of the Busy World," like Wordsworth himself in *The Prelude*, the Wanderer is by upbringing and habit sensitive to nature, whose objects are his earliest texts: impressions "lay / Upon his mind like substances" (lines 137–38), and as a child he turned "his ear and eye / On all things which the moving seasons brought / To feed such appetite" (lines 150–52) until he "attained / An active power to fasten images / Upon his brain" (lines 144–46). Consequently, books are initially only supplements to a ready supply of sermons in stones. Martyrologies, romances, the Bible, Milton, and geometry are his literary texts (a list almost identical to Wordsworth's own in *The Prelude* V). Books and nature complement each other: "Early had he learned / To reverence the volume that displays / The mystery, the life which cannot die; / But in the mountains did he *feel* his faith" (lines 223–26). He buys his volume of Milton at a town bookstall but he reads it, as if it were the sun itself, in the mountains: "Among the hills / He gazed upon that mighty orb of song, / The divine Milton" (lines 248–50).

A schoolmaster supplies geometry texts to help the boy pass an idle hour by imposing formal theorems on surrounding natural data that "clothed the nakedness of austere truth" (line 269). What he learns comes to life only when he applies it to the external world:

> His triangles—they were the stars of heaven,
> The silent stars! Oft did he take delight
> To measure the altitude of some tall crag
> That is the eagle's birthplace, or some peak
> Familiar with forgotten years, that shows
> Inscribed upon its visionary sides,
> The history of many a winter storm,
> Or obscure records of the path of fire.
> (lines 272–79)

By measuring altitudes, he reads both natural and literary texts and, not by chance, traces still another text in the vestiges of weather and disasters. The harmony of interaction—passivity merging into activity, abstraction into concreteness, potentiality into actuality, and impression into expression—rings in the biography's most moving lines. Watching the sunrise, sensing the cosmic unity between sky and earth and ocean, the growing youth is both spectator and participant:

> Far and wide the clouds were touched,
> And in their silent faces could he read
> Unutterable love. Sound needed none,
> Nor any voice of joy; his spirit drank

The spectacle: sensation, soul, and form,
All melted into him; they swallowed up
His animal being; in them did he live,
And by them did he live; they were his life.
(lines 203–10)[29]

From his possession by natural harmony and his reading of an unutterable script, the young Pedlar advances to new texts: he sees men, their passions and feelings, which "speak a plainer language" in rural scenes. He responds empathically to poverty and suffering. The love and absorption, through reading, of nature lead inevitably to fellow-feeling, a love of man, and to an "untamed eye" which "he had wondrous skill / To blend with knowledge of the years to come, / Human, or such as lie beyond the grave" (lines 431–33). In a passage originally intended for *The Ruined Cottage* and later revised for Book IV of *The Excursion*, Wordsworth generalizes from this paradigmatic figure to show how absorption, contemplation, and, at last, active intellection, evince both moral responsibility and understanding:

> Nor shall we meet an object but may read
> Some sweet and tender lesson to our minds
> Of human suffering or of human joy.
> All things shall speak of Man, and we shall read
> Our duties in all forms, and general laws
> And local accidents shall tend alike
> To quicken and to rouze
> (*PW* 5:401; cf. *The Excursion* IV, 1235–48)

It is a lesson of human suffering that the story of Margaret dramatizes and, significantly, it is the Wanderer, that paragon of readers, who teaches it to us, through the figure of the Poet-Narrator, a man who may possess the advantages "of culture and the inspiring aid of books" (line 83) but who, nevertheless, requires an advanced reading course. This is what the "tale" in the poem provides. Like the narrator of "Michael," the Wanderer is a memorialist: he explicates unnoticed natural objects and teaches their meanings. He claims that "'tis a common tale, / An ordinary sorrow of man's life, / A tale of silent suffering, hardly clothed / In bodily form" (lines 636–39), but he clothes the austerity, indeed the invisibility, of truth with the garb of language, representing Margaret to us, and re-dressing her naked walls and her bare suffering.

Cognition and recognition are the substance of the poem; repetition and reenactment are its dramatic form. The Poet is schooled in tragic art by listening to Margaret's biography; he is refreshed, literally by the well-water that the Wanderer, repeating the hospitality offered by Margaret of old, points him to, and spiritually by the lesson he has learned (in the original Coleridgean ending, the narrator rises "a wiser and a better man," like the Wedding-Guest). Even the poem's topographical details support these central themes. The first seventeen lines paint a picture of summer ease and indolence, dappling cloud-shadows and cooling cave-moss, as seen by a dreaming observer who is sheltered within the recesses of a cave from the heat of noon. This aesthetic and distanced perspective is not at all, we learn suddenly, the lot of the speaker, toiling "across a bare wide Common," on slippery turf, plagued by heat, thirst, and buzzing insects. A man in want of refreshment, he arrives at what seems at first an unlikely "port"—a roofless hut, four naked walls, and the "gloom" of an elm grove, the agreed-on rendezvous with his friend, whom he encountered the day before in the village. Since no reason is given for the Wanderer's selection of this spot for their meeting, we can assume that he intends, from the first, to instruct the young poet, and that Wordsworth is careful, also, to show that this lesson is the product of toil, discomfort, and not mere pastoral lolling about in "the light of things." It is the Wanderer who, we now learn, has found comfort in "covert," not in the imagined cave of line 11, but upon the cottage bench of the real scene. Far from being pestered by heat and insects, he is "for travel unimpaired" and at the same time "recumbent in the shade, as if asleep" (lines 34–36). Qualified for hardship, he knows also how to avoid it.[30]

As Wordsworth bequeaths "Michael" as legacy to his poet-heirs, so the Wanderer ensures his immortality by educating the Poet who now, reciprocally, records in verse "some small portion of his eloquent speech." And both will be requited:

> I will here record in verse;
> Which, if with truth it correspond, and sink
> Or rise as venerable Nature leads,
> The high and tender Muses shall accept
> With gracious smile, deliberately pleased,
> And listening Time reward with sacred praise.
>
> (lines 102–7)

It was the Wanderer who, years earlier, singled out the young boy from his friends for instruction in "abstrusest matter" and for nourishment with old songs and sweet sounds, "feeding the soul, and eagerly imbibed / As cool refreshing water." And it is he who points the direction, significantly out of "the public way," like the landscape of "Michael," to "a well / Shrouded with willow flowers and plumy fern." The summoning of the dead, for the sake of nourishing the living, has begun.

The Wanderer's opening words may strike us as gnomic, if not positively oracular: "I see around me here / Things which you cannot see" (lines 469–70). His tale begins with the evidence of physical decay, the shrouded well, "the useless fragment of a wooden bowl," emblems of the silent sympathies that unite people to places and then dissolve with the death of one, the neglect of the other. The bond between landscape and its human caretaker is, in fact, the same as that of reader and text: gardens, however humble, cannot tend themselves, and "very soon / Even of the good is no memorial left." Like the books in *The Prelude* V, man's self-begotten efforts at immortality, cottage and garden are doomed to perish: "She is dead, / The light extinguished of her lonely hut, / The hut itself abandoned to decay, / And she forgotten in the quiet grave" (lines 507–10). Lest she be completely forgotten so soon the Pedlar now rehearses the story of Margaret's abandonment, despair, malingering hope, and gradual fading into death. In so doing, he reknits with his audience the "bond of brotherhood" that was unraveled by Margaret's death and the ruin of her land.

The Poet's response to the tale progresses from passiveness to active participation, just as reading itself, whether in the library or upon a mountain top, moves from the impression of sensory data and the absorption of nourishing details to an active, imaginative grappling with them. For this reason the tale is broken midway (line 605). We observe its effect on the listener who, because of the mingled mildness and solemnity of the teller, temporarily forgets it. Unawares, he is simultaneously affected by it—like the Boy of Winander at his moment of bafflement, or the speaker in "Resolution and Independence," hypnotized by the magical presence and delivery of the leech-gatherer:

> that simple tale
> Passed from my mind like a forgotten sound.
> A while on trivial things we held discourse,
> To me soon tasteless. In my own despite,
> I thought of that poor Woman as of one
> Whom I had known and loved.
> (lines 609–14)

Nothing will satisfy him now but the rest of the story, as he matches the "active countenance" and the "eye so busy" of the teller, which make present, as they represent, "the things of which he spake." Only art can comfort and relieve the "heart-felt chillness" that it alone has aroused:

> I rose; and, having left the breezy shade,
> Stood drinking comfort from the warmer sun,

> That had not cheered me long—ere, looking round
> Upon that tranquil Ruin, I returned,
> And begged of the old Man that, for my sake,
> He would resume his story.
>
> (lines 620–25)

Empathy and curiosity, chill and excitement, the Poet's responses in the middle of the story, are replaced at the end by the catharsis of tragedy:[31] by weakness, inarticulateness, and the "impotence of grief" in which he silently blesses Margaret "with a brother's love." Having made his own peace with the dead, the Poet is capable of an independent act of reading:

> Then towards the cottage I returned; and traced
> Fondly, though with an interest more mild,
> That secret spirit of humanity
> Which, 'mid the calm oblivious tendencies
> Of nature, 'mid her plants, and weeds, and flowers,
> And silent overgrowings, still survived.
>
> (lines 925–30)

The deep truth is imaged for him; he has mentally cleared away the unkempt, unpruned evidence of disorder with which nature has confounded the reader.

Sensing his friend's achievement as well as his pain, the Wanderer now dismisses sorrow and grief, consoling the Poet with an assurance of finality: we shall find our peace as Margaret has found hers. Reciprocity is, once again, the note struck: "Why then should we read / The forms of things with an unworthy eye?" (lines 939–40), he asks, before delivering his famous benediction over the dead woman. Great art redeems and ennobles us, much as Margaret has been redeemed by the mere act of remembrance and learning at which Wanderer and Poet have jointly labored. Even the landscape participates in the new "worth" that results from this peacefulness. What were weeds and overgrowings are now emblems of natural harmony instead of neglect, as the Wanderer recalls his own earlier achievement:

> She sleeps in the calm earth, and peace is here.
> I well remember that those very plumes,
> Those weeds, and the high spear-grass on that wall,
> By mist and silent rain-drops silvered o'er,
> As once I passed, into my heart conveyed
> So still an image of tranquillity.
>
> (lines 941–46)

Nature and art continue to support one another at the poem's end. Margaret has been commemorated by the telling of her tale and by the learning of it; the Poet has been trained in reading the forms of things with a worthy eye and in empathizing with human frailty; the setting has been relieved of much of its barrenness by the vision of the two men, who prove the assertion of a later Romantic poet, Whitman, that "the process of reading is not a half-sleep, but, in highest sense, an exercise, a gymnast's struggle."[32]

Finally, the larger landscape itself is transformed from the unattractive, indeed treacherous threat it presented initially to the toiling Poet. Reminding us of the end of "Lycidas," another poem where artistic commemoration and human faith effect a redemption of the living and the dead, Wordsworth closes Book I with "the sun declining," its "mellow radiance" a foretaste of the sober coloring of another famous sun in the Intimations Ode (and a balance to the setting sun that the Pedlar was watching when the Poet encountered him the day before). The two men, now "admonished" by the sweet harmonies of evening and its population, rise to return to their village inn. Silent themselves, like the "silent walls," which they regard once more, they walk, the Wanderer "with sprightly mien / Of hopeful preparation," quite literally to fresh woods and pastures new in the remaining books of The Excursion. By learning to read with an eye keen to the hidden worth of things, the Poet has made himself worthy of his future career, one which will resemble, we assume, the career of

Wordsworth as we know it, not in Matthew Arnold's portrait of an artless, styleless poet, but in Walter Pater's picture of a hierophantic Wordsworth, the reading of whom is

> an excellent sort of training towards the things of art and poetry. It begets . . . a habit of reading between the lines, a faith in the effect of concentration and collectedness of mind in the right appreciation of poetry, an expectation of things, in this order, coming to one by the means of a right discipline of the temper as well as of the intellect. He meets us with the promise that he has much, and something very peculiar, to give us, if we will follow a certain difficult way, and seems to have the secret of a special and privileged state of mind. And those who have undergone his influence . . . are like people who have passed through some initiation, a *disciplina arcani.*[33]

The reading *of* Wordsworth proves exactly what the reading *in* Wordsworth does: that art teaches us how to live. Art that is both educative and elegiac is the highest: to read and comprehend its language and lessons is a noble and humanizing achievement.

3

Children:
Prophecy and Nostalgia

Childhood came of age in the nineteenth century, according to the sociologists and historians, and it did so through
the encouragement of poets.[1] Throughout the Renaissance
and most of the eighteenth century, children were depicted
in poetry only as objects to be mourned (Ben Jonson's elegies) or as symbols of Christian innocence. The eerie eroti-
cism of Marvell's "Picture of Little T. C. in a Prospect of
Flowers" stands out as exceptional. But in the works of
Wordsworth and Blake, among others, children figure in
spectacularly new ways. Indeed, Wordsworth is the pre-
eminent poet of childhood, the first poet to plumb the
depths and contradictions of a condition that was, before
him, largely ignored or passed over with condescending
Christian pieties. That childhood has attained a special status in our own century owes as much to the imaginings of
Wordsworth as to those of Freud.

To talk of Wordsworth's children as heroic figures, or
even as fully real creatures, is to raise certain difficult questions about their status—ontological, psychological, and
symbolic—within his poetry. Childhood epitomizes the
two principal dimensions of his poetic temper: the nostal-
gic and the prophetic. Moreover, unlike his ideas about old
age, which changed as Wordsworth reached the fullness of
maturity and the prospect of death, his feelings for and
treatments of childhood do not conform to any simple
chronological pattern. After his legitimate children were
born, starting with John in 1803, his feelings about chil-

dren were strongly focused but not poetically different from those of the prepaternal poetry. The losses of Catharine and Thomas added new poignancy to his naturally elegiac temperament, and after the death in 1847 of his beloved Dora, no longer young but still his child, he wrote no more poetry.

Yet even in his poetic beginnings Wordsworth granted to childhood special honors. Indeed, no other subject occupies such a range of generic territory: in first-person narratives, from *The Prelude* to slighter lyric reminiscences; in direct addresses to unresponsive, largely objectified infants; in descriptive lyrics based on travel incidents; in dramatic encounters with speaking children; and in the theoretical expostulations favored by the characters in *The Excursion*, children are nowhere far from the adult's memory or attention. Wordsworth's original contribution to the poetry of childhood was his uncanny ability to present the joys and perils of another life, one from which any adult is invariably separated yet which he has experienced distantly, and to weigh the loss against the gain without doing damage to the quite legitimate emotional claims of adults over children, however unbridgeable seems the gap between them.

Because they are the fathers of his men, Wordsworth's children are his first heroic figures, whom he invests with the heaviest symbolic trappings, which may seem ill-fitting, excessive, or unfashionable to contemporary tastes. In the period of childhood we can see the clearest images of some of the poet's abiding uncertainties concerning human life and growth. Wordsworth arranges his children, much as he does his adults, along the entire spectrum of human activity, from lively animation, playfulness, and doing, to tranquillity, sleep, and death. Even though he attributes to the child unique powers ("mighty prophet," "seer blest," "best philosopher"—all the exceptional apostrophes of the Intimations Ode), he alternately appeals to our sense of the organic continuity between infancy and adulthood. By leading off his series "Poems Referring to the Period of Childhood" with "My Heart Leaps Up," the poet insists upon his hopeful attempt to bind together two different selves even if conditionally: "And I could wish my days to be / Bound each to each with natural piety."[2]

Wordsworth projects upon his children either the condition of moral innocence, which he derives from both Lockean epistemology and Christian commonplaces, or of magical potency that the years will strive to abate. The self proceeds from richness to impoverishment of experience, or exactly the other way around, from depletion to fullness. Lastly, he conceives of childhood either as a Herculean power in a cradle, transferred later into boyhood activity, sometimes mock-heroic or marginally criminal, or as passive dependence, suffering, and weakness.[3] The first image is Wordsworth's response to the ideals of classical heroism that are never far from his mind when he thinks of simple "doing"; the second to Christian suffering and meditative calm, the very ground trod by all the stoics and endurers in his poetry.

We might begin with a characteristic poem, although one not popular with modern readers, the "Address to My Infant Daughter, Dora, on Being Reminded that She Was a Month Old That Day, September 16." The specific, and loquacious, ordinariness of the title belies the poem's probable debt to Virgil's fourth eclogue, the one poem that may have stood as an inspiration, if not an exact source, for Wordsworth's inflation of infancy. In this most unpastoral of poems, Virgil achieves the very union of tenderness and imagination that Wordsworth ascribes admiringly to Milton, in an 1801 letter to Charles Lamb (*EY*, p. 316). Paul Alpers has shown how certain elements of mystery, such as the identity of the real child, are deliberate and functional in the poem, where Virgil "consciously makes the child emblematic or mythical: that is, the birth and growth of a child represent the nature, value, and human proportions of the new age that the poem desires and foretells."[4]

Finding in Virgil a spiritual and intellectual mentor,

Wordsworth refrains from making large claims for a new golden age or for large sweeps of historical progress. Nevertheless, he uses the same mixture of sublime and commonplace tones that characterize Virgil's peculiar song; but where Virgil often sings of lofty things in a personal manner, Wordsworth simply reverses his predecessor's arrangement and elevates the ordinary to the level of the heroic. He even manages a nod, but nothing more, toward Virgilian historical cycles and evolutionary progress when he compares his daughter's condition with that of her "unblest coevals," Indian children born in the wilds, "Where fancy hath small liberty to grace / The affections, to exalt them or refine." For Wordsworth, the progress of civilization is measured by the growth of tender sympathies, not by the charting of empire. Included among "Poems of the Fancy" because of its organizing metaphors, the "Address" could stand as comfortably among the "Poems of the Affections."

Inflated in diction, the poem attempts to plot a path midway between grandeur and weakness for its central human and symbolic figure. The opening finds the father a little surprised that his child has even lasted so long:

> ——————Hast thou then survived——
> Mild Offspring of infirm humanity,
> Meek Infant! among all forlornest things
> The most forlorn—one life of that bright star,
> The second glory of the Heavens?—Thou hast
> (lines 1–5)

And the note immediately swells to one at once more pessimistic and more imperial:

> Already hast survived that great decay,
> That transformation through the wide world felt,
> And by all nations.[5]
> (lines 6–8)

But although the first section of the poem (lines 1–39) proceeds to distinguish the advantages of a "modern" baby, raised indoors where mother love rather than astronomical calculation can figure its age, the second part (lines 40–65) develops an elaborate comparison between child and moon, "to enliven in the mind's regard / Thy passive beauty." It is not only the child who is passive, however. By conferring metaphor as a gift, the father naturally animates both the infant and his own mind, which initially was as passive as the child. His initial exclamation and question indicate a forgetfulness in the adult, who himself must be jogged from his reverie into waking thoughts. The child occasions reflection.

In the extended simile, the poet first bequeaths to his daughter a superior position: both girl and moon are bright and sinless, but the moon ranges the heavens continually, "impatient of the shape she wears," whereas the baby, secure in a foreknowledge (which her father has projected upon her) that "one journey" alone will define her human life, sleeps contentedly. Suddenly the comparison undergoes (line 60) one of those manic-depressive peripeteias that make Wordsworth's transitions seem desperate even when they are natural and inevitable. The image, like the very moon on which it focuses, is undone:

> Alas! full soon
> Hath this *conception*, grateful to behold,
> Changed countenance, like an object sullied o'er
> By breathing mist; and thine appears to be
> A mournful labor, while to her is given
> Hope, and a renovation without end.
> (lines 60–65, emphasis mine)

An ambiguous reference creates a tense but perfect dialectical balance here. "Conception" is at once the daughter, who has frowned in her sleep—elsewhere she is addressed personally, never conceptualized as a distant item of the poet's mind—and the idea within the poet's imagination. Simultaneously, the simile in lines 62–63 recalls the earlier description of the moon itself, which "through gathered clouds / Mov[ed] untouched in silver purity" (lines 48–49).

The power of fancy that responds to, and yet also confers meaning upon, the sleeping child offers a double perspective on infant weakness and strength. Just as the child requires parental sustenance for survival, so she also seems to need adult poetic "conceiving" for the beginning of her relational identity; at the same time, the baby occasions the "conception" within her father's now active brain. A reciprocal, even a courteous, form of courting has developed, and the poem turns once more, in its conclusion (lines 66–78), to a double schooling: the baby's smiles, reminiscent of those of Virgil's boy at the end of the fourth eclogue, reassure the father that "heaven cheers / Thy loneliness" (does he means "cheers" as "mitigates" or as "encourages"?), while the poet blesses his daughter with hopeful prospects.

Still, his mental seesawing creates another poetic uncertainty; watching his daughter smile, he "reads" the effect in complementary ways. Either the smiles are signs of Heaven's pledge of support, or else perhaps, he wonders, their origin is from within. Might they be called

> Feelers of love, put forth as if to explore
> This untried world, and to prepare thy way
> Through a strait passage intricate and dim?
> (lines 72–74)

The genitive in English is always our amplest case, and "feelers of love" may be construed as either objective or subjective, as the feeling invoked is either responsive or self-creating. Ending, as he so often does, with the heightened language of eighteenth-century personification, Wordsworth reads Dora's smiles as tokens that in the future will be acknowledged by, and serve to provoke, Joy and Reason themselves. The moon has given way to the beams of the sun, in the finest and least insistent touch of all: Dora's smiles "are beginning, like the beams of dawn, /

To shoot and circulate." The poem, which began by awakening the adult's consciousness, ends with the dawning of a child's life.

A child, as Wordsworth says in "Michael," "more than all other gifts / That earth can offer to declining man, / Brings hope with it, and forward-looking thoughts." In Wordsworth's poetry, all children are gifts, as his Dora's resonant name suggests, and all adults are declining. Wordsworth's children often stimulate the presentation of that wisdom granted by bodily decrepitude, either dramatically, in those half-comic attempts to reason with the young where it is the teacher who is schooled ("We are Seven," "Anecdote for Fathers"), or else symbolically in their provocation of imaginative energy within the adult's discerning mind.

Wordsworth persistently considers maturity as both a fall from childhood integrity and a growth from relative emptiness to the fullness of the philosophic mind.[6] Even when addressing an actual child, his mind is capable of the most radical shifts in mood, as untoward thoughts and anxieties flood in. The "Address to Dora" is one example of a speculative balancing act: the poet goes through several versions of a metaphor until he finally accommodates himself to a positive one.[7] In an address to another child, written two years earlier and echoing the immediately preceding "Resolution and Independence," Wordsworth combines a ready glorification of childhood with his compulsive fears of growth and mortality.

What is most striking about "To H. C.," the address to the six-year-old Hartley Coleridge, is what is omitted. The poem begins with ten irregular lines of rapt, ecstatic apostrophe to a creature who seems only marginally earthly, before it settles with a thudding transition into its main subject: "O blessed vision! happy child! / Thou art so exquisitely wild, / I think of thee with many fears / For what may be thy lot in future years" (lines 11–14). As so often in such cases, Wordsworth mourns himself, not his ostensible subject. The child, whatever symbolic or emotional value Wordsworth has invested him with, becomes a mirror of the poet's worst fears. He reads his own fate projected elsewhere, while simultaneously depicting the vast distances between youth and maturity.

The tense shifts strangely at line 15 as the poet fears for the boy in the same way he worried about his own future in "Resolution and Independence":

> I thought of times when Pain might be thy guest,
> Lord of thy house and hospitality;
> And Grief, uneasy Lover! never rest
> But when she sate within the touch of thee.

Evidently confusing the boy with his father, or with himself, the poet snaps himself out of his sick fancies and blind thoughts by refocusing on the delicate living child before him. The only possibilities for Hartley's life, Wordsworth now asserts, are either instant death ("Nature will either end thee quite") or the almost unnatural prolongation of childhood's privileged joys:

> Or, lengthening out thy season of delight,
> Preserve for thee, by individual right,
> A young lamb's heart among the full-grown flocks.
> What has thou to do with sorrow,
> Or the injuries of to-morrow?
>
> (lines 22–25)

The one possibility deliberately denied the child is ordinary human growth; it is mysteriously important for Wordsworth to keep the little H. C. in a state of extended childhood, or else to release him. Although parents are unable to grant full adulthood to their own children, Hartley is another's child. Still more striking, the poet desperately dehumanizes a child no longer an infant, but a fully active six-year-old:

> Thou art a dew-drop, which the morn brings forth,
> . . . .
> A gem that glitters while it lives,

And no forewarning gives;
But, at the touch of wrong, without a strife
Slips in a moment out of life
                              (lines 27–33)

Poised between the views of childhood offered by "Blest the Infant Babe" (*The Prelude* II, 236–75) and other hopeful autobiographical passages, and the degenerative view partly entertained by the Intimations Ode, "To H. C." looks at the child as a fragile, precious vessel, unprepared for the weight of the world or its moral abuses.[8] Why, we might ask, does Wordsworth not offer this child the sensible, third alternative, of growing *into* life instead of being crushed by it? As when watching his infant Dora in her cradle, Wordsworth must have been struck by the remoteness of childhood and infancy from the rest of our days. At about the same time he wrote this poem, on a four-week holiday at Calais with Dorothy to visit Annette Vallon and his French daughter Caroline, Wordsworth expressed a fatherly interest, which continued throughout his life, in his child, still accented with feelings about her remoteness:

It is a beauteous evening, calm and free,
The holy time is quiet as a Nun
Breathless with adoration; the broad sun
Is sinking down in its tranquillity;
The gentleness of heaven broods o'er the Sea:
Listen! the mighty Being is awake,
And doth with his eternal motion make
A sound like thunder—everlastingly.
Dear Child! dear Girl! that walkest with me here,
If thou appear untouched by solemn thought,
Thy nature is not therefore less divine:
Thou liest in Abraham's bosom all the year;
And worshipp'st at the Temple's inner shrine,
God being with thee when we know it not.

The same motif recurs in the sonnet and the address to Hartley: both children are "untouched," in the one case by "solemn thought," and in the other by wrong (just as three years earlier Lucy "could not feel / The touch of earthly years"). Like Dora and Hartley, Caroline is bundled up in paradox: frivolous and thoughtless on the one hand, divine and devout on the other; active and playful, but also symbolically dead ("Thou liest in Abraham's bosom all the year"), and finally offered a consolation that is, strictly speaking, illogical and unwarranted: "God being with thee when we know it not." Does the poet claim extraordinary knowledge for himself denied to other mortals? Does he wish to console himself, not his daughter, because of the inevitable variance between appearance and reality? Is he recalling us to the necessity of faith? Even when blessing what the Intimations Ode labels "Delight and Liberty, the simple creed / Of Childhood," Wordsworth sees childhood fragility ambiguously as itself a kind of entrapment, and childhood, like any unthinking child himself, always represents for the poet a throwback to a simpleminded, however worthy, nostalgia that suckles pagans and moderns alike. We must not apotheosize the personal or historical past by projecting upon it a strength that the present lacks. Wordsworth remains simultaneously forward-looking and memory-laden.

From the very start of his poetic career, Wordsworth also understands childhood, in spite of its deathly blessedness, as the beginning of potential criminality.[9] The famous reminiscences in Books I and II of *The Prelude*, attempting to do justice to the child's unbridled freedom and active course, paint the lawlessness of his pursuits, as does "Nutting," originally intended for *The Prelude* but published separately and finding its ultimate place among the "Poems of the Imagination," as if to prove the correlation between the moral sense and childhood pleasures of stealth and rapine. Although Wordsworth wrote poems about all three of his daughters, he curiously wrote none about his sons, even Thomas who died at six in 1812. This is due perhaps to his view of childhood "action" as predominantly masculine, and associated thereby with his own life rather than with those of others.

In the final series of "Poems Referring to the Period of Childhood," "My Heart Leaps Up" is followed by "To a Butterfly," in which the contemplative adult recalls his dangerously active youth. The boy is the primitive destroyer; his sister holds the restraining and charitable hand of natural piety:

> A very hunter did I rush
> Upon the prey:—with leaps and springs
> I followed on from brake to bush;
> But she, God love her! feared to brush
> The dust from off its wings.[10]

The butterfly itself is now the historian of the poet's infancy, reviving the dead times and reminding him of past action. The mature adult, having been chastened, invokes both the insect and the past it represents; now that he has given up collecting butterflies, he can, pathetically, only recollect and importune them. The butterfly, a former victim, gets its revenge by abandoning the adult to his nostalgias.

Both in remembering his own youth and in depicting that of others, Wordsworth succeeds simultaneously in reviving and removing the spirit of humanity from his children.[11] He continually blurs the line between life and death, not only because it may be easier to love the dead than the living, but also because the permanent gulf between past and present selves forces memory to bridge it more strenuously even as time irrevocably enlarges it. As a past life, childhood holds the seeds for present action; and as a present reality—as in an adult's meetings with living children—it often bears unique evidence of human dignity. Childhood's resonant ambiguity makes its own claims on the adult's ideas of heroism.

❦

Children as objects of lyric description and observation occupy a major subgenre in Wordsworth's poetry. They are often different from those who appear unresponsively in apostrophic poems ("Address to My Infant Daughter," "It Is a Beauteous Evening"), or from the young Wordsworth in autobiographical verse. Whether energetic and buoyant, or dependent and tranquil, these children all bear marks of a ghostly fatality, a grandeur fated to die. In a short piece from his middle years, "Characteristics of a Child Three Years Old" (1811), written about Catharine Wordsworth a year before her death, Wordsworth tries to write a poem of definition, which turns into the literary equivalent of an eighteenth-century portrait. Generalization is his rule; specific detail and clear visualization are reserved for the metaphors and the natural landscape rather than for the human subject. The child is lost, so to speak, among the natural images that pretend to reveal her. Beginning with adjectives, proceeding to abstraction, Wordsworth's technique distances us from the girl and even seems to separate her from her own activity:

> Loving she is, and tractable, though wild;
> And Innocence hath privilege in her
> To dignify arch looks and laughing eyes;
> And feats of cunning; and the pretty round
> Of trespasses, affected to provoke
> Mock-chastisement and partnership in play.
> (lines 1–6)

Childhood play *is* play; there is something artificial or imitative about it (cf. stanza 7 of the Intimations Ode), as there is about the chastisement with which the delighted onlooker will wag a finger at the girl. We must wait until line 13 for the child to do something, to take action, here tied to a self-sufficient happiness, the Miltonic overtones of which portend the dangerous fragility of blithesomeness:

> And, as a faggot sparkles on the hearth,
> Not less if unattended and alone
> Than when both young and old sit gathered round
> And take delight in its activity;
> Even so this happy Creature of herself

Is all-sufficient; solitude to her
Is blithe society, who fills the air
With gladness and involuntary songs.
(lines 7–14)

The final movement, attempting to render the girl's light sallies in play, stresses their unsubstantiality more than their mere frivolity:

Light are her sallies as the tripping fawn's
Forth-startled from the fern where she lay couched;
Unthought-of, unexpected, as the stir
Of the soft breeze ruffling the meadow-flowers,
Or from before it chasing wantonly
The many-coloured images imprest
Upon the bosom of a placid lake.
(lines 15–21)

By the end, the child moves actively in an otherwise tranquil natural setting but is herself responsive to the wind's pressure, which comes, it seems, from behind her, impelling her lithe body forward even as it rustles and unsettles the previously stilled images on the lake. She is both of the landscape and apart from it.

This combination of delicacy and disruption makes the girl into a later, although younger, version of the Boy of Winander, himself mimicking the calls of owls to fetch a counterresponse from them, and associated like the girl with a humanized natural scene that at once subsumes and distinguishes the human presence:

the visible scene
Would enter unawares into his mind,
With all its solemn imagery, its rocks,
Its woods, and that uncertain Heaven, receiv'd
Into the bosom of the steady Lake.
(The Prelude V, 409–13)

Comparable disappearances occur in these two passages: in "The Boy of Winander," Wordsworth doubles the absorptions and reflections (a heaven received into the bosom of the lake is received into the boy's mind), and he ambiguously emphasizes the reciprocity of absorption ("his mind with all *its* solemn imagery"), as the boy himself becomes a deeper part of the landscape.

In "Characteristics of a Child," the similes "light as" and "unexpected as" promise a rhetorical balance that is denied in favor of a more complex animation. The first noun phrase ("light as a fawn's") with its passive participle ("startled") gives way to a longer and more active construction ("the stir . . . ruffling . . . chasing"), which ends in the stillness of the lake. The major activity, presented only at the poem's end, and at one remove owing to the similes, reduces itself to tranquillity, disappearance, an eerie reminder of final calm. "Unthought-of" gives us, perhaps, the child's point of view, while "unexpected" gives only the adult's perspective on child or breeze; the paradoxical conjunction of wanton chasing and placid lake in the last three lines, jarred ever so slightly by the phrase "from before it," makes the child into an unconscious co-conspirator in some frivolous but darksome interruption. Burial never seems far from Wordsworth's mind when he looks at water.

Nor, for that matter, is death far from his mind when he looks at children. This response may be an inevitable one during an age when infant mortality was an expected fact of life, but in Wordsworth's images of childhood it is also something more. The three-year-old girl and the eleven-year-old boy were both to die, one in life, the other in his own commemorative poem, yet even in life an insubstantiality clings to them that makes their deaths seem mysterious rather than grisly. When we consider other dead children in Wordsworth's poetry, this death-in-life posture stands out even more prominently. Aligning nostalgia with an acceptance of present hardship, his *Kindertotenlieder* are a different genre from the elegies, classical or Christian, of his predecessors.

"The Danish Boy" is the most chilling of these; if a single grammatical or imagistic turn kept the girl and boy in the two previous poems eerily unrealized, then the Danish Boy is, from start to finish, a macabre figure as well as a child of comforting calm. Within a sacral, secluded dell, close by a tempest-stricken tree and the last stone of a lonely hut, walks the eternal "shadow of a Danish boy," something visible and present. As genius of this solitary place, the Danish Boy survives as "a spirit of noon-day" yet "seems a form of flesh and blood." But as a noon spirit, he must be naturally shadowless, and even as a shadow his visibility is compromised by his bodilessness. And yet he seems to be alive. Throughout the five stanzas, Wordsworth insistently develops the boy's thoroughgoing duality—seen but unseen, attractive yet repellent (he is the darling and joy of flocks upon the neighboring hill, but his own dell houses no beast or bird of its own), and associated with a pastoral enclosure at once desolate and deathly.

From his opening immortality but corporeal uncertainty ("in this dell you see / A thing no storm can e'er destroy, / The shadow of a Danish Boy") through the intermediary animating details that flesh him out, the Danish Boy, a solitary singer, is progressively enlivened and simultaneously removed from humanity: "From bloody deeds his thoughts are far; / And yet he warbles songs of war, / That seem like songs of love." His *thoughts* are far from *deeds*, and his songs are of blood but seem just the opposite. He is the presiding genius of ambivalences, the most bizarre of which, his own ontological uncertainty, comes at the end in a simile:

> For calm and gentle is his mien;
> Like a dead Boy he is serene.

This last line is a shocking provocation. Do we hear it as an affirmation of his spectral immortality (he is serene, as any dead boy would be)? Or, is Wordsworth startling us with a blurring of our normal categories of perception (this living boy possesses all the gentleness we usually associate with a corpse)?

Living or dead, visible or invisible, militant or lyric, the

Danish Boy defies our knowing him. He lacks centrality. Wordsworth's fondness for marginal figures nowhere finds surer portraits than in his children. For an adult, from one perspective, all children are dead since they recall his former life, now buried; he then can project his sense of his own pastness onto the very living creature who has rudely provoked him to remember it. Especially when in repose, the Wordsworthian child is closest to death, as in the second poem "To a Butterfly," in which the dormant insect is infantile ("I know not if you sleep or feed") and corpselike ("How motionless!—not frozen seas / More motionless!"). But in its active stage, the butterfly reminds the adult of his own playful childhood, which fades away into layers of infinite, "frozen" sameness:

> We'll talk of sunshine and of song,
> And summer days, when we were young;
> Sweet childish days, that were as long
> As twenty days are now.

The rhythm of identification, sublimation, and alienation attends upon Wordsworth's treatment of, and response to, these children, alive or dead. In "The Pet Lamb" (where the erotic substitution of an animal for a human anticipates *The White Doe of Rylstone*), the lamb itself is an anthropomorphized child, tended by little Barbara Lewthwaite, "a child of beauty rare." Admiring the couple, Wordsworth endows the young girl with a song with which to nurture and cradle her pet. The poet marching homeward then repeats the song to himself, "And it seemed, as I traced the ballad line by line, / That but one half of it was hers, and one half of it was *mine*." Of course, the ballad, in its inception, is entirely his, but he has so thoroughly identified it with the girl that its repetition appears, in retrospect, a bequest *from* her. He now lays claim to what he originally owned. What was projected has been returned; the gift has repaid itself.

But the last stanza extends the speaker's generosity and yet withdraws from ampler relationships. Fear and kindness twin themselves in Wordsworth's responses to his children: repeating the song, the speaker decides that "more than half to the damsel must belong, / For she looked with such a look, and she spake with such a tone, / That I almost received her heart into my own." As the Boy of Winander receives the solemn imagery of woods into his mind, and as "Characteristics of a Child Three Years Old" ends with "images imprest" into the bosom of a lake, the dialectic of reception functions in the imaginary exchange with Barbara, but the mitigating "almost" assures the separation of child and adult. For Wordsworth a going out and a coming in should be one and the same—projection and introjection should function simultaneously, but they do not.[12] Common sense renders the union entirely fictive; humans always stay apart. Since separateness is unbridgeable, Wordsworth endows with heroic potential those figures who attempt or provoke its denial. The allure of the commonplace, inciting him to thoughts of communion, achieves momentary grandeur, but ultimately it fails tragically to deliver the hopeful promise with which he had invested it. Unlike the Solitary Reaper, who was mature enough to sing her own song, which the speaker carried away as his burden, Barbara Lewthwaite must have a song provided: the viewer's hope may be entertained, although it can never be satisfied.

Projection counters isolation, so much so that we may rightly wonder to whom the subtitle ("Solitude") of "Lucy Gray" justly applies. Although the second stanza dehumanizes and isolates the girl, and additionally personifies the dwelling from which she seems excluded, the bulk of the ballad gives us a Lucy who, in life, is very much at the center of human relationships. In her mysterious death-in-life middle state—another child absorbed rather than buried within a landscape—Lucy now transcends mere solitude. Instead, the speaker unintentionally isolates himself from typical human encounters and perception in the first three stanzas. He insists alternately upon Lucy's visibility and her ghostliness, or, perhaps, upon his own magical envisionings, which stem from isolation and are denied to the mundane viewer:[13]

> Oft I had heard of Lucy Gray:
> And, when I crossed the wild,
> I chanced to see at break of day
> The solitary child.
>
> No mate, no comrade Lucy knew;
> She dwelt on a wide moor,
> —The sweetest thing that ever grew
> Beside a human door!
>
> You yet may spy the fawn at play,
> The hare upon the green;
> But the sweet face of Lucy Gray
> Will never more be seen.

After tracing for us the mysterious quest, disappearance, and vestigial reminders of the girl, however, the speaker sounds less willing to remain in his own solitary state:

> —Yet some maintain that to this day
> She is a living child;
> That you may see sweet Lucy Gray
> Upon the lonesome wild.
>
> O'er rough and smooth she trips along,
> And never looks behind;
> And sings a solitary song
> That whistles in the wind.

Falling back uncritically on hearsay, and implicitly including himself as part of the "some" and "you" who constitute the vox populi, the speaker reabsorbs himself into common humanity, the community of the living and, more important, of the adult. Unlike her more famous namesake, Lucy Gray unknowingly permits her viewer a reentry into common life.

The young, like the dead, perform benefactions of which they are unaware; Wordsworth both teaches and learns from the children whom he continually meets. Most of the adults who encounter children in Wordsworth's po-

etry are capable of offering and receiving instruction. The
father in "Anecdote for Fathers" yearns to "teach the hun-
dredth part" of what he has just learned from his five-year-
old son, and the arithmetical Wordsworth in "We Are
Seven" will not confess to having learned from the eight-
year-old girl unconscious of death but deliberately allows
her "will" the last word. The children prefigure those
ghostly, usually aged characters who instruct the poet in
more humane concerns. The speaker is always less tire-
some when he takes action—as in charitable response to
Alice Fell's ruined cloak, in "The Norman Boy" where he
magically grants wishes for transport, or when he finds a
lost lamb in "The Idle Shepherd-Boys"—than when he
merely admonishes, as at the end of the same poem: "And
gently did the Bard / Those idle Shepherd-boys upbraid, /
And bade them better mind their trade." Likewise, in "The
Westmoreland Girl," a late poem to his own grandchildren,
he seizes the occasion to sermonize on will and duty,
equating poetic composition and grandfatherly preaching.

In addition to offering occasions for service or simple relationship, children frequently appear as agents of larger
spirits. Vessels of grace, whether in their quiet they seem
dead, or in their playfulness criminal, they remind the
adult of past blessedness and present removal from it.
Having once been a child is one thing all adults have in
common; all children can potentially speak to even the
most obdurate of grownups. By virtue of his very existence, a child corrects, and chastises, the adult's isolation.
Self-sufficiency in an adult means alienation, whereas in a
child (like the three-year-old) it symbolizes integrity. This
constant shifting of perspective, a rethinking and refor-
mulating of values, keeps Wordsworth's human figures,
the agents so often of his poetic thinking, alive and fluid.
He is not a poet of a single vision. The Intimations Ode, for
example, might be retitled "Several Ways of Looking at a
Child," because it is populated by an audible shepherd boy
(stanza 3), a bouncing Baby and children gathering flowers

(stanza 4), reminders of the speaker's own youth (stanza 1), and imagined versions of our common progress (stanzas 5 to 8). By the poem's last turn (stanzas 9 to 11), childhood and children have essentially disappeared, having been subsumed into natural images ("the innocent brightness of a new-born Day," line 195). Once again, children enter Wordsworth's world only to vanish from it. Because the adult has traveled farthest from the source of light and glory, his need for human solace is greatest; because the poem marks his coming to terms with loss and growth, the actual children are replaced by metonymic progeny, natural but personified images.

The poet begins by regretting a failure of both vision and appearances in all objects of sight. A celestial light has evaporated, whatever its internal or external source may have been. And yet the children of the Ode's first movement are defined entirely not as seers but as doers: the shouting shepherd-boy, himself not much superior to the beasts on holiday, the children culling flowers, and the leaping Babe. The poet is excluded from active natural joy and participates, by an effort of will, only vicariously; we hear a muted pathos in the anxious protests of the onlooker craving admittance to a party where his jollity would appear contrived, out-of-place, or potentially ludicrous:

> Ye blessèd Creatures, I have heard the call
>   Ye to each other make; I see
> The heavens laugh with you in your jubilee;
>   My heart is at your festival,
>   My head hath its coronal,
> The fulness of your bliss, I feel—I feel it all.
> (lines 36–41)

He thinks, like Prufrock, another prematurely old man, that the blessed creatures, beasts or humans, will not call to *him*.

Childhood action assures childhood communion and therefore joy. Even the sociologist's view of the child overwhelmingly depicts him by his "work," what he "shape[s]," "frames," "will fit," a vocation of imitations fast on one another's heels.[14] Childhood passivity, as stanza 8 demonstrates, however, opens to view the image of the six-year-old as best Philosopher. Here, in his contemplative guise, the child is, with three exceptions, the object of all action (the first active verbs for him are the fairly bland "dost keep" and "reads"): haunted truths "rest upon" him, Immortality "broods" over him, custom will soon "lie upon" and "crush" him. As we have seen, meditation or tranquillity so often leads Wordsworth's figures to the stillness of death. In stanza 8, the blind child teasingly "provokes" (the strongest verb) the years to kill the child within him. In his perplexity, uncertain whether to trace adult misery to childhood patterns of action or of nascent intellection, Wordsworth manages to blame the child in both of his roles.

With the major turn in the Ode, as rebirth miraculously occurs between the eighth and ninth stanzas, Wordsworth gives childhood its due ("that which is most worthy to be blest") and also turns away from it, even as his own childhood and its particular gifts and graces have naturally abandoned him. We might label the hiatus between these stanzas a mimetic bridge, a formal turn that duplicates the pattern in life it traces:

> Full soon thy Soul shall have her earthly freight,
> And custom lie upon thee with a weight,
> Heavy as frost, and deep almost as life!
>
> IX
>
> O joy! that in our embers
> Is something that doth live,
> That nature yet remembers
> What was so fugitive!
>
> (lines 127–33)

As suggested earlier, the paradox of childhood is its simultaneous separation from and connection to adult consciousness. We are distant from our past selves and yet they are always with us. In the Intimations Ode, Wordsworth reinvigorates himself by reassembling the past through the complete emotional refocusing that occurs in the break between the stanzas. Something lives in the embers: the implicit phoenix image establishes a continuity binding our days together.

The final song of thanksgiving is for the doubts, apprehensions, mental faculties not in themselves active, but leading to action and to elevation: those which, "a master light of all our seeing; / Uphold us, cherish, and have power to make / Our noisy years seem moments in the being / Of the eternal Silence" (lines 153–56). The adult, surely no Prufrock any longer, rejoices in his abandonment by and of childhood, and of action itself. The poem's last two and one-half stanzas reduce action to imagination (we travel, see, and hear the activities by the shore through the magical insight in our mind's eye) or to "thought," with which the speaker, newly contented in the isolation that had alienated him at the start, joins the vernal gaiety of birds and beasts.

Childhood, even its imitative aspects that are gently mocked in stanza 7, relies no less on habit, it turns out, than does the "more habitual sway" of the natural landscape to which the poet pledges himself at the end. The sober poet, no longer tripping lightly but keeping watch over man's mortality, looks with faint nostalgia to the activity of childhood, and reminds us as well of the origins of the Ode in Pindaric celebrations of athletic contests: the victor's palms, those won in sport or, taking sport as a metonymy, in life itself, are unsentimentally set down in favor of "thoughts," a new and sublimer reward (cf. the 1802 poem "I have thoughts that are fed by the sun," PW 4: 365). To the swift and to the young go the crowns of glory; to the adult come the pleasures and weight of consciousness.

❧

"Sweet is the holiness of youth," wrote Wordsworth in his 1801 modernization of Chaucer's "Prioress' Tale": it is a line

entirely his own. To his depiction of the lusty play of childhood, Wordsworth added what was to be sanctified among
Victorian pieties as a still more touching picture of the
child: the angel of our future hopes. At its best, in the image of Caroline ("It is a beauteous evening") this beatification is complicated by the death-in-life that blessedness
brings with it. The poems in which Wordsworth parades
his platitudes of childhood saintliness may embarrass us
with their album sentiments (and indeed few of them are
poetically interesting). But the joint embleming and em-
balming of childhood simultaneously involve other images
of blessedness. Thus, in an 1835 quatrain, written to a child
and in her album, Wordsworth sounds almost like an orthodox Blake, revising *The Book of Thel* for the delicate ears
of the young:

> Small service is true service while it lasts:
> Of humblest Friends, bright Creature! scorn not one:
> The Daisy, by the shadow that it casts,
> Protects the lingering dew-drop from the Sun.
> (*PW* 4: 178)

Wordsworth's most successful presentations of children
contain a slight edge that hones the soft delicacy of conventional sweetness: the premonitions of death in sleep, of
alienation in action, of obduracy in spirited playfulness.
Even at peace, Wordsworth's children seem larger than ordinary life. But in his less successful poems, the edge is
lost: the emblem and the sentiment count for most, and
the disturbing ambiguities of real life and heroic zest are
muted in favor of the unmitigated tones of docile acceptance. Even where he evokes "the placid innocence of
death" he soon passes it by in favor of a conventional religious icon, as in the 1824 sonnet about the daughter of
Thomas Monkhouse (*PW* 3: 46), which plucks images from
the standard Wordsworthian garden but then thought-
lessly ignores what it has culled. The girl has given up her
usual unquietness by a "special grace" through which nei-

ther temper sullies her cheek nor cries untune her voice. The child hypnotizes her gazer who

> Might learn to picture, for the eye of faith,
> The Virgin, as she shone with kindred light;
> A nursling couched upon her mother's knee,
> Beneath some shady palm of Galilee.
>
> (lines 11–14)

The will to believe has overcome the wish to praise; one would never commend Wordsworth for the individuality of his "characters," but by comparison to the "infant M. M.," Lucy Gray and the unnamed girl in "We Are Seven" have strikingly personal identities. The timid "eye of faith" gives this poem away, suggesting that childhood, with its special prominence in Wordsworth's sense of the life cycle, is less "signified" than "signifier." Seizing upon whatever possibility for orthodoxy awaits him, Wordsworth uses the child as the line toward actual worship. Only through the child, so to speak, can we approach the Mother. By picturing the Virgin through the living child (how unlike Yeats's "Among School Children" despite the similar provocation), the enrapt gazer justifies his own faith.

Another sure sign of Wordsworth's decline into something resembling orthodoxy is the way he is able to tame the wildness of many of his poetic children, perhaps hoping to allay the boy's savagery in the first books of *The Prelude* with the spiritual promise of salvation held out by the Monkhouse infant. "The Blind Highland Boy," a relatively early poem (1806), was placed in 1815 and 1820 among the poems on childhood, then refiled in "Memorials of a Tour in Scotland, 1803" (*PW* 3: 88) even though Wordsworth had not heard the story until after his return from that trip. We see what happens when the naked sublimity of childhood adventure is compromised by both the poet's sense of his audience (it is "A Tale Told by the Fire-side" and addressed to children) and the facts of the true story from which the poem grew. But more importantly, "The Blind Highland Boy" may stand as an example of Wordsworth's growing reluctance, after the completion of *The Prelude*, to recall or represent the dangerous and possibly tragic consequences of childhood bravado. As we can see, after *The Prelude*, childhood becomes both more spiritual and more harmlessly playful, as if the poet, now himself a father, and having exorcised his own boyhood, chooses to depict those children he might wish his own (or, retrospectively, himself) to be.

The Blind Highland Boy, beloved and deprived, blessed by God with "joy/Of which we nothing know," as compensation for his blindness, is haunted and tempted by the eternal roar of the waters by which he lives. The soul of infinite time lives within the sound of the waves' rhythms, and to the natural attractions of the sea are added the human allure of sailors' tales, "the bustle of the mariners/In stillness or in storm." Despite (or because of) maternal injunctions, however, the ten-year-old boy sets out for sea, Edward Lear–like, in a giant turtle shell, stolen from a neighboring house after he is inspired by an old tale of an English boy who had sailed in a similar bark to meet his father's man-of-war. Provoked by books, led on by childish hopes, prompted to an act of studied stealth and subsequent risk, the child is, to this point, a composite of other Wordsworthian children. But the boy remains blessed, overcome by neither fear nor guilt, nor human, divine, or natural retribution. Under the anxious eyes of mother and other adults on shore, the child triumphs exultantly in his skiff, as if angels protect his blind daring.

The protection takes the ironic form of the boy's capture by wily sailors (he is saved) and the simultaneous evaporation of his blind—in both senses—hopes. A Wordsworthian rite of passage, the same sort that in other contexts (e.g., the Simplon Pass) demands suffering, sublimation, and finally the passing of years to overcome, is here minimized in the ease of the transition—the boy seems never to be in serious danger—from childhood hopes to a return to the social life of human community. When the boy is saved, he has been, as it were, violated, and his inner visions destroyed; he is returned to that light of common day that he will never be able to see or to supplant with his own inner light:

> "*Lei-gha—Lei-gha*"—he then cried out,
> "*Lei-gha—Lei-gha*"—with eager shout;
> Thus did he cry, and thus did he pray,
> And what he meant was "Keep away,
>   And leave me to myself!"
>
> Alas! and when he felt their hands—
> You've often heard of magic wands,
> That with a motion overthrow
> A palace of the proudest show,
>   Or melt it into air;
>
> So all his dreams—that inward light
> With which his soul had shone so bright—
> All vanished;—'twas a heartfelt cross
> To him, a heavy, bitter loss,
>   As he had ever known.
>   (lines 201–15)

The boy has sustained a double loss. More important than his congenital sightlessness has been the inner light that once illuminated his soul, but has now fled. The bitterness of this loss, brought out in the double sense of "cross" as torment and betrayal, Wordsworth would have us believe, finds compensation in the return to social life. Precisely because the adult population (narrative bard aside) fails to understand the blessedness of the boy's condition, the sailors set out to rescue him. Given the narrator's earlier sympathy with his hero, this is a form of imaginative murder:

> And let him, let him go his way,
> Alone, and innocent, and gay!
> For, if good Angels love to wait
> On the forlorn unfortunate,
>   This Child will take no harm.
>   (lines 171–75)

Wordsworth's ambivalence—any adult's—informs this
conditional clause, for only in the minds of the faithful, the
credulous, or the naive, do good angels invariably protect
the adventurous, foolhardy young. Even the boy, snatched
from the perilous deep, tames himself in later years to the
maturer pleasures of adult life on shore, diminished
though it is from former sublimity: "though his fancies had
been wild, / Yet he was pleased and reconciled / To live in
peace on shore" (lines 243–45).

His life saved, the blind Highland boy lives, like his turtle shell, "preserved" as an inspiration to local color and
tradition. His adventurous life has been deflected; returned to social reality, he has been transformed into artistic inspiration. He lives paradoxically in spite of, and yet
because of, his visionary blindness: saved by the sailors, he
lives through poetry.

Increasingly in his orthodoxy, Wordsworth looks at
childish adventure, bravado, and sublime aspiration as the
unimaginable source of adult malfeasance. Vainly grieving
for Napoleon (PW 3: 110) in 1802, he wonders "what food /
Fed his first hopes?" The wise governor is not trained in
battles, nor even on the playing fields of Eton, but is nurtured maternally:

> Wisdom doth live with children round her knees:
> Books, leisure, perfect freedom, and the talk
> Man holds with week-day man in the hourly walk
> Of the mind's business: these are the degrees
> By which true Sway doth mount; this is the stalk
> True Power doth grow on; and her rights are these.

The emblems of ordinariness and the idylls of the commonplace begin, even in Wordsworth's prime, to gain his
strongest assent. Reared under the double fostering of
beauty and fear, Wordsworth seems to prefer, for his public figures at least, the consolations of a personified Wisdom, a rendition of the real mother too early snatched
away from him. Here knowledge is purchased at the price
of power—the very loss he wishes to prevent for his "race

of real children" in *The Prelude* V, 436–49; Wisdom becomes another name for maternal love.

The political claims of childhood as the foundation of adult heroism remind us that Wordsworth was concerned, almost in inverse proportion to his direct involvement, with national affairs throughout his life. This theme is developed in a not particularly distinguished poem, "The Italian Itinerant, and the Swiss Goatherd" in *Memorials of a Tour on the Continent, 1820* (*PW* 3: 181). Watching some mountaineers in a riflery contest, Wordsworth imagines the ghosts of Swiss heroes descending from their tombs to shed grace on their living representatives. But in an off-hand transition, the poet interjects an aside:

> But Truth inspired the Bards of old
> When of an iron age they told,
> Which to unequal laws gave birth,
> And drove Astraea from the earth.
> (lines 75–78)

One wonders about the connection, especially with the opening adversative "but," between the classical reference and what has preceded. These lines stand poised strangely between two observed scenes: the mountaineers at their sport and the eponymous goatherd who seems, by virtue of the classical allusion, at least at first a reminiscence of Virgil's magical baby in the fourth eclogue.

Instead, the boy offers a lesson in deprivation, an example of natural rather than human inequities, because he is described, at first parenthetically, as marginal, almost deathly like the Danish Boy:

> —A gentle Boy (perchance with blood
> As noble as the best endued,
> But seemingly a Thing despised;
> Even by the sun and air unprized;
> For not a tinge or flowery streak
> Appeared upon his tender cheek)
> (lines 79–84)

He suggests at last the ironies of Swiss heroics and democracy, an alienated figure in the midst of symbolic grandeur. The child, all "feeble innocence" to the poet's imagination, represents the disenfranchised, but he also calls into question the terms and efficacy of adult achievement, power, and politics:

> Heart-deaf to those rebounding notes,
> Apart, beside his silent goats,
> Sate watching in a forest shed,
> Pale, ragged, with bare feet and head;
> Mute as the snow upon the hill,
> And, as the saint he prays to, still.
>
> (lines 85–90)

A study in loss ("heart-deaf," "bare," "mute," "still"), the child is a figure of death-in-life who, unlike earlier such children in Wordsworth's poetry, inspires a political response:

> Ah, what avails heroic deed?
> What liberty? if no defence
> Be won for feeble Innocence.
> Father of all! though wilful Manhood read
> His punishment in soul-distress,
> Grant to the morn of life its natural blessedness!
>
> (lines 91–96)

Wordsworth remains faithful to his idealized "natural piety," here promoted to natural blessedness. The frailties of the Infant Babe in *The Prelude* II, the plight of orphans, outcasts, and beggars, are here rehearsed once more ("feeble Innocence") through a sudden allegorizing of visual evidence. The automatic emblem-making alone marks this poem as relatively late, but equally characteristic are the voice of social outrage and a heavenly Father as the object of that speech. Poetry has become the vehicle for the transmission of political worries. The polemicist has appropriated the children to his own ends.

We might speculate on the primary holds on the poet's imagination in the years between the composition of *The*

Prelude and 1820, when the "Memorials" of the European tour and the "River Duddon" sequence were published.[15] Who can ever say, Wordsworth asked when he began *The Prelude* in 1798, "this portion of the river of my mind / Came from yon fountain?" (II, 214–15). The stream as a figure of human life flows through his epic autobiography (e.g., III, 10–12; IV, 39–55, 247–68; XIII, 172–84), a tribute to both Wordsworth's symbolic imagination and the landscape of his childhood. But whereas the human element is central, the natural secondary or at least independent, in the River Duddon sonnets we can see the poet deliberately humanizing nature not for purposes of clarifying human life but for formal figuration. He personifies the Duddon through more than the conventions of apostrophe. To the natural course along which it flows Wordsworth applies a human analogue. Whereas in 1798 human life was like a river, in 1820, a river has a quasi-human life of its own.

The first eight sonnets of the Duddon sequence tackle the problem of origination, the one that baffles the poet's best efforts in creating his own image in *The Prelude*. Like the Wordsworthian child, the river itself reaches maturity through the joint agency of fear and beauty; its path parallels that of the paradigmatic Wordsworthian hero in *The Prelude*, and it is associated as well with national history and the course of empire. In the Duddon we see perhaps the last important Wordsworthian child, or, rather, his transformation. Turning his head unenviously from Horace's "prattling" Bandusia (sonnet 1), and "heedless" as well of Alpine torrents, turning away from both the pastoral and the sublime insofar as each resides on foreign soil, Wordsworth hails a native stream whose birthplace he seeks even as he, like Denham, takes poetic encouragement from its liquid measure: "Pure flow the verse, pure, vigorous, free, and bright, / For Duddon, long-loved Duddon, is my theme."

The second sonnet picks up the motif of the child's fearful lot from *The Prelude* I. The river's origin ("Child of the clouds") is as airy as the child's in the Intimations Ode, and its mountain sources free it, for the time being, from sordid industry and heat. The cradle is blessed by the poetry of "the whistling Blast" and the patronage of "Desolation," the ruthless power that spares little further below but obviously strengthens the child for its ongoing adventure. Unannounced, unacknowledged, the stream seems mysteriously fathered forth; self-generating, like the mists of imagination (*The Prelude* VI), the river offers its "Foster-Mother, Earth" (who cares equally for the human child in stanza 6 of the Intimations Ode), its self-created tribute:

> To dignify the spot that gives thee birth
> No sign of hoar Antiquity's esteem
> Appears, and none of modern Fortune's care;
> Yet thou thyself hast round thee shed a gleam
> Of brilliant moss, instinct with freshness rare;
> Prompt offering to thy Foster-Mother, Earth!
> (Sonnet 3)

By sonnet 9 ("The Stepping-stones"), the childlike stream has grown "into a Brook of loud and stately march"; throughout the first part of the sequence, Wordsworth not only humanizes the river as it pursues its growth up to liquid and heroic fullness, but also crosses the stream with references to human life, much the reverse of his typical procedure twenty years earlier. Thus, in sonnet 5, the river flows by a rude cottage, whose children "sport through the summer day, / Thy pleased associates:—light as endless May / On infant bosoms lonely Nature lies," where the loneliness of Nature and river is finely mitigated by the real mother keeping a careless eye over her flock, and by the comfort of human playmates.

In the eighth poem, Wordsworth begins his historical investigation by asking what primitive tribesman first quenched his thirst at this stream. The stream itself, a silent historian or mute babbler, can, murmuring, give no record of its beneficence (its little nameless, unremembered acts). It exists as pure, functional symbol, exactly as a child must give future hope to an adult: "Thy function was to heal and to restore, / To soothe and cleanse, not madden and pollute!" Raised in and by Nature, the quasi-human river now, in its adolescence, begins both to assume human obligations of charity and to become part of the greater power of Nature herself, which will heal and purify humankind. As it becomes more a river, the Duddon becomes, as well, more noticeably human in its charitable offices. In the antepenultimate sonnet 32, the majestic river is absorbed into the Thames and into the very spirit of English nationalism, freighted with commerce and military vessels; at last (sonnets 32 and 33), in its "radiant progress toward the Deep," it inspires its poet once more to a hopeful consideration of his own freedom and readiness to "mingle with Eternity."[16]

The "After-Thought" (sonnet 34), a justly anthologized poem that attests to the extent of Wordsworth's artistry well after his "great decade," looks back to the river, a "partner" and "guide," as to an emblem of past life. Having surveyed the course of the river from the mysteries of origination to the equally mysterious calm of final submergence, Wordsworth has almost explicitly followed the progress of the idealized human life that his poetry—whether nominally about himself or about others—continually depicts. In abstracting a message from the paradoxically moving yet constant river ("The Form remains, the Function never dies"), Wordsworth looks nostalgically to the days of early youth and to thoughts of heroic achievement that belong to youth:

> We Men, who in our morn of youth defied
> The elements, must vanish;—be it so!
> Enough if something from our hands have power
> To live, and act, and serve the future hour;
> And if, as toward the silent tomb we go,
> Through love, through hope, and faith's transcendent
>   dower,
> We feel that we are greater than we know.

Defiance or, to use another Wordsworthian word, obstinacy is that part of childhood development that gives birth, eventually, to the philosophic mind as well as to heroic ambition. Just as early terrors and miseries create, through some "dark invisible workmanship" (*The Prelude* I, 352) the adult's calm self-worth, so the turbulence of the infant stream eventually leads it to the fulfillment of a social and national destiny. But the "eagerness of infantine desire" (*The Prelude* II, 26) leads to and is matched by the quiet independence that also comes in childhood and evinces the self-sufficiency of mature solitude. A river, like a man, changes and grows. As Freud writes, in a simple ironic tautology to which Wordsworth would have assented, "Men cannot remain children forever; they must go out into 'hostile life.' "[17] But since the Child is forever Father of the Man, in the adult the child is always working to deliver hope and strength and to remind him of retreating innocence.

For the course of human life, a river serves Wordsworth as a limpid model, even as his own life, far from over in 1820, begins to resemble the Hermit's "Where hope and memory are as one" ("The Tuft of Primroses," line 289). Like the best Wordsworthian heroes, the Duddon finds an outlet in action (to "serve the future hour") and in mere being. Declining, like the river, into a broad low valley, Wordsworth became increasingly conscious not only of the unique privileges of childhood, whether in repose or tumult, but also of the special claims of age itself to heroic possibility.

4

The Necessity of Being Old

Thirty years ago, Robert Mayo steered readers of the *Lyrical Ballads* away from an unthinking belief in its revolutionary novelty and toward its contemporaneity.[1] According to Mayo's research on magazine verse of the 1790s, Wordsworth's poems were strikingly new in neither form nor theme; they are important for their superiority to, and not difference from, much of the decade's popular verse. The *Lyrical Ballads* was the distillation, not the fountainhead, of a tradition. Even the same sorts of characters—female vagrants, deserted mothers, derelicts, unfortunates in many guises—to whom Wordsworth returns incessantly in his efforts to humble the subjects and democratize the language of poetry, had been anticipated in those now-forgotten periodical pages. Of these types, however, there is at least one whose repeated presence in Wordsworth's oeuvre is significant for the subsequent course of poetry itself: Wordsworth is the first modern spokesman for old age.

Old age was rarely, before Wordsworth, a major subject for literature at all, and even after him, it is a territory better charted by novelists and dramatists than by poets. The great delineators of age are Sophocles, Shakespeare, Dickens, and Beckett; the handful of modern poets who may be added to the list—Tennyson, Yeats, Eliot, Stevens—all learned from Wordsworth. It is striking, too, that Wordsworth's interest in age takes many forms within his poetry: blank verse portraiture ("The Old Cumberland Beggar," the discharged soldier in *The Prelude* IV); symbolic lyrics ("To the Small Celandine," "The Thorn"); longer narratives

like "Michael"; crisis lyrics like "Resolution and Independence"; lyrical ballads (the Matthew poems, "Goody Blake
and Harry Gill"); and speculative philosophical passages in
The Excursion, which epitomize the crucial philosophical
and emotional tensions of his work. In all these poems,
many of them among his greatest, Wordsworth perma-
nently enlarges the human population of English poetry
and creates a peculiarly modern kind of hero. By depicting
the old, Wordsworth balances his hopes that an ascent to a
final eminence is our earthly due against his opposing
fears for what we may become. Years are supposed to bring
"the philosophic mind," but after a point they steal more
than they bestow and the old are left forlorn, doddering,
helpless, and comic.

Lewis Carroll had the last word on the inanity of these
figures; his parody depends not so much on the specific resemblances between his old man and Wordsworth's leech-
gatherer as on their potentially ridiculous senility for
which comedy is the sole remedy. "If I laugh at any mortal
thing, 'tis that I may not weep," as Byron wrote. Likewise,
Carroll chooses to scoff rather than to pity:

> I'll tell thee everything I can:
>   There's little to relate.
> I saw an aged, aged man,
>   A-sitting on a gate.
> "Who are you, aged man?" I said,
>   "And how is it you live?"
> And his answer trickled through my head,
>   Like water through a sieve.
>
> He said "I look for butterflies
>   That sleep among the wheat:
> I make them into mutton-pies,
>   And sell them in the street."
> . . . .
> And now, if e'er by chance I put
>   My fingers into glue,
> Or madly squeeze a right-hand foot
>   Into a left-hand shoe,
> Or if I drop upon my toe
>   A very heavy weight,

I weep, for it reminds me so
Of that old man I used to know—
Whose look was mild, whose speech was slow,
Whose hair was whiter than the snow,
Whose face was very like a crow,
With eyes, like cinders, all aglow,
Who seemed distracted with his woe,
Who rocked his body to and fro,
And muttered mumblingly and low,
As if his mouth were full of dough,
Who snorted like a buffalo—
That summer evening long ago,
  A-sitting on a gate.[2]

Such is the worst that Wordsworth can inspire. Carroll's response points to the real problem that Wordsworth faced: Is it possible to ennoble poverty, or glorify insipidity, to focus an unrelenting beam upon ordinariness and still convince us that the attention is honest, the ordinariness interesting?[3] Old men provide the hardest challenge of all.

At their noblest, Wordsworth's old men possess a rugged strength, physical and emotional, that has simultaneously kept them alive and been nurtured by their aging. But Wordsworth also paints pictures in which age combines the fragility of childhood with the isolation of maturity, lacking the glad animal movements of the first, and the moral conscience of the second. Wordsworth is troubled by the question of what, if anything, age possesses with which to protect itself against all other losses and "fallings from us." His responses, like his cast of characters, offer insight into a compromising and tentative, sometimes fearful mind.

Perhaps the best introduction to the old men is not a human hero at all, but a negligible flower, the lesser celandine, commonly called pilewort. Of three poems addressed to the celandine, published in 1807, only the last is included in the 1815 grouping, "Poems Referring to the Period of Old Age." The first two, both written in 1802, evince the same preference for a flower that is commonplace but unnoticed, unflaunting although "prodigal of itself." The celandine may suggest a new heroism; at least it replaces glorious floral bravado with simplicity and anonymity. Careless of its neighborhood, it grows everywhere: "there's not a place, / Howsoever mean it be, / But 'tis good enough for thee." Opening and closing itself according to light and temperature, the celandine keeps tenaciously alive. It is also the special care of the poet, who relinquishes primroses, lilies, and daisies, the usual figures in a poetic posy, to others. The special flower "shall be mine," he says, and he eschews greater adventures to become the spokesman for this small thing:

> Thou art not beyond the moon,
> But a thing "beneath our shoon:"
> Let the bold Discoverer thrid
> In his bark the polar sea;
> Rear who will a pyramid;
> Praise it is enough for me,
> If there be but three or four
> Who will love my little Flower.
>
> (PW 2: 146)

Wordsworth surely had this kind of object in mind when he wrote that his intention in the *Lyrical Ballads* was "to choose incidents and situations from common life . . . and, at the same time, to throw over them a certain colouring of imagination, whereby ordinary things should be presented to the mind in an unusual aspect" (PrW 1: 123). Focusing on humble beginnings, he seeks to redefine our ideas of greatness; a natural but small aristocracy will be won over to the celandine, which, in many ways, resembles another Wordsworthian *inconnue*:

> She dwelt among the untrodden ways
> Beside the springs of Dove,
> A Maid whom there were none to praise
> And very few to love.
>
> (PW 2: 30)

Two years later, Wordsworth sees the flower differently, now old and unlike the delicately hidden Lucy. Still responsive to the vicissitudes of weather, the celandine may be either open or shut, passive "like a Thing at rest." "Now standing forth an offering to the blast, / And buffeted at will by storm and rain," the flower resembles Peele Castle. It is beyond choice, not because it is unhuman, but rather because it represents the very last stage of human life:

> "It doth not love the shower, nor seek the cold:
> This neither is its courage nor its choice,
> But its necessity in being old.
>
> "The sunshine may not cheer it, nor the dew;
> It cannot help itself in its decay;
> Stiff in its members, withered, changed of hue."
> And, in my spleen, I smiled that it was grey.
>
> To be a Prodigal's Favourite—then, worse truth,
> A miser's Pensioner—behold our lot!
> O man, that from thy fair and shining youth
> Age might but take the things Youth needed not!
> (PW 4: 244–45)

Only one phrase in the poem, "in my spleen," explicitly states the speaker's emotions, but everything implies a major change from two years earlier. The celandine is now a forthright symbol of the human condition, beyond heroism and choice, bound only by the laws of necessity. If the flowers in the earlier poems suggested Lucy, this one is certainly like the leech-gatherer, "like a thing at rest" recalling "like a thing endued with sense" in stanza 9 of the 1802 "Resolution and Independence." Where the two earlier celandine poems substituted modest praise of a common flower for epic quest and "star y-pointing pyramid," this one replaces even willed stoic fortitude with mere acceptance. Heroism has been denied or redefined, depending upon our reading of the ambiguous last two lines, which enigmatically pose a central question in Wordsworth's poetry: What is taken away, what abides, and what is added during life? The speaker might regret that in age, fortitude and courage, perquisites of youth, are snatched away, or he might be sanguine that age will perpetuate ("take" as "continue") those qualities that youth does not need. But he does not say what youth needs or what is taken (away?

or along?) by Age. How does Wordsworth, a man at the height of creative and intellectual maturity, respond to this image of his own future failure?

We may find a hint of an answer in the Intimations Ode, in which "the meanest flower that blows" expresses Wordsworth's strongest feelings for mortality, which transcend or prevent articulation and emotion. Wordsworth began the ode in 1802, but after four stanzas and the formulation of a loss ("Whither is fled the visionary gleam? / Where is it now, the glory and the dream?"), he waited two years before attempting to complete it. The rhetorical problem at the end of the third celandine poem reappears at the center of Wordsworth's newly created strength in stanza 10 of the great ode:

> Though nothing can bring back the hour
> Of splendour in the grass, of glory in the flower;
> We will grieve not, rather find
> Strength in what remains behind.

The list of what remains behind spans a lifetime: "The primal sympathy," which we retain from youth; the "soothing thoughts" that spring from human suffering, which are a newfound solace in maturity; and "the faith that looks through death," the "years that bring the philosophic mind," which project us hopefully forward to new, not yet fully acquired powers.

"What remains behind," then, is both what we are left with of childhood glory (the intimations, not the immortality), and our memory of past strength, which will continue to inspire us, from afar, even as the old pleasures recede, because it is the very "fountain light of all our day." But memory itself can be painful, as one of Wordsworth's most articulate old men reminds us: in "The Fountain" (PW 4: 72), Matthew regrets the perseverance of memory and, he implies, of consciousness itself: "Thus fares it still in our decay; / And yet the wiser mind / Mourns less for what age takes away / Than what it leaves behind." Although the Intimations Ode moves toward a rejoicing in the acquisition of new powers, as Lionel Trilling points out,[4] there is still the nagging pressure upon Wordsworth's mind that what has disappeared from earlier unity is irreplaceable.

The first four stanzas bemoan the loss of the glorious halo that, in childhood, surrounded all objects of all sense. The verse, however, dramatizes a more important problem of advancing age, not the one that Wordsworth is consciously articulating: isolation from nature, an incapacity to bridge the gap between selves; a total loss of connection. Sharing the bliss of the children at play is possible only because the adult cannot himself play; hearing without really sharing their joy is his plight even at the end; joining the children's sport in thought alone suggests that isolation is never remitted. Both the problems and the solutions (or rationalizations) that the poet articulates are those of an old man. "Human suffering," present thoughts of which are supposed to soothe and chastise the adult, is the future he can anticipate. Consciousness of death as our earthly fate is progressively, in the poem, more important than the loss of the visionary gleam. Indeed, as concern for the loss of the gleam recedes gradually from the poem, a new focus on weakness, mortality, and survival itself, brightens. Human growth involves both a loss (if the metaphor of preexistence is taken seriously) and a gain in worldly experience, an acquisition that kills: the soul's "earthly freight" is the weight of custom, "heavy as frost, and deep almost as life."[5]

The state of philosophical maturity that begins stanza 9 is analogous to a rebirth from death, but with a twist: the new adult is already old. Early maturity, the time of crisis (like Wordsworth's life through much of 1802), is like a death from which arises, through the joint acts of memory and resolution, the new adult: "O joy! that in our embers/ Is something that doth live,/That nature yet remembers/ What was so fugitive." The thirty-four-year-old poet has here been born again, in maturity, from the "sullen" (line 42) and splenetic solitary, to the compensating, but still solitary, philosopher of the last three stanzas. The price for the new life, however, is an awareness of those feelings of suffering that in maturity prepare us for "palsied age": the sober eye keeping its watch over man's mortality is looking at itself. Recognizing those thoughts that lie too deep for tears is equivalent to seeing the necessity in being old; it is neither courage nor choice. *De te fabula narratur.* Because Wordsworth is obsessed with death, he can contemplate with envy the old men (or the old flower) in his poems. They are alive, if barely, and Wordsworth is afraid of dying. He does not think that he will survive, in 1798 when he addresses Dorothy at the end of "Tintern Abbey": "If I should be where I no more can hear/Thy voice, nor catch from thy wild eyes these gleams/Of past existence"; or in 1804, when he writes to De Quincey: "You have as yet had little knowledge of me but as a Poet; but I hope, if we live, we shall be still more nearly united";[6] or in 1805, while in the same breath planning to join Coleridge as "prophets of nature" at the resounding end of *The Prelude*:

> Whether to me shall be allotted life,
> And with life power to accomplish aught of worth
> Sufficient to excuse me in men's sight
> For having given this Record of myself,
> Is all uncertain.
>
> (XIII, 386–90)

The loss of consciousness that sometimes accompanies age, especially the loss of the knowledge of mortality, returns the old to a second childhood and, therefore, to the state whose loss, try as he might, Wordsworth never fully ceases to regret. But we cannot entirely accept some critics' arguments that Wordsworth prefers the dead to the living because of his innate misanthropy or nostalgia for lost unity.[7] On the contrary, his fascination with the old, especially in his own youth, reveals an unwillingness to apotheosize unthinkingly the unitary and harmonious stasis that only the grave bestows. In his portraits of the old,

Wordsworth can have it two ways at once: with one foot in the grave, the old men are reminders of our common future as well as presences in our midst to assure us that some, after all, do survive. Appropriately, the title character of "The Farmer of Tillsbury Vale"[8] is named Adam, a farmer now living in the city, "like one whose own country's far over the sea." Disenfranchised, perhaps, from Eden, old Adam proves the truth of what Wordsworth writes in a different context, that "diversity of strength / Attends us, if but once we have been strong" (*The Prelude* XI, 327–28). He smells the hay at Haymarket, and "he thinks of the fields he so often hath mown, / And is happy as if the rich freight were his own."

The old are the Wordsworthian equivalent of Yeats's golden Byzantine bird that sings of what is past and passing and to come. The Old Cumberland Beggar, for instance, is a history, reminding a rural population of past charitable offices, a daily presence and test in their midst, and a death's-head, a memento mori, forcing us all to look ahead. In a successful poem like this, Wordsworth does not sentimentalize the old. Even the late "I Know an Aged Man" (1846), which Cleanth Brooks uses as a foil for the early poem, poses essential questions about age, which relieve it of some of its potentially offensive lachrymosity.[9] An old man who is alone in the world maintains a "relationship" with a single robin, which he feeds daily, until they are separated by his entering a charity ward. Is the pitiful, even pathetic, camaraderie with a bird sufficient recompense for the man's loss of human connections, or is his ordinary condition (verging perhaps on senility) a token of an extraordinary strength? The poem does not say:

> Wife, children, kindred, they were dead and gone;
> But, if no evil hap his wishes crossed,
> One living Stay was left, and in that one
> Some recompense for all that he had lost.
>
> O that the good old Man had power to prove,
> By message sent through air or visible token,

That still he loves the Bird, and still must love;
That friendship lasts though fellowship is broken!
$(PW\ 4:\ 161)^{10}$

Whether or not we find the poem convincing, its theme—
the power of love to support an otherwise intolerable situation—lies at the core of Wordsworth's concerns. At its
profoundest we find it in "Michael," where "the comfort in
the strength of love" keeps Michael alive for a while despite the news of his son's ignominy.

As Brooks's analysis makes clear, it is not so easy to tell
why "The Old Cumberland Beggar" is deemed a success,
"I Know an Aged Man" a failure, apart, perhaps, from the
seriousness accorded to the subject by blank verse. Perhaps the deliberate complexity of the figure I have outlined
above explains the Beggar's hold over the critical imagination. The old man is a warning, just like another of his age
of whom Wordsworth wrote: "No book could have so early
taught me to think of the changes to which human life is
subject, and while looking at him, I could not but say to
myself—we may, any of us, I, or the happiest of my playmates, live to become still more the object of pity than this
old man, this half-doting pilferer" $(PW\ 4:\ 447)$. Especially
after Geoffrey Hartman's lessons on Wordsworth's funerary moments and epigraphical greetings, it is difficult not
to see the Beggar as a presence from the grave who halts
worldly travelers in order to educate them.[11] Even some of
the realistic opening details seem, in retrospect, symbolic,
by virtue of their accumulated force. The Beggar sits on a
piece of rude masonry, a place for rest after hardship that is
like a tombstone; the crumbs that he inadvertently shares
with the hopping birds fall "in showers," a small suggestion of higher things; the Horseman stops and the post-boy
"passes gently by," motifs very much on Wordsworth's
mind when he wrote "The Solitary Reaper" almost ten
years later.

Like a figure from the dead—*Et in Cumberland ego*—the

Beggar is a warning of our own deaths; ironically, "all pass him by," rushing on to get where he already is, like the mad rout depicted by Shelley in "The Triumph of Life." He is also like us *at this moment*. "Bow-bent, his eyes forever on the ground, / He plies his weary journey": throughout his apocalyptic poetry, Wordsworth thus depicts himself before the extreme moments in which revelations break through. In *The Prelude* XIII, ascending Mt. Snowdon, the poet "with forehead bent / Earthward, as if in opposition set / Against an enemy . . . panted up / With eager pace, and no less eager thoughts" (lines 29–32). Or, in the early "A Night-Piece": "the pensive traveller . . . treads / His lonesome path, with unobserving eye / Bent earthwards" (lines 9–11). We are all pilgrims, sharing an attachment to an earth that is both sustaining and hostile; the difference is that the Beggar has forgotten that our home is with infinitude and only there.

Because "we have all of us one human heart," Wordsworth stretches the human lineaments of this Beggar as thin as possible, as if taunting us to condemn the old man for selfishness, obliviousness, and uselessness. Brooks and Harold Bloom,[12] the poem's strongest defenders, still have difficulty with the "moral" values in the poem's middle section, which praises the Beggar as the occasion of human charity in others. At the bottom of the social heap, he makes even the poor who dole out scraps to him feel virtuous. The rural people "found their kindred with a world / Where want and sorrow were" (lines 115–16), and consequently they bless the Beggar because he is the agency by which they are themselves blessed. One-sided though it appears, Wordsworth wants to prove that a reciprocity exists even when the scales are unbalanced. We are related to the Beggar in more than a piously gratifying way. He is selfish, but the cause of charity in others; he is impervious and forgetful, but an agency of memory, reminding others of their "little, nameless . . . acts of kindness and of love," no longer unremembered.

The unbalanced reciprocity in the relationship is emphasized by the poem's imagery of sight, recognition, and eyes. The Beggar's eyes work badly, if at all; "the heaven-regarding eye," the salient feature of youth and maturity, has been replaced by a downward look. The eyes of neighbors look out for him while statesmen are willing to cast him "out of view" into a poorhouse. Wordsworth's own sober eye watching the "setting sun" at the end of the Intimations Ode recalls the vision of the old man:

> if his eyes have now
> Been doomed so long to settle upon earth
> That not without some effort they behold
> The countenance of the horizontal sun,
> Rising or setting, let the light at least
> Find a free entrance to their languid orbs.
>
> (lines 186–91)

As the climax of his benediction, Wordsworth rhetorically and aphoristically summarizes the interchange between Beggar and world: "As in the eye of Nature he has lived, / So in the eye of Nature let him die," Nature's eye here equated not only with the woodland birds and winter snows that have partnered him, but also with man's eye, which has cared for him.

The same problem, in tone and dramatic surprise, which complicates our response to and threatens the credibility of the old Cumberland Beggar, is seen more easily in "Animal Tranquillity and Decay," a poem that overflowed from the former:

> The little hedgerow birds,
> That peck along the road, regard him not.
> He travels on, and in his face, his step,
> His gait, is one expression: every limb,
> His look and bending figure, all bespeak
> A man who does not move with pain, but moves
> With thought.—He is insensibly subdued
> To settled quiet: he is one by whom
> All effort seems forgotten; one to whom
> Long patience hath such mild composure given,

That patience now doth seem a thing of which
He hath no need. He is by nature led
To peace so perfect that the young behold
With envy, what the Old Man hardly feels.

                                  (*PW* 4: 247)

Rhetorical and metrical evenness ("not with . . . but with";
"patience . . . patience") evinces the sheer monotony in a
life that has been led by nature beyond nature to a higher
neglect. The young envy what the old man is insensible of:
the peace that passeth all consciousness.

One version of this poem (1798) concluded with the following lines:

> —I asked him whither he was bound, and what
> The object of his journey; he replied
> "Sir! I am going many miles to take
> A last leave of my son, a mariner,
> Who from a sea-fight has been brought to Falmouth,
> And there is dying in an hospital."

Wordsworth's tinkering with the original ending shows the
problem that attends his presenting the old man. If the old
man speaks, Wordsworth risks plunging the poem into
bathos or matter-of-fact triviality after the relative stateli-
ness and grandeur of his description. Yet the man's speech
is humanizing; grand at a distance, he is not really different
from us in motive and behavior. The shock of strangeness
gives way to the shock of commonalty.

The discrepancy between sublimity and matter-of-factness, or distance and intimacy, is the substance of Coleridge's famous objections to "Resolution and Independence."[13] In the encounters with the aged—with beggar,
leech-gatherer, and even the discharged soldier in *The Prelude* IV (who is like an old man, although his age is not
given)—the repeated design is a homeopathic one.[14] By
projecting his deepest anxieties and fears of "solitude, pain
of heart, distress, and poverty" onto these figures and by
then learning from them lessons of patience and endurance, Wordsworth receives successive doses of advice for

emotional and spiritual health. Even the motif of repetition, the speaker's demand that the leech-gatherer retell his story, bespeaks not absentmindedness or stupidity, but his desire for repeated experiences of the same news. When he says that the leech-gatherer seemed "like one whom I had met with in a dream," the speaker implies that his own imagination has in some ways predicted the old man's appearance: the "peculiar grace, / A leading from above, a something given" is in fact born from the inner need of the poet, which leads without to an external agency. The 1850 *Prelude*, likewise, emphasizes the soldier as an embodiment of the power of "solitude" that returns us to "our better selves" when we have been dallying too long among worldly follies. The embodiment is, then, a projected image of our own solitude.

Just as his poetry produces the heroic out of the commonal, Wordsworth's mind develops the sublime from the subliminal. An idealized self, an old man who has endured, emerges from the poet's psyche to challenge, hold, and sustain him. The descriptions of leech-gatherer and soldier are of a piece with the Old Cumberland Beggar. The soldier is initially "ghastly," "lean," "meager," "faded," and "desolate," perhaps in pain, but then "stately," "steady," "solemn," and "sublime." The leech-gatherer, "not at all alive or dead," is bent double by the killing weight of life, at first rocklike in his immobility but later rocklike in his endurance, a man of "solemn" and "stately" speech (a natural poet), a model of religious perseverance. Both are seeming automata (the soldier speaks, "knowing too well the importance of his theme, / But feeling it no longer") who become fully human on closer inspection. Ultimately they are less important in themselves than in their effect on the young speaker whom we watch watching and responding to them. Through his shifting perspectives on these figures, we see him absorbing their healthful remedies.[15]

Like Coleridge's Ancient Mariner, the leech-gatherer

and discharged soldier rehearse autobiographical narratives that admonish and bless their listeners, and that finally are rendered by clichés. They defy articulation or reductive moralizing. ("He loveth best who prayeth best" is a moral that entirely fails to account for the Mariner's experience; thus is he fated to retell his story endlessly. Its meaning is itself.) Even in their shadowy status these apparitional figures, the living dead, redefine heroism for us. Both masquerade as creatures of the lowest social order but are emissaries from a higher world to the middle state of human doubts and turmoil. Again, like the Ancient Mariner and the Cumberland Beggar, even the Wandering Jew of whom they are all versions, the men hypnotize and penetrate their interlocutors by the magical power of their eyes, which are agencies of connection and feeling, not of perception alone. Wordsworth delivers the soldier to a cottage for food and rest, and warns him to keep off the road late at night. The soldier turns the admonishment against his would-be comforter: "My trust is in the God of heaven / And in the eye of him that passes me" (lines 494–95). His faith links sight and vision to charity and deliverance. To see is to comfort as well as to believe.

More than any other Wordsworthian solitary, the leech-gatherer is the deliberate double of the speaker.[16] The opening stanzas of "Resolution and Independence" picture a poet conscious of his own isolation from nature and humanity who willfully tries to cure his isolation by sensuous contact (he sees the hare, he hears the birds) as he did in the Intimations Ode. This provides a temporary distraction, but his hopeful and regressive pronouncement of happiness is immediately undermined by the welling-up of his frustrations: "Even such a happy Child of earth am I. / . . . / But there may come another day to me—/ Solitude, pain of heart, distress and poverty" (stanza 5). That future day is, in part, at hand now. The "untoward thoughts" with which he strives produce three distinct fears: that he has not cared for himself sufficiently and prepared for his own future; that consequently "all needful things" will not "come unsought"; that the inevitable end, "despondency and madness," and death may be close at hand. The meeting with the old man, which follows immediately, seems to be a matter of "peculiar grace," a chance event, but the poet's having already articulated a desire to "heed" for himself dramatically suggests that what he sees is what he needs, what he wants. Determination and destiny are co-workers in his salvation.

In this joint development, the leech-gatherer is both the hand of providence and a living example of hope and strength. Combining the features of luck, faith, and genial good with those of will (the endless, increasingly strenuous efforts in his work), the old man trusts both God and man: "Housing, with God's good help, by choice or chance." In confronting what he initially thinks is a sea-beast, a stone, a derelict, the fear of what he may become, the poet finds relief. The medicine has been administered from without, it is true, but only because the patient is ready for it. He needs both inner and outer support, because isolation may result from a merely self-willed recovery. Resolution, after all, can become obstinate and debilitating hope (the case of Margaret in "The Ruined Cottage"), and independence can lead to the isolation of the young solitary ("Lines Left Upon a Seat in a Yew-Tree" [PW 1: 92]), to "the self-reliance of despair" (The White Doe of Rylstone), or more precisely, to the despair of self-reliance. Thus God and the leech-gatherer provide an outward focus for a determination that comes from within. At the poem's end, the leech-gatherer becomes a figure already in the past, a diminished thing of use to the poet for what he symbolizes:

> I could have laughed myself to scorn to find
> In that decrepit Man so firm a mind.
> "God," said I, "be my help and stay secure;
> I'll think of the Leech-gatherer on the lonely moor."[17]

Just as Wordsworth cures himself by projecting out of his deepest fears and strengths an image of an old man who has suffered and still triumphed, in the figure of Matthew he combines the literal truth of early death (his own worst fear) with the confected biography of a fictitious old man. The Reverend William Taylor, Wordsworth's teacher and schoolmaster at Hawkshead, died in 1786 at the age of thirty-two; in a note to "Matthew" Wordsworth admits that "like the Wanderer in 'The Excursion,' this Schoolmaster was made up of several both of his class and men of other occupations" (*PW* 4: 415).[18] In the "Matthew" poems Wordsworth is clearly protecting himself from his own fears by changing this teacher from an early victim into a survivor, a venerable wise man whose long life is a lesson in the truths of sadness and the joys and pains of memory. As Mary Moorman's description of Taylor—"young, scholarly, poetic, kind, no one could have been better fitted than Taylor to be, all unknowing, the tutor of a great poet in his happy youth"—suggests, Taylor is another double.[19] If Wordsworth is to absorb his lessons and imitate his model before reaching venerability himself, he must conceive of his teacher as an older man. If the teacher dies before his expected time, and at an age approximating Wordsworth's own in 1799, when the poems were composed, then the pupil must confront the possibility of his own untimely death.

At the age of thirty, the tentative and uncertain Wordsworth would hopefully agree with Yeats's retrospective pronouncement that "bodily decrepitude is wisdom." Matthew's unique wisdom blends past and present gaiety, sadness, and a knowledge of the irreversibility of time and fate, a knowledge that the apprentice poet has yet to accept fully. In "The Two April Mornings" (*PW* 4: 69) "the village schoolmaster," like the leech-gatherer, seems both the double and the opposite of the young poet. The manic-depressive condition that will be the poet's alone in "Resolution and Independence" here belongs to Matthew who, blithe and merry on a holiday in the fields, suddenly changes mood and surprises the poet with an exclamation: "The will of God be done." The substance of the poem explains the reasons for this new despondence; Matthew has been reminded of a day thirty years before on which he encountered by his daughter's grave another "blooming girl." In her natural animal innocence, she is the dead Emma's double (much as this day is the "brother" of that distant spring day), but she is also the dead girl's opposite, merely by being alive. The struggle between particularity and universality triggers the momentary sadness in Matthew's sight. What is lost can never be replaced even by what most resembles it.

In "The Fountain," Wordsworth distances himself from unpleasant truths by placing them in the old man's mouth, and yet accepts them as true. We see the same tension between gaiety and sadness conditioned by memory as in "The Two April Mornings." Matthew is "the grey-haired man of glee," but repetition of experience reminds him of how he is no longer the same: the stream goes on forever but we, its observers, change. We are set apart from nature, from blackbird and lark, because our old age is not beautiful and free. Heavy laws, the knowledge of mortality, press upon us, and no love is enough to compensate for our knowledge of past happiness and present decay. His is the voice of a man who is willing to surrender as well as to laugh and sing his old witty rhymes. The joy of the old is both hypocritical—the pose expected of the man of mirth—and inevitable, for a residue of gaiety persists in those who have once been gay:

> "But we are pressed by heavy laws;
> And often, glad no more,
> We wear a face of joy, because
> We have been glad of yore.
>
> "If there be one who need bemoan
> His kindred laid in earth,

The household hearts that were his own;
It is the man of mirth.

"My days, my Friend, are almost gone,
My life has been approved,
And many love me; but by none
Am I enough beloved."

Although Anne Kostelanetz insists that the two viewpoints in this "conversation" poem are balanced, surely Matthew's argument has the edge over Wordsworth's somewhat naive offer to become a second son to him.[20] Doublings and repetitions there may be in nature, especially if we believe, like Wordsworth, in "a mighty commonwealth of things" that balance and reflect one another. Still, the irreversible linearity of human life, returned to over and again by the poet in his effort to understand the aging process and age itself, gives Matthew's voice a greater authority and finality.

"The child is life, the man death," G. Wilson Knight's somber summary of the Intimations Ode,[21] is an approximate truth that Wordsworth continued to modify as he aged and realized both that he *had* survived and that his own death was increasingly imminent. The morbid fear of early death gradually yielded to a sober autumnal perspective that, adjusted to the reality of his own situation, never forced upon Wordsworth a heavy or barren tone. A late letter to Aubrey de Vere, for example, is witty, gracious, and humane while admitting the truth of all the clichés about nostalgia in old age: "Old men's literary pleasures lie chiefly among the books they were familiar with in their youth. . . . It is in vain to regret these changes which Time brings with it; one might as well sigh over one's grey hairs."[22]

As Wordsworth's own star sinks into the light of common day, his poems continue to explore the compensations that age should (or does) provide for those losses man has sustained. His most lucid theoretical exposition comes in the last book of *The Excursion*, where the Wan-

derer discourses on the imaginative glories of old age. Asserting the primacy of activity in all living things, he suggests that the vigor and hope, "meditated action," of youth
are what cause us, in age, to "revert so fondly to the walks /
Of Childhood." Nostalgia is but half the story, for as we decline into the vale of years, the Wanderer conjures up a
happy picture of age as an ascent to a final Eminence, literal as well as figurative:

> though bare
> In aspect and forbidding, yet a point
> On which 'tis not impossible to sit
> In awful sovereignty; a place of power,
> A throne, that may be likened unto his,
> Who, in some placid day of summer, looks
> Down from a mountain-top.

(lines 52–58)

Poised like Chaucer's Troilus or Lucretius's philosopher
above "the vast multitude; whose doom it is / To run the
giddy round of vain delight / Or fret and labour on the
Plain below" (lines 90–92), the aged sovereign, a privileged
monarch of all he surveys, is gradually disencumbered of
sensuous ties with the earth: "the gross and visible frame
of things / Relinquishes its hold upon the sense, / Yea almost on the Mind herself, and seems / All unsubstantial-
ized" (lines 63–66). Seeing goes, but hearing remains, as
the "invigorated peal" of the river beneath him mounts,
like the Atlantic waters threatening the heavens in *The
Prelude* XIII. Gradually, even sound disappears, first the
"ever-humming insects," then "the murmur of the leaves,"
and finally and strangely from all willed bodily connection,
the "thousand notes / . . . / By which the finer passages of
sense / Are occupied; and the Soul, that would incline / To
listen, is prevented or deterred" (lines 71–80).

The program of sensory deprivation is redeemed by a
final lesson that our home is with infinitude; the severe
yet gentle loss of sense confers, he urges, "fresh power
to commune with the invisible world, / And hear the
mighty stream of tendency / Uttering, for elevation of our

thought, / A clear sonorous voice" (lines 86–89). How far this condition is from that of Matthew, Cumberland Beggar, and the anthropomorphized celandine! It is, moreover, a note that Wallace Stevens must have heard echoed in his own mind's ear when he pictured an old man at the end of summer in Oley's ripe hayfields:

> It is the old man standing on the tower,
> Who reads no book. His ruddy ancientness
> Absorbs the ruddy summer and is appeased,
> By an understanding that fulfils his age,
> By a feeling capable of nothing more.
> . . . .
>   It is
> A land too ripe for enigmas, too serene.
> There the distant fails the clairvoyant eye
>
> And the secondary senses of the ear
> Swarm, not with secondary sounds, but choirs,
> Not evocations but last choirs, last sounds
> With nothing else compounded, carried full,
> Pure rhetoric of a language without words.
>
> Things stop in that direction and since they stop
> The direction stops and we accept what is
> As good.[23]

The last choirs may be Keats's, but the old man himself, and the wishful "Credences" of the poem's title, point only to Wordsworth.

The major problem with the Wanderer's account of our final ascent is not that it is a hopeful theory, never proved, but that Wordsworth virtually undercuts it by the subsequent incidents in the poem. Unwilling either to surrender sensory control and pleasure (the gross frame of things *almost* but not fully relinquishes its hold upon the perceiving and imagining Mind), or to retreat into a monastery of the meditative self, Wordsworth emphasizes the communion of man with nature, and the community of man and man. Even the Wanderer's theorizing stands against his earlier admission of emotional resistance: "Life's autumn past, I stand on winter's verge; / And daily lose what I desire to keep" (IV, 611–12). Subsequently, there is no loss, only gain, in the shared excursion of Wordsworth's characters. Following the Wanderer's lecture on the necessity of civic education and "the discipline of virtue" in a democracy, the Pastor's wife remarks on the shining temptation of the evening landscape, and the whole group pursues its way to the margin of a lake, thence by boat to a *fête champêtre* upon a birch-fringed island. The tranquillity of nature, evening, and human contentment cannot be disturbed, even by the misanthropic Solitary, who puts to the test the Wanderer's earlier meditation on the benevolence of age. Looking back at the deserted and dying fire on the beach, the Solitary sees an emblem "of one day's pleasure, and all mortal joys! / And, in this unpremeditated slight / Of that which is no longer needed, see / The common course of human gratitude!" (lines 555–58).

The only answer to the challenge of skepticism comes in the dramatized ascent by the entire group of "a green hill's side," from which they see a valley preserved "from all intrusion of the restless world / By rocks impassable and mountains huge" (lines 578–79). The calm of this embrace, like that in "Home at Grasmere," is perfect because shared.[24] Far from suggesting the gradual removal from sense of worldly delight and human intercourse, the last scene describes each person as alternately quiet, and pointing out a favorite discovery, "merely from a wish / To impart a joy, imperfect while unshared" (lines 586–87). The final sunset counters both the Solitary's emblem of the dying fire and the Wanderer's depiction of sensuous decay; it epitomizes the dependency of imaginative and religious intimations upon specific, shared, visual details. The clouds "had become / Vivid as fire" as the lights of the declining sun shoot upward to the sky:

Innumerable multitude of forms
Scattered through half the circle of the sky;

And giving back, and shedding each on each,
With prodigal communion, the bright hues
Which from the unapparent fount of glory
They had imbibed, and ceased not to receive.
That which the heavens displayed, the liquid deep
Repeated; but with unity sublime!

(lines 601–8)

This is truly the natural rhetoric of a language without words, the sign of a covenant between man and man, man and nature, and the late philosopher with the child-father of his own earlier self.

In Wordsworth's poems after 1814, the earlier strategies of projection and sublimation with which he handled his simultaneous fears of early death and of bodily and mental decrepitude in age are replaced by a combination of stoic fortitude, Christian faith, and a revival of "the light of youthful glee" (*PW* 3: 86). Since the worst fears of "Resolution and Independence" were not realized, the desolation and hardship of the earlier old men give way to autumnal mellowness, an acceptance not only of mortality but of the need, even in age, "of ennobling impulse from the past, / If to the future aught of good must come" (*PW* 3: 212). The poetry is less dramatic; there are fewer "characters"; now his focus shifts to his own life in first-person meditations and lyrics. The true voice of feeling is considerably softer, less sullen, and less harried than in the earlier poems. At its least interesting, it adds bald piety to the usual Wordsworthian motifs, as in the 1835 "Written after the Death of Charles Lamb" (*PW* 4: 272), where we may hear echoes of Wordsworth's own early crises when he refers to Mary Lamb's intervals of sanity:

the remembrance of foregone distress,
And the worse fear of future ill (which oft
Doth hang around it, as a sickly child
Upon its mother) may be both alike
Disarmed of power to unsettle present good
So prized, and things inward and outward held
In such an even balance, that the heart

Acknowledges God's grace, his mercy feels,
And in its depth of gratitude is still.
(lines 112–20)

More remarkable is the refusal to mourn in the "Extempore Effusion Upon the Death of James Hogg" in the same year (*PW* 4: 276), a poem from whose ballad stanzas rolls a necrology of Wordsworth's poetic contemporaries—Lamb, Scott, Coleridge, Crabbe—all now outlived by him who was "earlier raised" and remains "to hear / A timid voice, that asks in whispers, / 'Who next will drop and disappear?'" For among "ripe fruit, seasonably gathered," over which the survivor will not cry, it is Wordsworth who has been left behind. Matthew's earlier words about how the wiser mind responds to what remains now become prophetic of Wordsworth's later life, from which children, siblings, and friends, moving "from sunshine to the sunless land," departed as the darkening shadows surrounded him.

The impressive "Elegiac Stanzas" (1805) steeled Wordsworth against excessive grieving until his beloved Dora died in 1847, when his own strength all but crumbled at the end. Nevertheless, the sense of imminent death heightens Wordsworth's pleasures in old age. The human past and present sorrow are both foils to set off the glow of his happiness, through either a conventionally pious acceptance of God's will or a somewhat heartier, more jovial spunk with which we rarely associate the poet in his "great" early decade.[25] In "Musings Near Aquapendente" (*PW* 3: 202–12) from the "Memorials of a Tour in Italy" with Crabb Robinson in 1837, Wordsworth sounds as if he is repeating, in the language of *The Prelude* I, the adventures of his escape from London more than forty years earlier. He gives thanks

That I—so near the term to human life
Appointed by man's common heritage,
Frail as the frailest, one withal (if that

Deserve a thought) but little known to fame—
Am free to rove
. . . .
                 free to rove at will
O'er high and low, and if requiring rest,
Rest from enjoyment only.

                          (lines 91–100)

Although conscious that the Stream of Time bears much away, "nor seldom is put forth / An angry arm that snatches good away, / Never perhaps to reappear" (lines 319–21), Wordsworth maintains throughout this poem a tone of strikingly youthful enthusiasm for the tour ahead of him, especially for Italy's ennobling influence on the individual tourist and the nations of Europe. When he says that we need more "heroic impulse from the past, / If to the future aught of good must come" (lines 349–50), we hear the personal dimension, as well as the historical and political ones, of his meditation. Wearing "a crown / Of earthly hope put on with trembling hand" (lines 110–11), the old sage speaks both of the blest tranquillity achieved by men at all ages and of the active principle that attends us only if we pursue it: "who would keep / Power must resolve to cleave to it through life, / Else it deserts him" (lines 115–17). (The Wanderer devotes the beginning of his meditation on age to this same topic, *The Excursion* IX.)

Instead of suggesting a diminution of sensuous perception, poetic vigor, or even personal energy, "Musings Near Aquapendente" shows the strength of old age which Wordsworth achieved in old age. The poem repeats or recalls expressions of freedom, self-reliance, and the joys that come from contemplating a landscape in "Tintern Abbey" and *The Prelude* I. Likewise, the 1831 "The Primrose of the Rock" (*PW* 2: 303) matches the third celandine poem of 1804, in its devotion to a rugged, ordinary flower. "A lasting link in Nature's chain," by virtue of literal tenacity the primrose exemplifies the vital principle of the universe; reborn annually, it betokens the speaker's continued affection. No longer splenetic, as he was years earlier when confronting a similar flower, the poet watches the lonely plant, unfearful of death, and blesses it with hope for the propagation of thousands like it. Even thistles become "types beneficent," as Wordsworth thinks ahead to the eternal summer after death instead of casting his eye to the ledger of what is lost and what gained in age.

Threatened by failing eyesight as early as 1805, Wordsworth retained a powerful "inner spirit" throughout his declining years, as well as "an ample sovereignty of eye and ear" like that of the old man in the 1807 sonnet "Though narrow be that old man's cares and near." Even when appropriating the words of Milton's Samson ("A little onward lend thy guiding hand") to begin an 1816 poem on his eye inflammation, Wordsworth depicts himself as strong "though not unmenaced." And still later, addressed by "the Spirit of Cockermouth Castle" (1833), when both man and building are "prepared to sink into the dust," the poet relies on his accustomed fortitude, which does not abandon him.

The equilibrium in Wordsworth's attitude toward old age appears in several small "poems of sentiment and reflection," originally published in 1820 and composed several years earlier. The "Ode to Lycoris" and the two lyrics dated September 1819 (*PW* 4: 94–101) epitomize the range of Wordsworth's feelings about his old age and Age itself. Not yet fifty, he calls himself "a bard of ebbing time" and appropriates to himself Macbeth's "sere and yellow leaf." But although the persona is old, the spirit is not. He gently mocks youthful melancholy, an affected guise when "twilight is preferred to Dawn, / And Autumn to the Spring."

We should, he continues, welcome our own and the year's decline without entirely succumbing, and in our own decay we should balance our souls by recalling the deity of youth within (and into) our breasts: "Still, as we nearer draw to life's dark goal, / Be hopeful Spring the fa-

vourite of the Soul" ("Ode to Lycoris"). The autumnal pair
that follows, however, yields to the harvest temptations of
"corn-clad fields," and hears in autumn's music "an impulse more profoundly dear / Than music of the Spring."
The "turbulence" and "impatience" of Spring's sounds recede as the spiritual ditties of fall touch a responsive inner
chord:

> This, this is holy;—while I hear
> These vespers of another year,
> This hymn of thanks and praise,
> My spirit seems to mount above
> The anxieties of human love,
> And earth's precarious days.

The conventional Christian sentiments in the first of the
two lyrics (the autumnal choristers, like seraphim, abide
with an all-providing God) and the backward glance, in the
second poem, at the history of poetry itself as a revelatory
and liberating power are two ways of confronting the autumnal beauties in the scene and their reflection within the
poet. Gracefully relinquishing youth and its triumphs
("Fall, rosy garlands from my head! / Ye myrtle wreaths,
your fragrance shed / Around a younger brow!"), Wordsworth, like the other autumnal singers, gathers in the harvest of his songs with a "timely carolling." He again finds
true liberty in the acceptance of narrowing boundaries, just
as at the end of *The Prelude* I ("a theme single and of determined bounds") or in *The Excursion* IV ("conscious that the
Will is free, / [We] Shall move unswerving, even as if im-
pelled / By strict necessity, along the path / Of order and of
good"). As he prepares to fade into winter himself, he witnesses the inner equivalent of surrounding natural unity:

> Yet will I temperately rejoice;
> Wide is the range, and free the choice
> Of undiscordant themes;
> Which, haply, kindred souls may prize
> Not less than vernal ecstasies
> And passion's feverish dreams.

Though much is taken, much abides: in that, at least, Wordsworth would agree with Tennyson's Ulysses. "Temperance" and willed self-limitation are the virtues of middle age and, as more is taken away, of old age, as the Fenwick note to *The White Doe of Rylstone* explains:

> Poetic excitement, when accompanied by more or less protracted labour in composition, has throughout my life brought on more or less bodily derangement. Nevertheless, I am at the close of my seventy-third year, in what may be called excellent health; so that intellectual labour is not necessarily unfavourable to longevity.
>
> (*PW* 3: 542)

In many of the late poems, the embers give a glow, if not much heat, and the temperance of Wordsworth's response to life's autumnal harmonies is evidence of creative impulse, if not fervor.

Far from being burned out, indeed far from death in September 1819, Wordsworth probably did not know that farther south, another, younger poet was confronting the same English fall and evoking it with tropes and images similar to his:

> Where are the songs of Spring? Ay, where are they?
>   Think not of them, thou hast thy music too,—
> While barred clouds bloom the soft-dying day,
>   And touch the stubble-plains with rosy hue;
> Then in a wailful choir the small gnats mourn
>   Among the river sallows, borne aloft
>   Or sinking as the light wind lives or dies;
> And full-grown lambs loud bleat from hilly bourn;
>   Hedge-crickets sing; and now with treble soft
> The red-breast whistles from a garden-croft;
>   And gathering swallows twitter in the skies.

Keats never reached even middle age, but in his last poems he seems to have learned age's lessons while overleaping its indignities. Ultimately, Wordsworth was lucky to have avoided them too, to have developed for himself the strength he had ascribed to his noblest old man in 1800.

Like Michael, Wordsworth "learned the meaning of all winds," and like Keats, looking over the stubble fields of Winchester in 1819, Wordsworth relinquished his worst fears and saw the world as good:

> Those fields, those hills—what could they less? had laid
> Strong hold on his affections, were to him
> A pleasurable feeling of blind love,
> The pleasure which there is in life itself.
>
> ("Michael," lines 74–77)

5

The Autobiographical Hero
in *The Prelude*

KNOWING, SEEING, DOING

The radical novelty of *The Prelude* is not, *pace* Wordsworth's assessment, that it "is a thing unprecedented in Literary history that a man should talk so much about himself" (*EY*, p. 586). The ample precedents of autobiography, confession, memoirs, all the genres of self-justification to God and men, require that a man talk about himself a great deal, and they take as their initial convention and their ultimate rationalization the unquestioned interest of their subject to both author and audience. Whether one considers *The Prelude* as preparatory to a great work never achieved or as a finished product in itself, the poem is most fruitfully analyzed as the effort of a man attempting to make of himself an epic hero.[1] Although the poem belongs, in part, to several genres—confession, meditation, verse epistle—it most self-consciously allies itself with the epic. Wordsworth's awkward dilemma is how to fit himself to traditional heroic status; navigating for himself a path midway between the spectatorial position Coleridge assigns him and the "egotistical sublime" Keats and Hazlitt burden him with, he retrieves his "self" from the depths of memory and presents it, in a new epistolary and Miltonic form, to an absent alter ego. Addressing himself to Coleridge in the Mediterranean, Wordsworth creates a life as bard and hero of a new epic.

Through a series of related antinomies we see this hero emerge, develop, and center himself in the poem: as an active man, engaged in tasks physical (climbing mountains, walking through the countryside) and creative (reading and writing), or as a passive man, feeling and suffering; as a participant in life or as a spectator of both life (at Cambridge, and in London and France) and art (considering the "self" as a distant, finished product); as a self clothed with accumulated experiences and developing through time, or as an unaccommodated man confronting peril, sublimity, and extremes of feeling and landscape; as a man concentric in the world whose primary method is analogy ("What one is, / Why may not many be?" XII, 91–92) and whose relationships with others are complementary (Coleridge and Beaupuy as ideal projections of contemplation and active involvement, respectively), or as man eccentric, for whom isolation seems the inevitable outcome of childhood solitude and criminality as well as the hoped-for condition of a man in retirement. These are the poles between which Wordsworth's self-presentation eddies, and it is a signal fact of Wordsworth's distinctive brand of "heroism" that he can sustain such paradoxical definitions, expanding and diminishing his main character, without apparent anxiety. Might we label the act of self-creation in *The Prelude* a feat of Keatsian negative capability? The mingled pride and self-effacement in his conscious turning away from "precedents" in the letter to Beaumont invites us to consider the poem as exactly such a creation.

Wordsworth's mission is fraught throughout with danger, and he understands the fact of abstraction as part of his agon: "Of Genius, Power, / Creation and Divinity itself / I have been speaking, for my theme has been / What pass'd within me. . . . / . . . / This is in truth heroic argument" (III, 171–74, 182). His heroism, thus, does more than follow the symbolic pattern many critics have traced: a life moving from harmony, through a fortunate fall into the chaos of experience, to a final imaginative or philosophical compensation, a higher innocence in maturity.[2] It is implicit in the arduous acts of remembering and recording with which he takes such pains and which have become, in subsequent autobiographical literature, conventional. We now accept the third-person narratives of Henry Adams or Norman Mailer not merely as a nod in the direction of a supposed objectivity, but as an acknowledgment of the real gap between past and present versions of a self. As Christopher Isherwood straightforwardly demonstrates in one of his memoirs, the writer may confess ignorance by using an authorial "I" for himself in the present, and a distanced "Christopher" for his thirty-year-old hero whose motivations, through the cloudy darkness of time, are simply irretrievable.[3]

Wordsworth frankly admits to his problem in "Tintern Abbey"—"I cannot paint what then I was"—and also embeds it in his claim that his recollections of the Wye Valley have had an unflagging influence on "that best portion of a good man's life, / His little, nameless, unremembered acts / Of kindness and of love." If moral identity is constituted by trivial and anonymous deeds, it is difficult to know the self, impossible to name what can be inferred but never seen. Action promotes worth, but knowledge alone confers meaning. The self doing and the self knowing seem to be, like power and knowledge, rival dispensations.

Namelessness is, in fact, not the least of *The Prelude*'s considerable variations on epic conventions. The poem never names its hero.[4] Proper names, those badges of singularity, belong to no more than a dozen persons, two of whom, Vaudracour and Julia, are fictionalized, not fully named, and removed from the poem in 1820. Among the others, Wordsworth names Coleridge, Beaupuy, and Raisley Calvert, the dead and the absent, but not Dorothy or Mary Hutchinson. To name is to memorialize.

At the start of Book II, Wordsworth confronts the "va-

cancy" between the present adult and the days of childhood that nevertheless seem present in his mind: "sometimes, when I think of them, I seem / Two consciousnesses,
conscious of myself / And of some other Being" (II, 31–33).
Later, he shadowily distinguishes between moods within
our intellectual life: "the soul, / Remembering how she felt,
but what she felt / Remembering not, retains an obscure
sense / Of possible sublimity" (II, 334–37). Finishing his
first year of university life, he confesses his problem: "I
cannot say what portion is in truth / The naked recollection
of that time, / And what may rather have been call'd to life /
By after-meditation" (III, 645–48).

"Hard task to analyse a soul" (II, 232) is Wordsworth's
worried confession to Coleridge, his intellectual mentor.
Hard are the problems of the origins and boundaries of
thought, and the perpetually dim befoggings and distor-
tions of memory, layered like the greater mind of which it
is a part, with recollections screening, augmenting, and ef-
facing one another. Because one is always "naked" and
clothed, one is always double: Wordsworth has a proto-ex-
istential sense of human alienation when he distinguishes
" 'twixt man himself . . . and his own unquiet heart" (XI,
18–19), and a sense of fragmentation: "the Man to come
parted as by a gulph, / From him who had been" (XI, 59–
60). As reading is Wordsworth's metonymy for knowing,
memory is his synecdoche for soul itself, a palimpsest
whose inscriptions are rarely clear and never possible to
date accurately.

For these reasons, "seeing" occupies in the poem a crucial middle position between knowing and doing. Significantly, the mere handful of extended similes in *The Prelude*
all embody its hero's perceptual and poetic development.
The comparisons that follow the revelations at the Simplon
Pass and on Mt. Snowdon in Books VI and XIII are inevitable meditations on those landscapes that have halted the
traveler, but in Books IV and VIII the poet interrupts the
narrative to analyze the difficulties of perception; quasi-

epic similes are his tool. The pleasures of nostalgia and the willful misinterpretation of reality, like the presence of metaphor, deliberately falsify the named truth by supplementing it with fanciful doubleness:

> As one who hangs down-bending from the side
> Of a slow-moving Boat, upon the breast
> Of a still water, solacing himself
> With such discoveries as his eye can make,
> Beneath him, in the bottom of the deeps,
> Sees many beauteous sights, weeds, fishes, flowers,
> Grots, pebbles, roots of trees, and fancies more;
> Yet often is perplex'd, and cannot part
> The shadow from the substance, rocks and sky,
> Mountains and clouds, from that which is indeed
> The region, and the things which there abide
> In their true dwelling; now is cross'd by gleam
> Of his own image, by a sunbeam now,
> And motions that are sent he knows not whence,
> Impediments that make his task more sweet;
> —Such pleasant office have we long pursued
> Incumbent o'er the surface of past time
> With like success; nor have we often look'd
> On more alluring shows (to me, at least,)
> More soft, or less ambiguously descried,
> Than those which now we have been passing by,
> And where we still are lingering.
>
> (IV, 247–68)

These "new employments of the mind," as he calls them (line 269), are nevertheless no aid, but rather an impediment; in spite of them Wordsworth is conscious of loss of power and self-diminution through his participation in worldly life. The same kind of halt in the narrative occurs in Book VIII (lines 711–41) in a section whose first part alludes to *The Aeneid* (6: 454, "Aut videt, aut vidisse putat") through *Paradise Lost* (1: 783–84), a section that, in March 1804, when it was composed, defined Wordsworth's disappointment in the Simplon Pass:

> As when a Traveller hath from open day
> With torches pass'd into some Vault of Earth,

The Grotto of Antiparos, or the Den
Of Yordas among Craven's mountain tracts;
He looks and sees the cavern spread and grow,
Widening itself on all sides, sees, or thinks
He sees, erelong, the roof above his head,
Which instantly unsettles and recedes
Substance and shadow, light and darkness, all
Commingled, making up a Canopy
Of Shapes and Forms and Tendencies to Shape
That shift and vanish, change and interchange
Like Spectres, ferment quiet and sublime;
Which, after a short space, works less and less,
Till every effort, every motion gone,
The scene before him lies in perfect view,
Exposed and lifeless, as a written book.
                              (VIII, 711–27)

In the final version, however, Wordsworth places this
extended metaphor about the difficulties of reading the
world in the middle of his recollection of arriving in London (itself a repetition from Book VII), when the weight
and power of history and of "aught *external* to the living
mind" (line 701) presses upon the newly arrived traveler.
Burdened, then metaphorically confused and blinded,
then peopling the vacancy with new imaginary projections
until the whole becomes "a Spectacle to which there is no
end" (line 741), Wordsworth reduces the external world
that threatens him to a projection within his mind, and he
fills the stage of his mind with grim forms and spectres
such as one might hallucinate in a Platonic cavern. A swell
of feeling and of thinking is "follow'd soon / By a blank
sense of greatness pass'd away" (lines 743–44). But emptiness and fullness, absence and presence, inner and outer
dimensions vie with one another in heroic proportions, as
the youth is prepared for the paradoxical symbol which he
projects onto, and simultaneously accepts from (or reads
into and reads from) the vast metropolis, "the Fountain of
my Country's destiny / . . . / Chronicle at once / And Burial-
place of passions and their home / Imperial and chief living
residence" (lines 747–51). The language of paradox devel-

oped in metaphor is the surest sign in *The Prelude* of heightened witnessing, or of those numinous moments in which the self is either challenged or raises itself to heroic pitch. These similes seem to validate a middle position for the self, between active subject and recollected or passive object. The very grounds for the hero's identity differ from those in earlier epics, but it is not simple self-consciousness that separates Wordsworth as hero and author from Achilles and his creator. Rather, the author makes himself a hero by placing himself on the stage, in the middle of a heroic drama of his own conscious construction. It is as if Wordsworth has fashioned the entire poem in the key that Virgil strikes when he has Dido placing herself not only within a myth but even as a character in a mythic tragedy, a figure from Aeschylus or Euripides.[5] The extended similes, a stylistic heightening of recollection through an epic device, raise the speaking self to a heroic level. Throughout the poem, the poet shifts to this mode at moments when action, or any human control, begins to be thwarted.

The Prelude is a poem of characters and "character," the multifold meanings of which are interwoven throughout and point to the heroic achievement of the speaker by way of the runes and inscriptions he encounters and makes. "Characters," whether engravings, the words of one's written language, or the roles one assumes and the people one meets, build character.[6] Moral status is the result of such encounters. The development of the poet's mind and character are literally dependent both on what he may read in the universal text of nature and subsequently inscribe in a text of his own, and on the roles he has assumed or had cast upon him while growing up. Henry James asked, "What is character but the determination of incident? What is incident but the illustration of character?"[7] To which a reader of Wordsworth might well reply: Character is moral worth drawn from characters, witnessed, read, and dramatized.

The human connections, however unlikely or ghostly,

proved by Wordsworth's confrontations with emissaries
from different ranks and orders, allow for the development
of the self by a mirroring of one character through or in
others. All repetition, whether the challenge of human
mirroring or the rote recitation of catechism and formula,
strengthens the self. As Robert M. Adams observes, we
may define the self either by addition (what the individual
accumulates or, in Wordsworth's phrase, "the freight of
earthly years") or by subtraction, what exists at the core of
being after layers of veils and masks are stripped away.[8]
Repetition, like confrontation, augments the self by forcing it forward and establishing connections with the past.
In contrast, moments of loss, confusion, or deprivation,
which may be labeled in one guise the experience of the
sublime, have their origin in the mingled fear and pleasure
of terror, and paradoxically test the self by rendering it
speechless, helpless, or affectless. After great pain comes
the formal feeling in which reconstitution begins with the
self-in-meditation deliberating upon the self-in-action.
Hence what Wordsworth refers to as the "wholesome separation of the two natures, / The one that feels, the other
that observes" (XIII, 330–31). But while he always suggests dichotomies such as this, the poetry constantly undermines simple polarities.

In action and in observation the self may be either active
or passive: it responds to external stimuli, it stamps its
own mark on the world; and in contemplation it is both
subject and object. Wordsworth understands the paradox
of autobiography as the Romantic dilemma of a will divided by self-consciousness, which Coleridge characteristically solves by saying that the spirit must be an act:

> Again the spirit (originally the identity of object and subject)
> must in some self dissolve this identity, in order to be con-
> scious of it; *fit alter et idem*. But this implies an act, and it fol-
> lows therefore that intelligence of self-consciousness is impos-
> sible, except by and in a will. The self-conscious spirit
> therefore is a will.[9]

So knowledge and power may not be rival dispensations after all.

HEROISM AND MOCK-HEROISM

The rhythmic flow of *The Prelude* allows us to see both the hero and humanity in general in terms of the related, but certainly not identical, antinomies of grandeur-pettiness and activity-passivity. In the summarizing eighth book, for instance, Wordsworth paints a picture of Grasmere Fair, attended by the rural population whom he venerates because they were his first examples of humankind:

> Immense
> Is the Recess, the circumambient World
> Magnificent, by which they are embraced.
> They move about upon the soft green field:
> How little They, they and their doings seem,
> Their herds and flocks about them, they themselves,
> And all that they can further or obstruct!
> Through utter weakness pitiably dear
> As tender Infants are: and yet how great!
> For all things serve them; them the Morning light
> Loves as it glistens on the silent rocks,
> And them the silent Rocks, which now from high
> Look down upon them; the reposing Clouds,
> The lurking Brooks from their invisible haunts,
> And Old Helvellyn, conscious of the stir,
> And the blue Sky that roofs their calm abode.
>
> (VIII, 46–61)

Although the people are first depicted in action and in their puniness (lines 49–54), their true greatness comes when they are presented as objects of natural obeisance and respect (lines 55–61). The dialectical force of this paragraph strikes at the heart of Wordsworth's conception of man and therefore of himself, the main region of his own song.

Before attending to the poem's antitheses, we must return to the premise that the poem's subject is heroically conceived, both as an individual and as representative of all humanity *in posse*. From the start, Wordsworth models himself on a heroic ideal compounded equally of classical valor and stoicism, and Christian Romance, or what Milton calls "heroic martyrdom" (*Paradise Lost* 9: 32). It is an ideal in which struggle and *aristeia* have been internalized but are bodied forth through the language of heroic activity: his freedom and escape from the city bring "the hope / Of active days, of dignity and thought, / Of prowess in an honorable field, / Pure passions, virtue, knowledge, and delight, / The holy life of music and of verse" (I, 50–54). The work of glory he intends to perform or compose in Grasmere is progressively reconceived from 1805 to 1850. "Prowess" becomes "punctual service high" and leisure comes to predominate over the "trial of strength" accorded to the poet's soul that (1805 MS, line 139) is struggling to "grapple with some noble theme," yet failing to do so because the recreant mind is the enemy or impediment to its own achievement.

But just as *The Prelude* wrestles with its own formation as its author revises it for close to fifty years, and revising, through it, himself, so also is classical literary heroism continually tested, found wanting, and therefore satirized, throughout the poem.[10] Card-playing (I, 534ff.), like other childhood games, is a mock-heroic preparation for adult life; as Wordsworth reminds us in the Intimations Ode, a child develops "as if his whole vocation / Were endless imitation."[11] Although the awkwardness of Wordsworth's style and his temperamental inability to rival Pope attest to his uncertainty about the card game itself, he tells us that in cards there are no neglected soldiers, thereby readying us for the discharged soldier in Book IV and the ways in which reality is bound to disappoint our feelings for justice and truth throughout the poem. Military service, the heroism of the active life (in the discharged soldier and Michel Beaupuy in Book IX), meets with only ingratitude and shame.

The scenes at Cambridge in Book III tend likewise to the mock-heroic and the claustrophobic. Though Wordsworth is "not for that hour, / Nor for that place" (lines 80–81) he transcends the limitations of domestic, social coziness by isolated walks through the adjoining fields, where he finds fittest speech and stimulation as he is "awaken'd, summon'd, rous'd, constrain'd," searching for universals in nature and in the mind, "ascending . . . to such community with highest truth" (III, 109–20). The first "act" (line 259) in the new life is the setting to sleep of Imagination. The image of a new Wordsworth, lazy, unprofitable, and boisterous, running tipsy to Chapel from Milton's rooms at Christ's College, embarrassingly enforces the poetic problems he has with self-definition through action and the discovery of appropriate models or language for heroic imitation. Based on his distrust of action, the university is a parody of a parody since it is a model for the greater world: "here, in dwarf proportions, were express'd / The limbs of the great world" (lines 615–16), a mock-heroic tourney of less than mortal blows.

Looking back, Wordsworth now realizes this *was* a part of life, not only a preparation for it, embodying normal hopes and fears, but he presents them as propped-up abstractions on show, a list of Spenserian personifications in a pageant: "Feuds, Factions, Flatteries, Enmity, and Guile" (line 636). Although some things were enjoyed, learned, or suffered, the "labouring time" (line 670) of nine months resulted in a progeny stillborn, since ardor was secondary to "submissive idleness" and the figure of the youth as passive loiterer or mock-heroic egoist in quest of undesired objects deprecates to mere time-serving his apprenticeship. Both vocation as imitation and university life as self-indulgent and self-dramatizing act without self-motivated action reduce heroic worth by rendering performance insignificant.

For Wordsworth, heroic enterprise always comes in going naked, but the effort, to be glorious, must involve a stripping away. Thus, toward the end of his poem, in a major moment of revelation, he remembers how he restored imagination and harmony following the period of psychic disturbance and moral doubting of the mid 1790s:

> I had felt
> Too forcibly, too early in my life,
> Visitings of imaginative power
> For this to last: I shook the *habit* off
> Entirely and for ever, and again
> In Nature's presence stood, as I stand now,
> A sensitive, and a creative Soul.
>
> (XI, 251–57, emphasis mine)

The image of Wordsworth standing like St. Francis to greet the sun is compounded by another, which originates in an earlier description of himself, during his crisis, as "a Monk who hath forsworn the world" (line 76; in 1850 MS, a "cowled monk"). At his climactic moment, then, the self-warring and destructive Wordsworth rips off his workaday "habit" to reveal his heroic nature.

But to be naked one must first have been clothed, unless one is lucky enough to have an education like that of the Boy of Winander, and doubly lucky to have survived. (Surely one of the hidden possibilities in this story is the murderous dangers of those mimic hootings.) Yet the infant prodigy of our modern day is "fenc'd round . . . in panoply complete" (V, 314) and therefore untouchable by Fear. Since fear itself, along with Beauty, is the prime ingredient of and preparation for heroic testing, and since self-forgetfulness, not self-consciousness, is the basis for childhood learning, Wordsworth can again suggest the parody of a parody by comparing the "mighty workmen" of modern educational theory to Sin and Death in *Paradise Lost*.

Just as the sham labor of college days mocks heroism, so the long description of London life throughout Book VII mocks sublimity. Whereas the traumatic Simplon Pass episode in the preceding book presents the characters of the great apocalypse, and the poet assumes his rightful place as reader of those characters and, later, as one among their band (in XIII, 231, he describes his soul as "a rock with torrents roaring"), here in the lurking passages of the city there is naught but show, masquerade, and deception. Infinity becomes a catalogue, and even landscape is replaced by landscape painting (lines 244–89). Wordsworth's first exposure to a shameful woman makes him realize that domestic tragedy or pathos is not far from mock heroism, since both disappointingly divorce the human form from humanity itself. He watches theatrical spectacles and reminds *his* audience of earlier apocalyptic moments in the Alps and elsewhere: "how eagerly, / And with what flashes, as it were, the mind / Turn'd this way, that way!" (lines 468–70).

Indeed, if London in part resembles a chaotic pseudo-infinitude, it comes later to signify Hell itself (lines 695–706), containing "all freaks of Nature, all Promethean thoughts / Of Man" (lines 688–89). Like Milton's underworld, it is undifferentiated and jumbled, a "blank confusion," a "perpetual flow / Of trivial objects, melted and reduced / To one identity, by differences / That have no law, no meaning, and no end" (lines 695, 701–4). All variety without distinctiveness, London allows for no integrity because it lacks simplicity. Wordsworth's achievement, he assures us, was his quickness in penetrating the hurly-burly appearance of urban life; the spirit of Nature had diffused, to his eyes at least, "composure and ennobling harmony" throughout "the press of self-destroying, transitory things." Still, as he recalls retrospectively in Book VIII, London is a paradoxical weight, seemingly full, but actually empty and destitute.

BOOK VIII: THE REAL
AND THE ABSTRACT

These negative or parodic moments in *The Prelude* suggest that Wordsworth is working vigorously to establish a context for heroism, for the presentation of a self in action and in meditation, or in working and being wrought upon, as he defines "higher selves" in Book XIII. The poem's "images of interaction," as Herbert Lindenberger calls them, are not only its symbolic heart; they also clothe and embody the naked self that is its subject. Wordsworth focuses on both himself and an abstraction, Man, both of whom he places heroically in a middle isthmus: "instinct / With Godhead, and by reason and by will / Acknowledging dependency sublime" (VIII, 638–40).

Book VIII is the theoretical justification for the self-representation of the poet throughout the poem. At the heart of the epic, this retrospect looks forward as well as backward, to prepare reader and writer for the dangers of the French books, and it allows us to see the poet as a single, but representative, heroic example of the entire species. Written before Book VII, which details the greater vulgarities of the city, the Retrospect is a reminder to poet and reader of the "slow gradations towards human-kind" on which Nature has steadied the young Wordsworth but that are still weak when compared, he says, to his ongoing commitment to Nature's own objects.

"Why should I speak of Tillers of the soil?" (line 498) he asks in the middle of the book, and the whole provides an ambiguous answer to the question. He poses a similar question in Book IV: "Why should I speak of what a thousand hearts / Have felt, and every man alive can guess?" (lines 33–34). Wordsworth routinely uses rhetorical questions when on the verge of apologizing for commonness or generalizing from himself: "What one is why may not many be?" or "It might be told (but wherefore speak of things / Common to all?)" (VIII, 665–66). Throughout Book VIII Wordsworth bases a love of man not on real human contacts, but on the images of man-as-species that flicker through the mind, or on the abstracted ideas of suffering and nobility that he has witnessed.

"Plain imagination and severe" (line 512), the equivalent of moral sternness, was in youth superseded by a spectatorial impulse that exaggerates, fancifully ornaments, and otherwise misreads details of human reality. It embellishes the "ordinary human interests" (line 167) that Wordsworth claims as the basis for his own development, for the novelty of his poetry, and for the potential for heroism among the shepherds who populate his memory and his landscapes. Although he avers his contact with real shepherds, not such as Spenser fabled, who are wedded both to labor and "majestic indolence" (line 389), Wordsworth objectively distances these figures so as to make them, whether in retrospect or in actuality during his childhood, into symbolic presences rather than named or full-bodied persons. The crux, then, is how he abstracts the idea of Man, early on, from specific individuals whom he types within his mind so that he can imagine a tragic or stoic sublimity for the most ordinary. Thus, the shepherd is radiant, gigantic, "a solitary object and sublime" (line 407), seen figuratively if not actually at a distance. Wordsworth merely substitutes the grandeur of the mundane for the pastoral graces belonging to earlier myths of Corins and Phyllises. Men are present to him as figurines "purified, / Remov'd, and at a distance that was fit" (lines 439–40), even though he is in daily contact with them. The poet confers distance upon the proximate in order to fill the stage with worthy dramatic characters.

The need to distance or purify to render "fit" explains the absence of real figures from Book VIII (and from the bulk of the poem as well). The Matron's Tale, written in 1799 and included here (lines 222–311) as an example of paternal love and duty, was eliminated by 1850, as was the description (lines 81–119) of the shepherd and his dog. By transferring the tender scene of father and sick child (lines 837–59) to Book VII, Wordsworth gradually denuded Book VIII of its characters, as if humans were no longer necessary once the idea of the Human rooted itself in the poet's mind.

The closeness to real shepherds, followed by the distancing or eliminating of them, epitomizes Wordsworth's treatment of himself throughout the poem. As both subject and object, he is plagued by the ordeal of remembering, correcting, and recreating his self, and in offering himself as his own hero he makes himself a dramatic character, now internalized as a spectacle in his own mind. He is hero and witness, and his memory is both the receptacle of the past and the theater at which he attends his own performance. In making himself an actor within the drama, he is literally enacting a self. He forms himself by his performance.[12]

THE FALL INTO HEROISM

Wordsworth becomes his own subject and, more specifically, his own hero, in spite of himself, since his opening impulses to find a theme for his poem are constantly thwarted by self-induced impediments. "I want a hero," Byron's exasperated plea, is equally Wordsworth's, who slides, as if accidentally, into his subject. "Was it for this / That one, the fairest of all Rivers," he asks, gave him birth and nurture (I, 271–72)? And from his early self-doubting and recrimination he falls naturally into a self-analysis, which, by the end of Book I, has persuaded him to continue his tale to Coleridge, seeing that he has attained a self-revival of interest and enthusiasm.

"Falls" is not too strong a verb to apply to Wordsworth's invention of a subject. The epic cast of the poem as the story of a postlapsarian and post-Miltonic Adam is announced by the poet's early proclamation of freedom: "The earth is all before me" (I, 15) and is reaffirmed in an ironic variation at the end of Book I when he has alighted upon his true subject, hardly choosing to do so: "The road lies plain before me; 'tis a theme / Single and of determined bounds; and hence / I chuse it rather at this time, than work / Of ampler or more varied argument" (lines 668–71).

Once the wheels of memory have begun to impel the poet on his mental journey, however, it is not as Adam that he calls attention to himself. Rather, the frisking play of childhood is riddled with suggestions of malice, criminality, and at several points, with muted echoes of satanic fall and vengeance. As a five-year-old, swimming in the stream, Wordsworth recalls how he "Made one long bathing of a summer's day, / Bask'd in the sun, and plunged, and bask'd again / Alternate all a summer's day" (I, 294–96); and we recall the fall of Mulciber as it was related erringly in Ausonian land (*Paradise Lost* 1: 738–47). "I was a fell destroyer" (line 318), he announces in 1805, although he mitigates his rapaciousness in the 1850 text; and he corrects the earlier misdating of his age (from nine to ten) although the earlier age would have heavier satanic implications. In 1850 he tends to spread, as well as to soften, his guilt: "was I a plunderer then" (line 336) becomes "moved we as plunderers."[13] Even as the Knaves in his mock-heroic card game (line 558) are like Vulcan cast down from Heaven, so Wordsworth calls into question the inherently fallen condition of all human endeavor. ("Hard task to analyse a soul" [II, 232] recalls Raphael's lament that it is "sad task and hard" to relate the War in Heaven.)

Throughout, even childhood action is treated as dangerous, risky, or criminal. While preparing his soul for future achievements, these early actions produce only guilt at the time. Since action is always tainted—all human activity may potentially imperil tranquillity or blessedness—heroic achievement is especially to be regarded skeptically. In this regard, Wordsworth's clearest literary affinity is with Virgil, especially with his insistence in the fourth eclogue that human adventure is *priscae vestigia fraudis*. Although Wordsworth returns at the end of Book I to his hope that thoughts from former years may invigorate him and "spur me on, in manhood now mature, / To honorable toil" (lines 652–53), by the start of Book II he resumes his mitigation of heroic language. The mock battles of childhood games end in exhaustion: "We rested in the shade, all pleas'd alike, / Conquer'd and Conqueror" (lines 68–69), but nature's ministry to the single child teaches him the perils of aloneness; his "quiet independence of the heart" proves to him ("perhaps too much") "the self-sufficing power of solitude."

Individual strength, a theme to which the poem repeatedly returns, is tempered throughout by the poet's knowledge of its attendant risks: alienation from one's kind, hubris, or the willed tyranny of the rational mind. Although solitude gives birth to the visionary power (II, 320ff.), Wordsworth wavers between crediting the isolated mind and praising the equality of interaction, the "heroic alliance" between infant and mother that becomes a paradigm for an intercourse between self and external object (climactically witnessed and experienced in the Snowdon episode in Book XIII). Paradoxically, heroic accomplishment is best ensured through a shared, relational experience.

The role of recollection and creative imagination in the poem are Wordsworth's "descents," his efforts to create his own character; as Richard Onorato notes, "the poet who recollects the child in his experiences of solitude presents at the same time the artist's heroic determination to pursue his recollections and imaginings in solitude in order to find again the 'special' sense of himself in his experience, and perhaps to determine its meaning."[14] According to Kierkegaard, "recollection has the great advantage that it begins with the loss, hence it is secure, for it has nothing to lose."[15] But as we shall see, Wordsworth is both agent and sufferer, both the active recollector of his own childhood and the passive screen for memory's flashings, as well as the heroically active pursuer (a role sometimes treated parodically or with satanic overtones), and the passive, sometimes victimized, recipient of natural or maternal sustenance. The child is orphan and victim, his mind the docile collector of external sensations, until intellectual control, at an early age, extends actively from it. Hence, with "growing faculties" (line 338) the soul aspires to possible sublimity: we may hear "growing" as both transitive and intransitive. For Wordsworth, only mental activity can be untainted by the stigma of action; it alone, but not always, offers heroism and redemption together. Although public life may test heroic stamina (II, 443–62), it certainly destroys heroic temper except, Wordsworth believes, in those who were properly raised *beyond* public life. For this reason, Wordsworth's early Sabine fare and the Spartan regimen he recalls from or retrojects into childhood (II, 80) enable him to understand the foolish wastefulness of life at Cambridge. In the old days, heroes were made and tested through acts of primitive plainness: "Princes then / At matins froze, and couch'd at curfewtime" (III, 467–68); but now amid the butterflies and popinjays of university life, there is neither plain living nor high thinking. "Learning" becomes a heroic abstraction, attempting to rouse the sodden youth to intellectual toil enforced with abstemiousness. With some degree of self-satisfaction, Wordsworth retroactively saves himself from the mass of depraved wastrels with whom he shared his university days. He was not, he says, so badly off as some others: "Far more I griev'd to see among the Band / Of those who in the field of contest stood / As combatants, passions that did to me / Seem low and mean" (III, 511–14). He seems priggish, although in retrospect he can call himself a "pretty Prisoner" (IV, 48) in whom "smooth enthralment" should have prompted self-satire.

ANGELS AND EPIPHANIES

During summer vacation (Book IV), as during term itself, Wordsworth continues to see the losses suffered, "the inner falling off" exacted by gauds and revelry that he mistook for "manliness and freedom" (line 277), and that seduced him "from the firm habitual quest of feeding pleasures." In a vocabulary that mingles the domestic and the heroic, Wordsworth vibrates between a heroic victimization (his very garments are preying upon his strength) and abstract analysis: "Something there was about me that perplex'd / Th'authentic sight of reason, press'd too closely / On that religious dignity of mind, / That is the very faculty of truth" (lines 295–98). But at the same time, Book IV presents two major moments that reaffirm the poet's grandeur. In both cases—his commitment to poetry (lines 330–45) and the meeting with the discharged soldier (lines 363–504)—the young Wordsworth is, *contra spontem*, and indeed against his own knowledge, first pledged to a vocation during his nominal holiday from scholarly or literary endeavors, and next schooled by an emissary who functions like a Homeric messenger (beggars and strangers come from Zeus). In the book of vacation, the self at rest is steadied and challenged for future growth and commitment.[16]

Other than the passages in Book IV, this artist's autobiography makes few overt references to the poet's work or even to his thoughts of a career, and a similar reticence precludes the divulgence of significant information about his chronological and psychological development.[17] Wordsworth scrupulously avoids the "merely personal," as Lindenberger suggests, because the poem is working toward a typological presentation of heroic possibility, not the growth of *this* individual's soul. For this reason, Wordsworth carefully stresses the general inadequacy of consciousness in forming character, career, and moral sensibility; in Book VI, some fourteen years after the major imaginative disappointment at the Simplon Pass, he addresses his "Soul," recognizing its glory only retrospectively.

The passivity of classical heroes in the face of the gods' actions has its peculiar analogue in Wordsworth's heroic self in *The Prelude*.[18] Just as *areté* may depart from and return to Achilles, just as any virtue derives equally from divine will and natural capacity (an "action from within and from without," XII, line 377), the major components of the Wordsworthian will to greatness are themselves unwilled but natural, in the sense either of "automatic" or "in the nature of things." Like Homer, Wordsworth "leaves you with the mystery of behavior, with a modern sense that a decision, like an emotion, is something that happens *to you*. You are responsible, but then again you are not."[19] Thus, recalling first his rural walks, "worthy to be priz'd and lov'd" (IV, 121), themselves reminiscent of earlier childhood meanderings with a favorite dog, Wordsworth describes the revelation of a powerful vocational direction that itself is barely clear. In a raw, cold, sunset hour, the soul, like Moses on Sinai, "gently . . . put off her veil, and self-transmuted, stood / Naked as in the presence of her God" (lines 140–42). Further, the experience is marked by the paradoxical rhetoric expressive of the ambiguity of self felt by the eighteen-year-old:

> As on I walked, a comfort seem'd to touch
> A heart that had not been disconsolate,
> Strength came where weakness was not known to be,
> At least not felt; and restoration came,
> Like an intruder, knocking at the door
> Of unacknowledg'd weariness. I took
> The balance in my hand and weigh'd myself.
> I saw but little, and thereat was pleas'd;
> Little did I remember, and even this
> Still pleas'd me more; but I had hopes and peace
> And swellings of the spirits, was rapt and soothed,
> Convers'd with promises, had glimmering views
> How Life pervades the undecaying mind,
> How the immortal Soul with God-like power
> Informs, creates, and thaws the deepest sleep
> That time can lay upon her; how on earth,
> Man, if he do but live within the light
> Of high endeavours, daily spreads abroad
> His being with a strength that cannot fail.
>   (IV, 143–61)

Naked yet full, restored but uncertain, the mind is pervaded by godlike power and itself constitutes that power. Man is the arena in which the immortal soul makes itself felt, and where it contends with time's deep weighty sleep; but mind is also the subject that defines its character by an act of going out, spreading itself and stamping its character with unfailing strength. The offhand simile of the intruder (lines 147–48) internalizes the Homeric insistence on hospitable entertainment and delicately maintains the classical tone.

A complementary visitation or heavenly message comes several hundred lines later, following Wordsworth's confession of his "inner falling off," and right before the image of his mind as a "strange rendezvous," "A party-colour'd show of grave and gay" (lines 346–47). After an evening of festive music and dancing, the young Wordsworth retires at dawn and begins his two-mile walk homeward:

> Magnificent
> The morning was, a memorable pomp,
> More glorious than I ever had beheld.
> The Sea was laughing at a distance; all
> The solid Mountains were as bright as clouds,
> Grain-tinctured, drench'd in empyrean light;
> And, in the meadows and the lower grounds,
> Was all the sweetness of a common dawn,
> Dews, vapours, and the melody of birds,
> And Labourers going forth into the fields.
> —Ah! need I say, dear Friend, that to the brim
> My heart was full; I made no vows, but vows
> Were then made for me; bond unknown to me
> Was given, that I should be, else sinning greatly,
> A dedicated Spirit. On I walk'd
> In blessedness, which even yet remains.
>
> (IV, 330–45)

From the sublimity of the opening alliteration to the elevated natural description, with its Miltonic overtones and the mingling of majesty and delicacy, Wordsworth paints himself into a landscape, stationing himself and preparing for an epiphany that comes, like most of the visionary moments in this most unmythological of poets, without an attendant form. The landscape itself seems to distill the message and to embody in its own emblems the boundaries of Wordsworth's future endeavors.

Epiphanic moments such as this, a smaller example of the major revelations in Books VI and XIII, internalize the directions traditionally delivered to heroes by divine messengers. The angelic function in Wordsworth may, as here, be subsumed into the landscape or into a gestalt impressed upon a mind unknowing. But at other moments heavenly emissaries do appear, and the discharged soldier, like the leech-gatherer and other admonitory figures, may be best understood as a vessel of grace, the stranger who is a god, or a god's surrogate, in disguise. Although the pattern of this episode does not resemble the form of classical epic descents, its function is remarkably similar: to direct or admonish the hero at a literal or figurative crossroads. Indeed, in one special way, the Wordsworthian encounter scene fulfills one of Thomas Greene's crucial claims about the shape of epic: "The most important recognition scenes in epic are not between two people but between the hero and his mortality."[20] If so much else in Wordsworth, as in Romantic poetry generally, represents an internalization of events or phenomena that were previously available externally, then the meeting with the discharged soldier tests the poet and reminds him, as do other human dealings in *The Prelude*, that this is the world of all of us, the place where in the end, we find our happiness and define our own presences.[21]

The soldier's spectral qualities ally him to angelic figures, but Wordsworth varies the classical epic pattern by presenting his messenger as one who seems, initially, not alive at all, and whose status throughout borders on both the ghostly and the abstract. For example, the 1850 revision retains a nice ambiguity in the subject of the verb "appeared": "He stood, and in his very dress appeared / A desolation, a simplicity" (lines 401–2); the man either embodies those qualities or is clothed by them. A further variation is that the poet greets the soldier, not vice versa; he initially finds himself spying on the man from his privileged place in the shade, "my self unseen." The experience unfolds as a series of miniature epiphanies: first the shock of the "uncouth shape," then a withdrawal to examine it, a stepping out to encounter the man, the dialogue between them, and the final action of the poet and admonition by the soldier. In the interplay, the comforter or guide and the recipient of his advice exchange places.

The meeting is prepared for by the oddness of the setting, by the poet's mind and his responses to the landscape (1805 MS, lines 364–99). He begins with paradox, alliteration, and a melting enjambment in his love of walking "alone / Along the public Way" which at night "assumes / A character of deeper quietness / Than pathless solitudes." As it happens, both poet and soldier are characters absorbed by the setting, and silence and sound unite in a typically mysterious way, as Wordsworth stresses the utter stillness of the place and the time, a stillness that numbs and nurtures:

> Thus did I steal along that silent road,
> My body from the stillness drinking in
> A restoration like the calm of sleep
> But sweeter far. Above, before, behind,
> Around me, all was peace and solitude,
> I look'd not round, nor did the solitude
> Speak to my eye, but it was heard and felt.
> (lines 385–89)

Like the leech-gatherer, the soldier is the poet's double, an image of what he may become, and regardless of his objective reality in the poet's experience, a projection in part from within the abyss of imagination. Just before he notices the man, he says, beautiful images "rose / As from some distant region of my soul / And came along like dreams" (lines 393–95). Into this hallucinated state of tranquil dreaming, a new figure intrudes and is presented as it is experienced, a synecdochic catalogue of parts (lines 405–13). Faded yet entire, spectral but unyieldingly steady, the figure has lips that seem to murmur sounds not quite heard. Stepping from his covert, the poet questions the man, and hears his simple words of ordinary life in the laconic style of one subdued or suffering, and then takes it upon himself to direct the soldier to hospitable lodging. On the walk backward to a peasant's cottage (cf. the return backward at the Simplon Pass), the poet makes conversation, and learns more about the soldier's life, which he does not report to us.

The encounter reminds us of the inefficacy of action; the soldier is characterized by his endurance, not his accomplishment, and we do not hear him speak directly until his epigrammatic admonition at the very end—he is stretched as thin as possible on the frame of humanity. In the man's peculiar senescence, we may also hear an echo of Wordsworth's earlier failure to distinguish between how and what the soul felt (II, 334–37):

> He, all the while, was in demeanor calm,
> Concise in answer; solemn and sublime
> He might have seem'd, but that in all he said
> There was a strange half-absence, and a tone
> Of weakness and indifference, as of one
> Remembering the importance of his theme
> But feeling it no longer.
>
> (IV, 472–78)

This sublimity or humanity manqué is the sternest possible test of one's own human measure. Conversation subsides again to silence; the "shades, gloomy and dark" are, possibly, metaphorical reminders of a Virgilian population in a subterranean landscape; the poet charitably delivers up his charge to the figure of a helpful peasant.

Up to this point, the episode is remarkable only for the oddness of the local effects and the self-congratulation attendant upon an act of Christian, or even classical, charity. But then the poet startlingly corrects his own self-righteousness by changing positions with his soldier. Having assumed for himself the comfortable role of Aeneas's Sybil, or Dante's Virgil, the psychopomp now finds himself berated, his peace of mind jarred. The soldier has profited from a human charity that he has refused to solicit, but his legacy of thanks to his guide turns out to be an eerie warning. For his part, Wordsworth, having indulged his customary melancholy in solitude, has been abruptly halted and now chastised by the soldier's example as a survivor who schools the young man in the virtues of suffering and resolution. The reproof of the soldier to the young know-it-all who advises him to keep off the streets at night undercuts his adolescent wisdom: "my trust is in the God of Heaven / And in the eye of him that passes me." Indeed, through the eye, agent of perception and feeling, Wordsworth first encountered the soldier who now thanks him for his service.

The effect of seeing, aiding, and finally being admonished by, the discharged soldier is a catharsis: having learned a lesson in patience, and having his own superior strength subverted, the young Wordsworth returns home with a "quiet heart." Chastened and subdued, the boy, as participant and witness, has absorbed a lesson from another character.

The episode of the discharged soldier stands out in *The Prelude* not only because of the presence of another person but also because for a brief moment Wordsworth lifts himself from his usual spectatorial position to a higher or complementary one of active involvement. The characteristic mode of the poem is a double seeing: both *of* the past from the present, and also *within* the past, where the poet is primarily a witness, especially in those books when he presents himself as remote from the lives and scenes he sees but rarely touches. The conclusion to Book VI, however, manages to have it both ways. After the momentous mountain episode, the melancholy and meditations provoked by the Simplon Pass, Wordsworth makes two different claims: the first (lines 661–80) that the mind was not a mere "pensioner," dependent on outward forms, and the second (lines 681–705) that he was a disinterested observer who "was touch'd . . . with no intimate concern." Indeed,

passivity is both the condition of traveling youth, enthusi-
astically permitting itself to be wafted by one breeze or current, or another, and the defense Wordsworth typically invokes as a kind of self-protection.

FRANCE: PUBLIC LIFE,
PRIVATE OBSERVATION

When the spectatorial guise becomes too difficult to wear
the man must either raise himself to a higher level of active
involvement or fall into anxious confusion, as he does in
the two dense books about France (Books IX and X). The
psychological and stylistic problems of these books lie in
Wordsworth's inability to integrate the personal and public
details in the autobiography: a problem both at the time
and in the retelling of it. Even as a spectator he seems often
at second hand, reporting news of, and from, other
sources; nor do his reflections originate at the time of the
events but in their recollection. With a "reality too close
and too intense" (X, 642) that might "profane the sanctity"
of his verse, the poet makes a strategic retreat for self-pres-
ervation. From the start, France seems as illusory as London did before it. When confronted by the seething city,
the poet resorts to catalogue, suggesting Miltonic chaos
and ending with moral abstractions (IX, 40–62). Initially
unmoved by public fervor ("I look'd for something that I
could not find, / Affecting more emotion than I felt," lines
70–71), the young man escaping family pressure to decide
upon a career is more touched by Le Brun's painting of
Mary Magdalene than by political ideas. (The book is
neatly framed by the Le Brun portrait and Wordsworth's
pathetic tale of Vaudracour and Julia.) He is a spectator
who has arrived late at a play in "a theatre, of which the
stage / Was busy with an action far advanced" (lines 93–94)
and because of age, temperament, and language, he is
without a program to the plot or the dramatis personae.

But worn out at last by frivolity, gaming, and the "puncti-lios of elegance" (line 118), the young tourist "gradually withdrew / Into a noisier world" (lines 122–23), a curious phrase that attests to Wordsworth's deep reluctance to re-gard the public sphere as a step upward, and he becomes a patriot. Thus ends (line 125) the prelude of his adventure. Even after he has become a Republican, Wordsworth continues to clothe his zeal beneath aesthetic cloaks.[22] His primary knowledge, he says, comes from "Tales of the Poets," which "fill'd my fancy with fair forms, / Old He-roes and their sufferings and their deeds" (lines 209–11). He sees one Royalist officer (line 148) as a Miltonic archan-gel, faded and fallen; ultimately, his path to political liber-alism is a *via negativa*, an aesthetic response to his distaste for the Royalists, which awakens within him his sleeping zeal.

Into the adventure comes Michel Beaupuy, himself a character from romance—meek, aristocratic, gracious when offended—one of Wordsworth's happy warriors and, with Coleridge, one of the absent deities who inspire *The Prelude*. In the midst of the reactionary Royalists, maimed and spiritless, Beaupuy stands out as a participant who has been "call'd upon to embody his deep sense / In action, give it outwardly a shape" (lines 408–9). He is an-other aesthetic projection—of the Revolution's ideals and of the poet's need for some closer connection to foreign events—the new model and the new guide covered with "radiant joy" (line 321) who leads the poet through the Loire Valley and who invests truth with hope and desire.

"A spirit was abroad / Which could not be withstood" (lines 520–21) is Wordsworth's sole comment upon his les-sons from Beaupuy at the moment when an impoverished girl, knitting and leading a languid heifer, comes into view. "'Tis against *that* / Which we are fighting" (lines 519–20), says Beaupuy, and it sums up all that Wordsworth learned during the first part of his stay in France. The poet continues merely to respond; he is still the audience at a spectacle, sometimes near at hand, sometimes distanced by space, time, or indirect and abstract discourse. The "spirit" of liberty is embodied for Wordsworth in the symbolic image of the knitting girl and in his discussions with Beaupuy; in both cases, his own sentiments are attenuated by a spectator's or student's stance. Beaupuy gains symbolic heroic status: "He thro' the events / Of that great change wander'd in perfect faith, / As through a Book, an old Romance or Tale / Of Fairy, or some dream of actions wrought / Behind the summer clouds" (lines 304–8). Even their discussions assume the status of artistic enterprise: "painting to ourselves the miseries / Of royal Courts" (lines 351–52); "We summon'd up the honorable deeds / Of ancient Story" (lines 371–72). No mere academic refreshment, their talks resemble heroic Platonic dialogue, because Beaupuy has become a participant in the great Trial of Nature at hand:

> One devoted, one whom circumstance
> Hath call'd upon to embody his deep sense
> In action, give it outwardly a shape,
> And that of benediction to the world;
> Then doubt is not, and truth is more than truth,
> A hope it is and a desire, a creed
> Of zeal by an authority divine
> Sanction'd of danger, difficulty or death.
>
> (lines 406–13)

The paean to Beaupuy's exemplary achievement resembles the language of the magisterial triumphs in the Simplon Pass and on Mt. Snowdon, only here the glory precedes, rather than follows, catastrophe, shock, or disappointment. Characteristically, Beaupuy is named only at this point, moments before Wordsworth metaphorically kills him (lines 430–36), commemorating him at the moment of reference to his death, itself the firmest proof of the inefficacy or pathos of action.[23] But the anticipated death of the hero is then followed by more description of their "frequent walk" and "earnest dialogues" on the Loire; Wordsworth frames the moment of Beaupuy's death in battle with reminders of the preferable irreality of fanciful discussion. The very woods, he says, are peopled for him by characters from Tasso, Ariosto, or Spenser (lines 449–67).

The poet's aesthetic temperament, mitigating his political involvement with flights of fancy, accounts for the episode of Julia and Vaudracour with which the book ends. It is beside the point to speculate on its connection to Wordsworth's guilt about his affair with Annette Vallon or to conjecture that its removal from *The Prelude* once the episode was separately published in 1820 represents the elimination of that guilt. Above all, the tale is a testimony to the power of private life over public events, exactly what Wordsworth's involvement with Beaupuy has already hinted at. Thwarted in love, Vaudracour wastes away, a figure in a lyrical ballad. Reclusive, mute, then imbecile, he is impervious to the glorious tidings of Revolution abroad in the land. Cut off, in "solitary shades," himself the cause of his child's death, Vaudracour becomes a living shade who in his extreme solipsism is a version of what Wordsworth could easily fear for himself. Beaupuy, the vessel of nobility in life and death, is balanced by Vaudracour, the embodiment of the pathetic futility of action in private life. Early death, tragic or pathetic, unites these two opposing figures: unlike causes produce identical ends.

Book X further proves Wordsworth's difficulty in taking or even depicting action without distancing it in some fashion. He finds himself separate from the Revolution, as an Englishman in France, and, later, as a Republican in a hostile England; he recounts public events "only as they were storm / Or sunshine to my individual mind" (X, 104–5). At the same time, he is implicitly connected to those events he witnesses when he adopts the guise of Old Testament prophet or intransigent Lear belligerently confront-

ing a hostile nature (lines 382–440). The utter horror of the
Revolution is softened, but heightened as well, by a distancing metaphor, which cripples the observer still further:

> upon these
> And other sights looking as doth a man
> Upon a volume whose contents he knows
> Are memorable, but from him lock'd up,
> Being written in a tongue he cannot read,
> So that he questions the mute leaves with pain,
> And half upbraids their silence.
>
> (lines 48–54)

By construing the events of 1792 through 1794 along the
lines of Miltonic epic or Shakespearian tragedy, Wordsworth implicates himself as a witness doomed to reenact or
internalize the spectacle that has assumed such outwardly
grandiose proportions. We see his involvement most mag-
nificently in the early apocalyptic lines that foretell the engulfing by the Revolution of its own children and that then
merge with the nightmarish reflection of Wordsworth as an
insomniac witness of regicide, projecting himself into Macbeth's guilty voice:

> "The horse is taught his manage, and the wind
> Of heaven wheels round and treads in his own steps,
> Year follows year, the tide returns again,
> Day follows day, all things have second birth;
> The earthquake is not satisfied at once."
> And in such way I wrought upon myself,
> Until I seem'd to hear a voice that cried,
> To the whole City, "Sleep no more!"
>
> (lines 70–77)

The shocking visions that disturb sleep and general tranquillity provoke in Wordsworth the observer an equivalent
to the Reign of Terror, "a sense / Of treachery and desertion
in the place / The holiest that I knew of, my own soul"
(lines 379–81), just as war between France and England divides still further his own political sympathies.

His mind is now an internecine battleground on which

political forces are arrayed. Inwardly stung at "how much the destiny of man had still / Hung upon single persons (lines 138–39), he also reminds himself of natural monarchies: "one nature as there is one sun in heaven," and thinks perhaps that "the virtue of one paramount mind" (line 180) might have saved all. The "mind" is a strong ruler (although Wordsworth is not without doubts about strong men, e.g., lines 168–76) and a single political intelligence stronger than his own divided instincts.

Wordsworth both exculpates himself—"I was as far as Angels are from guilt" (line 128)—and accuses himself (line 875ff.). At his lowest moment, he "Endeavoured with my best of skill to probe / The living body of society / Even to the heart; I push'd without remorse / My speculations forward; yea, set foot / On Nature's holiest places" (lines 875–79). He comes gradually to internalize those satanic crimes of Robespierre and the Terror, and to rehearse intellectually the immoral Jacobin excesses. His mind becomes the arena of an epic but anonymous battle, "a conflict of sensations without name" (line 266). Indeed, had he stayed in France, he fears he might have been killed as a Girondist sympathizer (line 195); and early death would have deprived him of both Coleridge's friendship and his own poetic vocation.

When he finds the events of the Terror too horrifying for response, he relies on his habit of negotiation through diminution and distance. All fall beneath the guillotine's blade, he says, just as a child, "if light desires of innocent little Ones / May with such heinous appetites be match'd" (lines 339–40), runs ever more quickly with a toy windmill to make it spin. Action is reduced to child's play, even if the child is, like the new Republic, godlike: "the Herculean Commonwealth had put forth her arms / And throttled with an infant Godhead's might / The snakes about her cradle" (lines 363–65; the English leaders are later described as children attempting to imitate giants, line 648).

Just as Robespierre is satanic overreacher ("Moloch,"

line 469), and the Revolution fails by the weight of its own excesses, the poet's individual heroic mind is tempted by the glittering fruit of Godwinian reason; it plucks, eats, and falls into the original sin: judgment. Amid the mock-heroic public sphere Wordsworth himself is "a child of Nature" (line 753), first giving himself up to the idealism of Beaupuy, but then done in by gluttony and strangulation when he tenaciously holds on to his principles (line 804) after the French become oppressors and he feels these old opinions "cling" round his mind. Rationalism seduces him and denudes him of grandeur; seeing "the human reason's naked self," Wordsworth parodies the earlier apocalypse of Imagination in Book VI by mocking Godwinian reason:

> The freedom of the individual mind,
> Which, to the blind restraint of general laws
> Superior, magisterially adopts
> One guide, the light of circumstances, flash'd
> Upon an independent intellect.
>
> (lines 826–30)

Ultimately a vivisectionist—probing the "living body of society / Even to the heart" (lines 876–77)—Wordsworth desperately abandons moral questions, having himself enacted the role of judicial tribune and found himself wanting: "Thus I fared, / Dragging all passions, notions, shapes of faith, / Like culprits to the bar, suspiciously / Calling the mind to establish in plain day / Her title and her honours" (lines 889–93).

When reality becomes "too close and too intense" (line 642) and threatens not only to profane the sanctity of verse but to undermine the poet's sanity as well, he retreats to a more remote vantage point. Wordsworth finds his psychological and poetic strengths in moments of elegiac contemplation: the two most memorable sections of Book X are his recollection of hearing of Robespierre's death (lines 467–567), and his closing address to Coleridge in Sicily (lines 905–1039). Confused by both the immediate political situation and abstract ideas, Wordsworth comes to see the dead as heroic by comparison to the disappointments provoked by the living. Present failures, personal and political, ennoble the dead.

The news of Robespierre's death reaches Wordsworth at a distance, in the Lake District in August 1794. The setting, although domestic and natural, is, however, theatrical: passing by the River Leven, Wordsworth sees the pastoral vales beneath "this show" (line 484), a "fulgent spectacle" (line 487) on which he gazes as on his jocund daffodils, but with a renewed pleasure, having chanced that morning upon the grave of his schoolmaster, William Taylor. From the early death of the man who foresaw that Wordsworth might be among the English poets, the narrative passes to that of him whose excesses the young man internalized. Stationed at a distance from the scene, observing a crowd fording a shallow stream, Wordsworth pauses, "Unwilling to proceed, the scene appear'd / So gay and chearful" (lines 531–32) when a traveler chances by, from whom he learns the news that Robespierre has been executed.

This episode is a complicated memory, looking backward to a time when, amid tranquil scenes, Wordsworth was comforted and surprised by two deaths, so to speak, and was primed to look forward to both his own poetic achievement and the cause of liberty. After reminding us of his sister's role in restoring him to "strength and knowledge full of peace" (line 926) by proving that his mind was like a moon clouded rather than waning, he ends his book with the long address to Coleridge which looks equally forward and backward, without and within.

Coleridge is simultaneously absent and present, living and dead; Wordsworth ends by explicitly recalling his own situation in Book I when he assures his friend that in exile he will find a home and will "linger as a gladsome Votary, / And not a Captive, pining for his home" (lines 1038–39). But within the address, the tone is complicated by Wordsworth's depiction of Sicily and what it represents, and by his transformation of Coleridge into a Lycidas figure. Sicily is a fallen land to which Coleridge's Malta journey has taken him; it is a "wreck of loftiest years," once glorious and virtuous, now decayed (a metonymy for Coleridge himself perhaps), but it is equally a place of refreshment, the traditional pastoral homeland. Nature will spread imperishable thoughts there; the sirocco will turn into a healthful breeze. Because Wordsworth used to dream of Sicily as a sacred island, he says, Coleridge, an absent alter ego and his own projection, will be restored. The one great society, of the noble living and the noble dead (line 970), from which Coleridge will derive his sustenance and into which Wordsworth seems already to number him, bridges the most basic of all chasms, that between life and death. Wordsworth keeps his friend alive, but in his distance and in the strange weavings of echoes from "Lycidas," Coleridge assumes a ghostly presence in the poem.

In lines 981–86, Coleridge-as-Lycidas occasions the poet's sympathy for him, himself, and the loss to the race:

> To me the grief confined that Thou art gone
> From this last spot of earth where Freedom now
> Stands single in her only sanctuary,
> A lonely wanderer, art gone, by pain
> Compell'd and sickness, at this latter day,
> This heavy time of change for all mankind. [24]

Lamenting the lessening of all pleasures in Coleridge's absence, Wordsworth addresses the Sicilian fields and requests for his friend a comfort that seems equally a burial (the same language used for himself in "Home at Grasmere"):

> Oh! wrap him in your Shades, ye Giant Woods,
> On Etna's side, and thou, O flowery Vale
> Of Enna! is there not some nook of thine,
> From the first playtime of the infant earth
> Kept sacred to restorative delight?
>   (lines 1002–6)

Wordsworth redeems a fallen Coleridge in a fallen Sicily through a sympathetic and imaginative self-extension. He simultaneously revives himself, his friend, and a landscape, and elegy gives way to prophecy as he finally stations Coleridge on a mountain peak, himself a resurrected inspiration:

> Thou wilt stand
> Not as an Exile but a Visitant
> On Etna's top; by pastoral Arethuse
> Or, if that Fountain be in truth no more,
> Then near some other Spring, which by the name
> Thou gratulatest, willingly deceived,
> Shalt linger as a gladsome Votary,
> And not a Captive pining for his home.
>
> (lines 1032–39)

In restrospect, this conclusion balances Wordsworth's swing to his final self-evaluation at the end of Book XIII. Indeed, the multiplicity of echoes between the two passages suggests that one end awaits both "workers" in the heroic destiny that Wordsworth paints for himself at the end of the poem:

> Anon I rose
> As if on wings, and saw beneath me stretch'd
> Vast prospect of the world which I had been
> And was; and hence this Song, which like a lark
> I have protracted, in the unwearied Heavens
> Singing, and often with more plaintive voice
> Attemper'd to the sorrows of the earth;
> Yet centring all in love, and in the end
> All gratulant if rightly understood.
>
> (XIII, 377–85)

The double motif of rising and gratulating ensures the unification, even in absence, of Wordsworth and his co-worker.

THE ARMING OF THE HERO

Whatever else is accomplished by the final passage in Book X, it marks Wordsworth's revival, or his readiness to describe the recovery from his mental crisis, which occupies the remainder of *The Prelude*. Significantly this end is achieved, the hero is armed, as it were, by the complicated and ambiguous murder and revival of his alter ego, the friend who is collaborator, teacher, and partner in his life's great enterprise. Just as Wordsworth named Beaupuy only at the moment when he commemorated his death, a moment framed by reminiscences of their many dialogues, so he essentially steadies himself by killing Coleridge and yet reanimating him among the regenerative details of a Miltonic landscape (that fair field of Enna) within the pastoral elegy that itself elevates to the very degree that it laments.[25] Wordsworth reminds us, strikingly, that absence is a necessary condition of epistolary writing (some would say of all writing), and that such absence, by definition, is a form of death; he proves as well that elegy, which Coleridge called "the form of poetry natural to the reflective mind," is a constituent of heroic or epic poetry.[26] Naming Beaupuy immortalizes him; invoking Coleridge as Lycidas places him among Wordsworth's secularly solemn troops and sweet societies.

Far from being exclusively the egotistical poet, Wordsworth has blurred the edges of personal lives and Wordsworth/Milton/Coleridge/Lycidas become a complex, interwoven figure in which community replaces individual identity. This characteristic twinning of self, or the use of projection from the self to other necessary figures, permits the community in which "we have all of us one human heart" and is the final step in creating one's character. Freud contended that "social feelings rest on identification with other people, on the basis of having the same ego ideal."[27] It is for this identification that Wordsworth is now ready to describe the supposed restoration from despair that he owed to nature's subtle thwarting of the tyranny of the bodily eye, to Dorothy's ministering kindness, to the example of Mary Hutchinson's simple blessedness, and to the spots of time as instruments of grace and sources of power. His elegiac feelings, as expressed in the France books, are at the heart of his feelings for contemporary affairs, for what happened to him and to the world around him. As Onorato says, "Unconsciously drawn to the subject of crisis in his poetry, unconsciously resisting its meaning, Wordsworth is at the same time seeking a revised and acceptable image of himself, and the composure in telling his story that he has begun to feel in living his life."[28] Like Coleridge, in his "Reflections on Having Left a Place of Retirement," Wordsworth, in the final movement of his poem, steadies himself to fight the bloodless fight along with his friend, restored to him at the end of Book XIII, as prophets of nature, pedagogues going forward to combat darkness and ignorance.

The arming of the hero for his anticipated struggle occupies the remainder of the poem. We may conceive the spots of time politically, as demonstrating the proper relationship of mind to outer reality, or aesthetically, as James Averill does in reminding us that originally they showed how the mind responds to suffering—either way, they reinstate power once it has apparently been lost.[29] As the classical hero is wounded, then revived by the timely intervention of mother or goddess with divine armor or medicinal salves, so the Wordsworthian hero describes, at this point, the restoration of his own mind, spirit, and courage.

The recovery of imaginative strength, and psychological recuperation generally, are shocking but virtually automatic. For all his reliance on duty, Wordsworth has an almost Homeric sense of how little the self controls its own constitution. In this regard, far from exemplifying Stoic resolve or epitomizing the Romantic will, Wordsworth allows the self its salvation through the grace or benevolence that it has sheltered within itself, all unknowing and all along.[30] If saved once, one is saved always and maintains a "secret happiness" (XI, 34) although one does not realize it. The shaking off of the monkish habit, the refusal to sit in judgment, the thwarting of the tyrannic bodily eye are all achieved with ease not because Wordsworth has an insuf-

ficiently developed sense of agon but because "blessedness" is a condition that the soul never senses unless under shock and degradation.

The common piety of Mary Hutchinson (XI, 196–223) is
not Wordsworth's own, but is exemplary for its unitary harmony. More complex, Wordsworth refers to his wife with
mingled condescension and envy, just as he addresses
Dorothy in "Tintern Abbey" or the shepherds in Book VIII
of *The Prelude*. In his own kind of salvation, contraries
maintain the dialectical struggle Blake depicts as the con-
tinual warfare of heaven: the last three books of *The Prelude*
contain more intense examples of Wordsworthian paradox
than the rest of the poem, and the ability to sustain and
profit from this paradoxicality gives the truest measure of
the Wordsworthian hero.

Some readers are disappointed that Wordsworth described the power of the spots of time successively as "fruc-
tifying," "vivifying," and "renovating," finding the last epithet the weakest because the most general. But the notion
of renovation as repetition alludes to the presence of previous salvation, which the two other verbs do not, and
constitutes a power that is nourishing, reparative, and sexual (it "penetrates" us, line 267). Redemptive in a way that
distinctly blurs the lines between Christian grace and pa-
gan divine intervention, it "enables us to mount / When
high, more high, and lifts us up when fallen" (lines 267–
68). And yet, the redemptive power comes, like the correspondent breeze, or like Shelley's inspirational wind in *The
Defense of Poetry*, from the inner passages of self and memory. Acting like an external agency, the path of salvation
has entirely relocated itself within the corridors of the
mind. And these are corridors of power.

Thus self-love precedes both love of nature and love of
man, and the two recorded spots of time, while abstruse
examples of the mind's excursive or controlling power,
show how the mind can "invest" the external world with
meaning and reap the accumulated dividends of this in-

vestment as accumulations of identity. There is a divine economy in Wordsworth's idealized self as well as in his universe, and the double motif of investment-as-clothing and investment-as-savings comes to bear on the growth of the character. Pleasure derives from fear, comfort from vexation, later plurality from early singularity, as the scene of gibbet, beacon, and girl is revised when reviewed, into "the spirit of pleasure." The transformation of an early, fearful, and solitary experience, into a later, shared one on which "radiance more divine" glows halolike comes from the early "remembrances, and from the power / They left behind[.] So feeling comes in aid / Of feeling, and diversity of strength / Attends us, if but once we have been strong" (XI, 324–28). Attended at Penrith by his future wife and by the repeated accumulations of memory, which alone constitute psychological strength, Wordsworth is, paradoxically, most defined when most attended: most "naked," in other words, when most "invested."[31]

Restoration has a double grammatical object when he goes on to his second spot-of-time, his recollection of anticipating the Christmas holidays, followed by his father's death and his subsequent feelings of guilt and despair: "I would enshrine the spirit of the past / For future restoration" (lines 342–43). To maintain or restore the past, it must be marmoreal, entombed; to restore the self requires the constant revival of past moments and constant withdrawals from the bank of memory in which the self's investments reap their interest. The poet restores harmonies to the past that will simultaneously restore *him* in future periods of crisis.

The language of paradox continues throughout the last two books: rhetorical balance is the surest sign of the hero's psychological strength. Wordsworth's equivalent for the ancient commerce between men and gods is his use of Nature as inspiration, source, or muse. *Arete* is given because deserved, and earned where bestowed; as Athena explains to Achilles at the beginning of the *Iliad*, "I have come to soften your anger, if you will allow yourself to be persuaded" (1: 206–7). Having announced at the end of Book XI (lines 326–34) that man's greatness stands on the base of "simple childhood," and having preempted Coleridge's language (from "Dejection: An Ode") by confessing that "this I feel, / That from thyself it is that thou must give, / Else never canst receive," Wordsworth begins Book XII by depicting Nature as the Earth to which Man or his spirit must, Antaeus-like, return for sustenance. From her "sister horns" come the twin gifts of elevation and peace, which balance aspiration and passivity:

> from her [genius] receives
> That energy by which he seeks the truth,
> Is rouzed, aspires, grasps, struggles, wishes, craves,
> From her that happy stillness of the mind
> Which fits him to receive it when unsought.
> (XII, 10–14)

Here the intense interaction of antinomies governs even the way syntax tends to melt or collapse: "craves" both blends into "From her" and stands as the last of the series of acquisitive desires before the final two lines, which replace appetite with tranquillity. (The 1850 version emends these lines so that man enjoys first the energy to seek the truth and then the stillness to receive it.)

"Words find easy way" (line 18), Wordsworth can now proclaim, having regained confidence and discovered a language apposite to the paradoxical heroic status he wishes for himself, one that will involve "the frame of life, / Social and individual" (lines 39–40), the self alone and in relation, and will encourage the building of the heroic from the commonplace. His newfound wisdom, following his recovery:

> seeing little worthy or sublime
> In what we blazon with the pompous names
> Of power and action, early tutor'd me
> To look with feelings of fraternal love

Upon those unassuming things, that hold
A silent station in this beauteous world.
                              (XII, 47–52)

Likewise, having found "in man an object of delight" (line 54), Wordsworth prepares himself to write a poem about "the dignity of individual Man . . . the man whom we behold / With our own eyes" (lines 83, 86–87), whose course is identical to the one the poet has traversed. Human relationships, however attenuated—on naked moors, "if we meet a face / We almost meet a friend" (lines 141–42)—are one fountain of power for the poet. Having moderated and composed himself, he reminds us of Odysseus faring on final voyages; Wordsworth returns to the "public road," which holds out, like the Alps, a conspicuous invitation to ascend and wander. And the merest country walk becomes, as in "Stepping Westward," "a guide to eternity, / At least to things unknown and without bound" (lines 151–52). It is of and to the people he meets on rural walks that Wordsworth wishes to write, "my theme / No other than the very heart of man" (lines 239–40).

But what is this man and of what is his heart? As usual, when he comes to expand a theme or definition, Wordsworth achieves a noble rhetorical balance through the interaction of paradox and redundancy, the one a stylistic sign of Wordsworthian sublimity, the other of Wordsworthian simplicity:

> thence may I select
> Sorrow that is not sorrow, but delight,
> And miserable love that is not pain
> To hear of, for the glory that redounds
> Therefrom *to humankind and what we are.*
>   (lines 244–48, emphasis mine)

And as an ideal audience, he selects not merely rustics but those whose inarticulateness masks a sublimest vocabulary, and who are Adamic in rural innocence as well as in omniscience:

> There are among the walks of homely life
> Still higher, men *for contemplation framed*,
> Shy, and unpractis'd in the strife of phrase,
> Meek men, whose very souls perhaps would sink
> Beneath them, summon'd to such intercourse:
> Theirs is the language of the heavens, the power,
> The thought, the image, and the silent joy;
> Words are but under-agents in their souls;
> When they are grasping with their greatest strength
> They do not breathe among them.
>
> (lines 265–74, emphasis mine)

Power is the base, the beginning, language merely the refinement or clothing of civilization, which the poet is able to deploy in the service of common man for whom he is the muse of desire, the principle of articulate energy.[32]

Thinking of himself as spokesman for, as well as representative of, the "universal heart," Wordsworth elects a vocation as pedagogue that demands a simultaneous identification with and separation from his audience, similar to his earlier dual attitude towards Mary Hutchinson. He said to Crabb Robinson in 1837 that "he did not expect or desire from posterity any other fame than that which would be given him for the way in which his poems exhibit man in his essentially human character and relations—as child, parent, husband, the qualities which are common to all men as opposed to those which distinguish one man from another."[33] Character is "exhibited" in the roles one assumes, and these are universally recognizable.

But Wordsworth always manages to have it two ways at once: he can address Dorothy as the image of himself at an earlier stage ("Tintern Abbey"), seeing in her "what once I was" only because now he is struck by the distance between them and by the differences between their roles. Likewise, in the Preface to *Lyrical Ballads* a common humanism marks his definition of the poet as a "man speaking to men," but Wordsworth then proceeds to list in great detail the differences between poet and human species. Although he says they are of degree, not of kind, it is difficult to take him at his word, for these maintain the secret sense of salvation for the poet-hero throughout his work. The adventurous sentiments of the famous manifesto from *The Recluse*, which Wordsworth uses as a prospectus to *The Excursion*, are repeated in *The Prelude* immediately after Wordsworth's claims to democratic commonalty:

> Be mine to follow with no timid step
> Where knowledge leads me; it shall be my pride
> That I have dared to tread this holy ground,
> Speaking no dream but things oracular,
> Matter not lightly to be heard by those
> Who to the letter of the outward promise
> Do read the invisible soul.
>
> (XII, 249–55)

SINGLENESS AND PLURALITY

Wordsworth adheres to a double allegiance: first, to the superiority of a single hero, and next to a spiritual democracy. The first comes from his hieratic or aristocratic leanings, and constitutes his legacy from classical literature, whereas the second stems as much from his political radicalism and his rural upbringing as from the Christian doctrines of salvation. This tension, never fully resolved, can be adduced or articulated only by the strongest paradoxes. For this reason the second mountain ascent, of Snowdon by night, was intended for the end of the poem as early as the five-book *Prelude* of 1804.

Indeed, the entire conclusion to *The Prelude* is the most powerful demonstration of those currents and eddies in which the whole has been supported: between the hero as spokesman for commonalty and as divine seer; between man as social being and as splendidly isolated Adam; between a glance backward for support and investiture for present obligations, and a proleptic hope for future achievement and restoration. In mood and structure, all of Book XIII may be taken as a gloss on the concluding lines of Book XII concerning the ennobling epistemic commerce between outer and inner worlds. Recalling his keen sighting in 1795 of a "new world . . . that was fit / To be transmitted and made visible / To other eyes," he reminds us as well of the foundation of man's power in the depth of childhood:

> having for its base
> That whence our dignity originates,
> That which both gives it being and maintains
> A balance, an ennobling interchange
> Of action from within and from without,
> The excellence, pure spirit, and best power
> Both of the object seen, and eye that sees.
>
> (XII, 373–79)

Snowdon and what follows synthesize and clarify this balance. Many critics have struggled gallantly with the Snowdon ascent, but the episode resists the keenest attempts at analysis because in neither the 1805 nor the 1850 version is it consistent in its references and applications.[34] What happens is clear enough, but what it means is less certain. The poet's response to the infinite sea of mists is baffling:

> The universal spectacle throughout
> Was shaped for admiration and delight,
> Grand in itself alone, but in that breach
> Through which the homeless voice of waters rose,
> That dark deep thoroughfare, had Nature lodg'd
> The Soul, the Imagination of the whole.
>
> A meditation rose in me that night
> Upon the lonely Mountain when the scene
> Had pass'd away, and it appear'd to me
> The perfect image of a mighty Mind,
> Of one that feeds upon infinity,
> That is exalted by an under-presence,
> The sense of God, or whatsoe'er is dim
> Or vast in its own being.
>
> (XIII, 60–73)

What is the "it" in line 68 that is "the image of a mighty mind"? What is feeding upon, or threatening, what? Are the real waters of the Atlantic, which he hears at a distance from the place he is standing, an under-presence that simultaneously threatens and exalts? How does Wordsworth expect us to transfer this metaphor to the relationship between the imagination and the outer universe?

We may question the meaning, but not the majesty, of the vision. Wordsworth as participant and observer—both in retrospect and at the time of the event—emphasizes heroic action and theatrical spectacle, and their intertwining. Breasting the ascent, he is progressively more cut off from his comrades by his silent musings: "with forehead bent / Earthward, as if in opposition set / Against an enemy, I panted up / With eager pace, and no less eager thoughts" (lines 29–32). In an enterprising and actively heroic posture, the participant here is far different from the passive and solitary speaker of "I Wandered Lonely as a Cloud," but the same thing happens to each. Both witness infinity, in the lyric a graceful and sprightly dance, in the epic a cosmic battle. On Snowdon, as at Ulswater, he sees a "shew," a "universal spectacle," and a "scene" (lines 52, 60, 67), which falls like a dazing flash, stuns him, and leaves him like the speaker in "A Night-Piece" to contemplate afterward the meaning of the vision.[35]

As befits the epic nature of *The Prelude*, the scene has been of battle. The real waters of the Atlantic threaten to usurp the power of the metaphorical sea of mists lying at his feet (which themselves, as metaphor, have in some sense already usurped the presence, or power, of real waters); the clouds in the sky darken the light of the moon, which, when revealed, momentarily obliterates the lesser lamps of the stars and hangs "naked." It is a scene of "mutual domination" and "interchangeable supremacy" (1850 MS, lines 81 and 84) to which the "grossest minds" cannot fail to respond, but which only "higher minds" actually embody. Everyone is a spectator; only the few participate symbolically in a struggle in which the mind may be an equal partner to the world. Wordsworth obliquely acknowledges his own power to send "abroad / Like transformation," in verses that epitomize the conflicting, or at least complementary, qualities of his heroes:

> They from their native selves can send abroad
> Like transformation, for themselves create
> A like existence, and, whene'er it is
> Created for them, catch it by an instinct;
> Them the enduring and the transient both
> Serve to exalt; they build up greatest things
> From least suggestions, ever on the watch,
> Willing to work and to be wrought upon.
>
> (lines 93–100)

The power of higher minds is both excursive ("can send abroad") and automatically receptive ("catch it by an instinct").

The lucky few exist as objects of natural obeisance (lines 97–98) and subjects of strenuous action (line 98); the rhetorical symmetry of line 100 deliberately images the ideal balance between the joy of exertion and that of self-surrender.

According to Wordsworth's note to "The Thorn" in 1800, imagination is "the faculty which produces impressive effects out of simple elements." Analogously, Wordsworthian heroism develops symbolic action from the simple elements which it witnesses and of which it partakes. Observation becomes the joint process of noting and of enacting, as a ritual is carefully *observed* by its participants. Seeing and doing, responding and asserting mingle dangerously, until Wordsworth relieves the tension with his tautological characterization of heroic souls: "In a world of life they live" (line 102). The verbal simplicity testifies to potentially rigorous activity at the simplest of levels.

Wordsworth's balance fluctuates between action and reception, high minds and grosser ones; the rhythms of Snowdon continue through Book XIII as Wordsworth more personally considers his individual strength and his debts or connections to other people. He rehearses the limits of his dependency and of his freedom. Although the superior minds maintain a communion with the invisible world (the source of those things of which Milton boasted of telling), they also acknowledge their power as contingent: "Such minds are truly from the Deity, / For they are Powers; and hence the highest bliss / That can be known is theirs, / The consciousness of whom they are habitually infused / Through every image" (lines 106–10). This statement has been misconstrued by some as a version of Coleridge's definition of the primary imagination or as praise of self-consciousness.[36] But, as the capitalization of "whom" in the 1850 version specifies, Wordsworth is here talking about divine reliance, about belonging to the deity, and not about knowing who one is. Greatest comfort derives from dependency.

And so, ironically, does greatest freedom. Communion with God and acceptance of divine authority, at the end of the Snowdon meditation (lines 104–19), are followed immediately by an equation with liberty, another conventionally Christian paradox, which has gone unremarked by those who wish to see Wordsworth, in 1805 at least, as more radical than he actually is:

> Oh! who is he that hath his whole life long
> Preserved, enlarged, this freedom in himself?
> For this alone is genuine Liberty.
>
> (lines 120–22)

His justification for self-worth, relying on divine dependency, derives from the same amazement Milton's Adam feels for God's grace: "goodness infinite, goodness immense! / That all this good of evil shall produce, / And evil turn to good" (*Paradise Lost* 12: 469–71). For Wordsworth, reviewing the progress of his life to this point, fear and love, or pain and joy, have been the sublime forms whence come strength.

Knowing now both who and of whom he is, Wordsworth can round his poem to a conclusion by acknowledging human dependency that will ready him for further imaginative independence. Just as imagination has been treated as both autonomous and dependent, so Wordsworth oscillates at the end between the inevitable obligations that human contact entails and the isolation of self-support. Love is one thing ("have thou there / The One who is thy choice of all the world," lines 157–58), but "intellectual love," also called "spiritual love" in 1850, is another. The equivalent of imagination, and "reason in her most exalted mood" (line 170), it has been a major current, arising from darkness and proceeding waywardly throughout the poem as a theme and a form. And it is the mark of solitude. But even when he attempts to define its crucial nature, Wordsworth resorts to a punning and paradoxical rhetoric:

> Imagination having been our theme,
> So also hath that intellectual love,
> For they are each in each, and cannot stand
> *Dividually*. —Here must thou be, O Man!
> Strength to thyself; no Helper hast thou here;
> Here keepest thou thy *individual* state:
> No other can *divide* with thee this work,
> No secondary hand can intervene
> To fashion this ability.
> (lines 185–93, emphasis mine)

Vital joy exists, darkly, inwardly, or not at all. And once possessed, nothing more seems necessary.

It comes as a surprise, then, that Wordsworth ends his poem with human acknowledgments and a hope that he and Coleridge will divide their labors in the future as prophetic pedagogues. As is typical in the organization of Wordsworth's verse paragraphs, the transitions mark the unconscious transferal of one set of ideas to another through overt similarities in diction. Wordsworth says that the man who has developed a "feeling intellect"

> Shall want no humbler *tenderness*, his heart
> Be *tender* as a nursing Mother's heart;
> Of female softness shall his life be full,

> Of little loves and delicate desires,
> Mild interests and *gentlest* sympathies.
> (lines 206–10, emphasis mine)

But he then addresses Dorothy, the very cause, it turns out, of those characteristics he has just praised as the offshoots of inner, and individual, strength:

> Child of my Parents! Sister of my Soul!
> Elsewhere have strains of gratitude been breath'd
> To thee for all the early *tenderness*
> Which I from thee imbibed. And true it is
> That later seasons owed to thee no less;
> . . . .
>   thy breath,
> Dear Sister, was a kind of *gentler* spring,
> That went before my steps.
> (lines 211–15, 244–46, emphasis mine)

A similar series of reversals seems to occur toward the end when Wordsworth, having remembered Raisley Calvert's legacy and having thereby made an epitaph to his youthful benefactor, turns once again to Coleridge, addressing him as if present. As Wordsworth's complementary principle, Coleridge has become a co-worker in the poem's destiny, as well as the invoked source of inspiration whose memory is drawn from the same springs of youthful strength as Dorothy's beneficence. Wordsworth rises to review his life and his poem, both lying distant beneath him like the "vast prospect of the world which I had been" (line 379)—where, however, the undercurrent of futurity in "prospect" balances against the literal pastness of the life—and then looks forward to the achievement of his great task.

As in Book X, the figure of Coleridge is the bridge between opposites: life and death, past and present, weakness and strength. Here, recollection spreads out into an anxious anticipation as Wordsworth worries about his own "power to accomplish aught of worth" (line 387) to excuse the self-indulgence of *The Prelude*, and he once more looks back, projecting his recollection into Coleridge as both his audience and his collaborator:

> beloved Friend,
> When, looking back, thou seest in clearer view
> Than any sweetest sight of yesterday
> That summer when on Quantock's grassy Hills
> Far ranging, and among the sylvan Coombs
> . . . .
> When thou dost to that summer turn thy thoughts,
> And hast before thee all which then we were,
> To thee, in memory of all that happiness
> It will be known, by thee at least, my Friend,
> Felt, that the history of a Poet's mind
> Is labour not unworthy of regard:
> To thee the work shall justify itself.
>
> (lines 390–94, 404–10)

The effort and achievement of "justifying"—a turn on Milton's assured pronouncement that begins, rather than ends, *his* epic venture—focus singly on the man who most resembles the author, his partner on Quantock's hills when they devised the *Lyrical Ballads*, but who, now distant, assumes the otherness necessary for approval or confirmation. He is a small, but fit, audience whose symbolic status lies midway between public applause and private self-confidence.

The conscious limitation of audience is also a self-limitation, just as the litotes of line 409 dramatizes the modesty of Wordsworth's Miltonic hopes: both are equivalent to the narrowing of poetic theme in Book I, the exuberance of "The Earth is all before me" yielding to the more guarded assurance of "the road lies plain before me." Perhaps the most distinctive part of Wordsworth's character formation throughout his poem is his self-accommodation to fluctuations in mood, which however extreme they appear to be, range themselves gracefully along a scale of developing tones and shades. As co-worker and audience in Wordsworth's heroic enterprise, Coleridge has provided inspira-

tion as an intellectual superior; he has also prompted feelings of superiority, as Wordsworth comes to treat him
symbolically as the distant invalid or the weaker vessel
who will be restored by and to the poet, even as Wordsworth has restored himself through the poem. Coleridge's
return will encourage Wordsworth to enter the major
phase of his enterprise. His penultimate hope is

> that Thou art near, and wilt be soon
> Restored to us in renovated health;
> When, after the first mingling of our tears,
> 'Mong other consolations we may find
> Some pleasure from this Offering of my love.
>
> (lines 423–27)

But then, with a final and ironic moment of self-doubt,
Wordsworth once more buries Coleridge by imagining the
climax of his life's work as a tombstone and, simultaneously, as ammunition for yet more remote battles:

> Oh! yet a few short years of useful life,
> And all will be complete, thy race be run,
> Thy monument of glory will be raised.
> Then, though, too weak to tread the ways of truth,
> This Age fall back to old idolatry,
> Though men return to servitude as fast
> As the tide ebbs, to ignominy and shame
> By Nations sink together, we shall still
> Find solace in the knowledge which we have,
> Bless'd with true happiness if we may be
> United helpers forward of a day
> Of firmer trust, joint-labourers in a work
> (Should Providence such grace to us vouchsafe)
> Of their redemption, surely yet to come.
> Prophets of Nature, we to them will speak
> A lasting inspiration, sanctified
> By reason and by truth; what we have loved
> Others will love; and we may teach them how.
>
> (lines 428–45)

The initial fear gives way to hope, as elegy in Wordsworth
is always the other side of panegyric. To praise, one re-

quires a real or symbolic corpse, but hope demands futurity and heroic ambition itself. For salvation, there must first be a fall; for rebirth, an antecedent death. So nations will sink and ebb, and then be redeemed; Coleridge, and implicitly Wordsworth, have their useful lives cut short, only to return as "united helpers forward"; skepticism ("if we may be," "Should Providence . . . vouchsafe," "we may teach them") alternates with confidence ("blessed," "surely yet to come," "others will love"), and the past with the future. It is a measure of Wordsworth's self-confidence and belief in the success of his poetic career that between 1805 and 1850 he replaced "we may teach them how" with "we will teach them how." As he revised his poem, he retrojected a confidence that at the original moment of composition he clearly could not entertain with complete faith. Paradoxically, assurance and futurity belong to retrospective glimpses. Only the achievement of his career allowed Wordsworth to rearrange his earlier tones and to recognize that he had fulfilled his mission after all. He has, in fact, taught us, and has fashioned out of discursiveness a tool for heroic pedagogy.

The tonal and rhetorical seesawing at the end of his epic bespeaks not so much an intellectual wavering as an implicit understanding and absorption of the limits of heroism. Thinking of Achilles, Cedric Whitman suggests that "heroism is the paradox of permanence abiding in the ephemeral; the transcendent will is like a tall tree, but once it has blossomed, the human soul from which it grew takes on a new and unexpected beauty."[37] The phrase "permanence abiding in the ephemeral" probably betrays an unconscious recollection of Coleridge's famous definition of the literary symbol, in *The Statesman's Manual*, as "characterized by a translucence of the special in the individual, or of the general in the special, or of the universal in the general; above all by the translucence of the eternal through and in the temporal." Whitman's observation happily, if coincidentally, balances the ancient and the modern not only by echoing the latter in the description of the former but also by updating the classic to include the contemporary within it. The paradoxes of heroism are Wordsworth's as well as Homer's. As the idealized projections of self onto other characters in *The Prelude* admit, no single man can ever fully embody the heroic ideal. So the poet came to rely increasingly on a splintered focus that illuminates equally distinctive individuals, all of whom represent, in poems as different as *The White Doe of Rylstone* and *The Excursion*, partial and separate claims to the status of heroism that even *The Prelude* never reserves entirely for its main character. The egotistical sublime, always shared, becomes progressively less egotistical after 1805. Even the posthumous title of the poem on his life betrays more than the self-aggrandizement of performance: "Growth of A Poet's Mind" has followed one possible path. *Quot poetae, tot viae*: other paths remain untrod.

6

The Mysterious Heroic World
of *The White Doe of Rylstone*

In 1837 Wordsworth appended some lines from his only play, *The Borderers*, written forty years earlier but unpublished, as an epigraph for a new printing of the 1815 edition of *The White Doe of Rylstone*:

> Action is transitory—a step, a blow,
> The motion of a muscle—this way or that—
> 'Tis done; and in the after-vacancy
> We wonder at ourselves like men betrayed:
> Suffering is permanent, obscure and dark,
> And has the nature of infinity.[1]

The sublime contrast that the villainous Oswald uses to rationalize murder and self-exile introduces a narrative that, more than anything else Wordsworth ever wrote, distills his complex feelings about human action and the efficacy of suffering. *The White Doe* is a major poem of dichotomies, establishing oppositions, and then razing or blurring them, as if to prove that the world is initially easier, and at last more difficult, to understand than we might have imagined.[2] Heroic action is played off against passive endurance and unlike gestures, postures, and modes of behavior come gradually to resemble one another. Two other lines from the play could have served as well as introduction to the romance: "So meet extremes in this mysterious world, / And opposites thus melt into each other" (lines 1529–30).

At first reading, these oppositions seem crystalline.[3] We have a story of the abortive Catholic uprising of 1569 against Elizabeth I, in which the patient, Protestant Emily Norton, sole daughter of a Yorkshire family, learns the virtues of suffering and sublimation: in the face of her heterodox family's rebellion, she merely stands and waits. Against the banner, which Emily has sewn, borne into battle by the Nortons, stands the mysterious white doe, emblematic of quietude, gracefulness, innocence, and otherworldly aspiration. Against the language of upward movement (the "rising" in the North, the apotheosis of Emily and her doe), there is a counterinsistence on images of falling and failing (the defeat of the rebels, Emily's sinking into peace), which suggest the framework of Aristotelian tragedy. And against the rhetoric of pathos, the grand and public schemes associated with battle and the poem's political subject, there is what Herbert Lindenberger, borrowing his terms from Quintilian, identifies as Wordsworth's language of ethos, used for Emily's humility and her meditative calm.[4] By providing a context for holiness in the public parts of the poem, Wordsworth is able to write of piety without plunging into bathos. By keeping the two areas distinct but always abutting, he makes us accept the Protestant Emily's almost Catholic sainthood and her brother's martyrdom as well.

Most readers have taken Wordsworth at his word and judged *The White Doe* a poem of pure imagination. Geoffrey Hartman, by labeling it a lyrical ballad, plays up the "singular nakedness" to which Emily is progressively reduced and the imaginative victory she wins over self-consuming stoicism by her faint connections with the world in the figure of the mysterious doe; he consequently dismisses the narrative action and the public dimension of the poem.[5] All the critics follow Wordsworth's interpretation of the poem, which deliberately focuses on Emily, the doe, and those passive qualities that distinguish the narratives of suffering

(*The White Doe* resembles *The Ruined Cottage*, but Margaret is given no choice but to crumble along with her house) from the action-packed thrillers of contemporaries like Scott: "Everything that is attempted by the principal personages in 'The White Doe' fails, so far as its object is external and substantial. So far as it is moral and spiritual it succeeds."[6] The "Apotheosis of the Animal," the "pure and lofty Imagination," rendered by the exquisitely limpid clarity of the "Christabel"-style versification and Drydenic diction[7]—everything seems to support Wordsworth's assertion in 1836 that "the true action of the poem was spiritual—the subduing of the will, and all inferior passions, to the perfect purifying and spiritualising of the intellectual nature."

To accept readily these claims at face value is to ignore the complexities of the romance, which is deliberately plotted to focus alternately on Emily's inner struggle and the public political conflict; further, the work urges us to see both the oppositions and the resemblances between major forces aligned along different columns. Thematically, the poem concerns types of heroic behavior, one active, the other passive, and refuses to acknowledge the superiority of either. Generically, it charts a road between Romantic narrative balladry, with overtones of Virgilian epic, and Wordsworth's meditative lyricism, here tinged by Ovidian metamorphosis. As such, *The White Doe* comes a close second to Keats's "Lamia," which Allen Tate claims is the most original narrative poem of the century.[8]

Wordsworth referred to the "action" scenes as the "mere business parts" of his poem, but they caused him much trouble, and as late as 1837 he was still fussing with them, unsatisfied with something nominally worthless. Although he berated Charles Lamb for not understanding the differences between the "gross and visible action" of dramatic poetry and the "victories in the world of the spirit" celebrated by *The White Doe*, we recall that it was

Wordsworth who first criticized Coleridge's Mariner for his passivity, for the apparent lack of willed action in that poem of "pure imagination," which, like *The White Doe*, presents a conquest over sorrow (and crime) "forwarded by communion with a creature not of [the human] species." In fact, the political and dramatic action in the poem, based on the old border ballad in Percy's *Reliques*, is as serious and moving as the depiction of Emily and her doe.

In an 1819 letter to Francis Wrangham, Wordsworth remarked: "As to the Nortons, the Ballad is my authority, and I require no more. It is much better than Virgil had for his Aeneid." This is a telling juxtaposition, because the "public" parts of the poem are among the most Virgilian in all of Wordsworth. In them we hear one of the poem's strong, authentic notes, one sounded faintly in the second epigraph, from Bacon's essay on atheism: the quest for a definition of true courage, and of the relationship between nobility in action and Spenserian "magnanimity," or as Bacon terms it, "the raising of humane Nature." The echoes from *The Aeneid* within the poem attest to Wordsworth's sympathy for the values of classical epic, especially the Virgilian ones to which he was naturally partial.[9]

In this regard, the story's central figure is Francis Norton, eldest son of nine and, with Emily, the inheritor of their dead mother's reformed Protestantism. Where the eight younger sons support their father's Catholicism and join him in battle and death, and where Emily is urged to abandon hope and await a heavenly victory, Francis alone must choose between two courses of action, either of which would compromise his values. He is tensely, classically poised between violating either his religious and political beliefs, or his filial duty. Like the seventeenth-century Republicans whom Wordsworth praises in the "Poems Dedicated to National Independence and Liberty" (*PW* 3: 116–17), Francis must unite action with composure, strength with restraint. Sacrifice and labor are the conditions of nobility: Roman stoicism, a discovery of hope in the abandonment of hope, colors his portrait, but Wordsworth's deeper feelings about the commonplaces of heroic behavior darken the picture. Francis is the spokesman for stoic fortitude. His farewell charge to Emily (lines 521–87), before his surreptitious accompaniment of the Nortons into war, is a pastiche of Virgilian reminiscences from the fall of Troy:

> The time is come that rings the knell
> Of all we loved, and loved so well:
> Hope nothing
> . . . .
> for we
> Are doomed to perish utterly:
> 'Tis meet that thou with me divide
> The thought while I am by thy side,
> Acknowledging a grace in this,
> A comfort in the dark abyss.
>
> (lines 528–37)

His admonition conflates Panthus's desperate finality— "fuimus Troes, fuit Ilium et ingens / gloria Teucrorum; ferus omnia Iuppiter Argos / transtulit" (*Aeneid* 2: 325–27)—with Aeneas's subsequent unstoic rush into insane battle: "una salus victis nullam sperare salutem" (2: 354).[10] The echo is tainted, for Francis, like Aeneas, is impetuous and unheeding. In the face of sure disaster ("For we must fall, both we and ours") that will transform landscape and household into "one desolation, one decay," Francis enjoins Emily to feminine acceptance: "Espouse thy doom at once, and cleave / To fortitude without reprieve."

Francis does not take his own nostrum; the poem operates on an ethical double standard. A "soul of conscientious daring," we see him act at three crucial moments. Twice he impulsively grabs a weapon; first, in a trance of agony, it is a lance, which he subsequently spurns "like something that would stand / Between him and the pure intent / Of love on which his soul was bent" (lines 518–20), as he decides to accompany father and brothers, naked and hidden, a dedicated Edgar or Kent to his father's Lear. Next, at the climax of canto 5, Francis meets the cruel taunt of Sussex's order to have the banner borne before the men on their way to execution: "with a look of calm command / Inspiring universal awe, / He took it from the soldier's hand" (lines 1331–33), and attempts to fulfill his father's last request to return the banner to Bolton Priory. Fleeing, he is impervious to everything but the banner, which functions as the agency of hypnosis much as the moon does in "Strange Fits of Passion": "All but the suffering heart was dead / For him abandoned to blank awe, / To vacancy, and horror strong" (lines 1386–88). It is *his* suffering here that echoes the cautionary remarks in the epigraph to the poem. Seeing the banner before him, Francis feels betrayed but committed. At last, surrounded by enemy soldiers who have reneged in their previous pardon of the one unrebellious Norton, he becomes, with a final gesture, a martyr. Snatching a spear (this time consciously) from an enemy's hand, he is himself struck down. The lance falls, but the banner, in his other hand, does not, until the very end. A soldier

> Seized it, as hunters seize their prey;
> But not before the warm life-blood
> Had tinged more deeply, as it flowed,
> The wounds the broidered Banner showed,
> Thy fatal work, O Maiden, innocent as good!
> (lines 1494–98)

An unintended victim, Francis Norton combines and surpasses the pious waiting of his sister and the strong, though futile, principled sacrifice of his father. His blood literally mingling with the depicted wounds of Christ, he enacts an *imitatio Christi*; his body remains uncovered and unrecognized for two days, and on the third is discovered and finally laid to rest. Mortality and transcendence are Janus-like twin figures in the romance.

This doubleness is explicit from the start of the poem. The seven lines Wordsworth added to the original fragment from *The Borderers* expand the opening tension:

> Yet through that darkness (infinite though it seem
> And irremoveable) gracious openings lie,
> By which the soul—with patient steps of thought
> Now toiling, wafted now on wings of prayer—
> May pass in hope, and, though from mortal bonds
> Yet undelivered, rise with sure ascent
> Even to the fountain-head of peace divine.[11]

Light opposes darkness, and salvation, damnation. More instructive is the paired contrast of "thought," with its active, participial "toiling," and peace. Such doubleness corresponds to the joint heroism of brother and sister in the poem. The poet's plea for inspiration at the end of the introductory first canto braces us for an equally paradoxical combination: "To chant, in strains of heavenly glory, / A tale of tears, a mortal story." (At the end, before the last moments of redemption, the same paradox is repeated: "A mortal Song we sing, by dower / Encouraged of celestial power.")

Francis's encouragement of his sister begins with a lengthy subordinate, conditional clause, which neatly telescopes their past through the double lenses of action and suffering:

> If, when at home our private weal
> Hath suffered from the shock of zeal,
> Together we have learned to prize
> Forbearance and self-sacrifice;
> If we like combatants have fared,
> And for this issue been prepared.
> (lines 575–80)

The paradox is capped by his admonition to "Be strong." Falling hopes are balanced by a rising fate:

> be worthy of the grace
> Of God, and fill thy destined place:

A Soul, by force of sorrows high,
Uplifted to the purest sky
Of undisturbed humanity.
                    (lines 583–87)

The Nortons, father, son, and holy daughter, form a triune image of Wordsworth's Happy Warrior, duplicating the virtues listed in that poem and those of the "Ode to Duty" (1804), written before the death of his brother, which critics usually label the entrance to his middle period of fortitude and mature, even preacherly, stoicism. Longing "for a repose that ever is the same," Wordsworth in the ode embraces duty "through no disturbance of my soul, / Or strong compunction in me wrought, / . . . / But in the quietness of thought." To accept duty is willingly to abandon uncharted freedom, "the weight of chance desires," those same qualms and frustrations that burden the poet in the beginning of *The Prelude* and constitute the customary freight of earthly years in the Intimations Ode. Duty is the limiting, and therefore liberating, muse of moral rectitude; she is the habitual mistress whom he seeks like a lover in order to achieve the automatic benevolence suggested by the ode's Senecan epigraph: "jam non consilio bonus, sed more eo perductus, ut non tantum recte facere possim, sed nisi recte facere non possim" ("Now, at last, I am not consciously good, but so trained by habit that not only can I act rightly, but cannot act otherwise than rightly"). The "confidence of reason" (line 55), here combined with Miltonic "lowly" wisdom, provides him with a strength similar to that sustaining Emily at the end of *The White Doe* where "strength of Reason," her lessons from Francis, coupled with "memory of the past," especially embodied for her in the figure of her animal, both sustain and ultimately release her.[12]

Wordsworth's seventeenth-century Republican faith in reason as law and solace is the keystone of his image of an idealized Nelson in the "Character of the Happy Warrior," and of the moral failure of Laodamia in the poem that, he later said, cost him more pains than anything else he had written.[13] This problem, as usual, stems from his seeing more complexly than a philosopher might and from being consequently incapable of adequately defining *reason*, of distinguishing its proper bounds from the cold, desiccated rationality of characters like Oswald or the talented young man in the early "Lines Left upon a Seat in a Yew-Tree."

The Happy Warrior combines the gallantry of Francis with the piety and patience of Emily. His "moral being" is his "prime care," and he is "pure" and "more alive to tenderness" as he is "more able to endure, / As more exposed to suffering and distress." His "Law is Reason"; like the leech-gatherer, he does not wait for worldly rewards, which will come, if at all, as "a constant influence, a peculiar grace." Whether famous or obscure, he "finds comfort in himself and in his cause."

Except that he mistakenly deems his allies' motives as pure as his own, Richard Norton is such a Warrior. Fearless but headstrong, he speaks "bare truth" to the gathered rebel forces, praying in the hopeful enthusiasm of rebellion for a return to the old customs: "To you a suffering State complains, / And ye must raise her from the dust" (lines 648–49). The North rises in arms, the rebellion catches fire as it moves to Durham, where the leaders "sang mass,— and tore the book of prayer,— / And trod the bible beneath their feet" (lines 713–14). There is no evidence in the poem that Wordsworth disapproves of the insurrection merely because, as Barbara Gates asserts, his own political and religious views were conservative and Anglican.[14] On the contrary, everything about Norton, even his Lear-like intransigence in spurning Francis until the very end, bespeaks his nobility. Surrounded by eight ripe and worthy sons, Norton is physically stationed so as to embody grandeur and ordinariness, a perfect mingling of Wordsworthian contraries:

> no steed will he
> Henceforth bestride;—triumphantly
> He stands upon the grassy sod,
> Trusting himself to the earth, and God.
> . . . .
> The monumental pomp of age
> Was with this goodly Personage,
> A stature undepressed in size,
> Unbent, which rather seemed to rise,
> In open victory o'er the weight
> Of seventy years, to loftier height;
> Magnific limbs of withered state.
>
> (lines 728–31, 737–43)

Outnumbered and disillusioned, Norton and his sons, in an admirable, desperate gesture, try to scale the walls and plant their banner within Barnard Castle. They are caught, imprisoned, and executed by the Queen's troops. The messenger's description to Emily stresses the pathos and religious martyrdom of their end: the Moon "hath witnessed their captivity" (line 1125); "marks of infamy and shame, / These were their triumph, these their pride" (lines 1225–26); "cruel Sussex, unrestrained / By human feeling" (lines 1328–29). Francis has inherited his Christian militancy legitimately. The Nortons' death is their apotheosis; their destruction is, rhetorically, a rising, and they go to martyrdom with stoic grace: "They rose—embraces none were given— / They stood like trees when earth and heaven / Are calm; they knew each other's worth, / And reverently the Band went forth" (lines 1318–21). Wordsworth's note about Emily could stand as well for her father and brothers: "How insignificant a thing . . . does personal prowess appear compared with the fortitude of patience and heroic martyrdom; in other words, with struggles for the sake of principle, in preference to victory gloried in for its own sake."

However foolhardy, the stately, reasoned action of the Nortons is one pole to which the wavering Francis leans. The other is Emily's pious quietism, which augments a living martyrdom in her, and to which Francis encourages her. As I have suggested, the moving portrayal of Emily is not the sole repository of value in the moral and emotional scheme of the poem. Balancing the masculine decisiveness of her brother and father, Emily's stoic resolve is undermined by her natural hope for her brother's safety, by Wordsworth's hints that stalwart, splendid isolation is as willfully, selfishly perverse as self-aggrandizing political rebellion, and by the ultimate formality of feeling after her great pain, which symbolically petrifies her. She sits like Patience on her own monument, a *soror dolorosa* joined in prayer by the otherworldly doe, her sole stay and comfort.

In attempting to apotheosize his heroine, Wordsworth comes dangerously close to rendering her less than human: Does the relinquishment of the rights of "feeble nature" (lines 1192–93) to hope produce as well the relinquishment of natural piety? Does the denial of Christian hope and the transference of love to an unhuman partner in her sorrows' mysteries beatify Emily or merely etiolate whatever vigor she once had through a purgation that is really a withering? These questions are at the heart of the poem's mysterious melting contraries. Distinct certainties constantly give way, under the tension of the drama, to blurred resemblances.

Emily gets the lion's share of attention only at the end. We see her briefly, silently receiving her brother's farewell in canto 2; we witness her uncertainty and struggle in canto 4 as she awaits news of the rebellion, but she does not occupy center stage until the dramatic action itself is over. She comes upon Francis's funeral at the end of canto 6, "and with her breast / Upon the ground received the rest,— / The consummation, the whole ruth / And sorrow of this final truth" (lines 1547–50). Her canto is the seventh, which stands outside the main action, and consequently balances the prelude of the first canto, enclosing and deflecting the five-act drama in the bulk of the poem. Emily both is and is not part of the romance, just as she is and is not tied to the public world of human behavior. She is both central and ancillary.

We feel the full weight of Emily's "unmerited distress" as the aftermath to the public tragedy of the piece: *The White Doe*, like Book I of *The Excursion*, is a lesson in how to read tragedy, only now we are schooled directly by the narrative, without the intervening filter of Wanderer and Poet whose discourse enacts for us an education in Wordsworthian truths. In the middle of the poem, Emily appears for a moment in a blessed, Coleridgean pleasure-garden, bathed by moonlight. From the doe, a "lonely relic" of earlier time (a curiously Catholic term for this symbol of the consecrated Protestant imagination), Emily passes into "a goodly spot, / With lawns and beds of flowers, and shades / Of trellis-work in long arcades, / And cirque and crescent framed by wall / Of close-clipt foliage green and tall" (lines 984–88). Soothed by the landscape, and ignoring but comforted by the animal, Emily now has a vision of her dead mother, "that blessed Saint," who first taught her the Protestant faith. Evoked ambiguously, like the doe (the line between the Reformed faith and Catholicism is hard to see), the vision of the mother is urged to redeem Francis from "that most lamentable snare, / The self-reliance of despair" (lines 1055–56).

Emily's inner drama is a struggle between committing the sin against the Holy Spirit, the abandonment of hope, and disobeying her brother's order to resign herself, wait, expect the worst, and thus to "finally secure / O'er Pain and Grief a Triumph Pure." It is the struggle between Christian and Stoic ethics, and Emily is eloquently reminded of her Christian obligation by her family servant—"Hope . . . must abide / With all of us, whate'er betide" (lines 1092–93)—whom she forbids to tempt her and sends off as an observer to return with news of the uprising.

In canto 7, we witness Emily's final transformation, first into a genius loci, at one with the unweeded desolation that has overtaken Rylstone Hall, and, second, into an evaporating spirit whose tenuous connection with life, in the shape of her companion Doe, both redeems her from the surrounding decay and dissipates her life while her soul, we assume, achieves the paradoxical harmony of "heavenly glory" through the tears of mortality with which canto 1 ended. In an extraordinary ending, Wordsworth paints a picture of grace separated from hope, love, and human connection.

For seventy lines (1568–1638), from her first appearance until she "melts into tears" at the approach of the radiant Doe, Emily sits transfixed, like a character out of Dickinson or like Stevens's Snow Man. The sign of Wordsworth's absolute control is the taut ambiguity of his tone in this portrait, flecked as it is with shadows that keep us from a clear emotional sighting of its subject. The "joyless human Being" (line 1580) is also "a virgin Queen" (line 1590), a strange enough reminder of the ruling monarch against whom the Nortons rebelled, sitting upon "a primrose bank, her throne / Of quietness," in a state of rigorously willed dejection, which is muted and humanized only by a Miltonic echo and by the ineradicable tenderness in her face, which grief has not entirely overshadowed. At first we are reminded that self-governance, a chaste control, is the key to this Happy Warrior:

> Behold her, like a virgin Queen,
> Neglecting in imperial state
> These outward images of fate,
> And carrying inward a serene
> And perfect sway, through many a thought
> Of chance and change, that hath been brought
> To the subjection of a holy,
> Though stern and rigorous, melancholy!
> (lines 1590–97)

The "holy/melancholy" rhyme from the opening lines of "Il Penseroso" may suggest a tempering of despair, but the following lines insist on Emily's unnatural attempt to envelop and freeze herself:

The like authority, with grace
Of awfulness, is in her face,—
There hath she fixed it; yet it seems
To o'ershadow by no native right
That face, which cannot lose the gleams,
Lose utterly the tender gleams,
Of gentleness and meek delight,
And loving-kindness ever bright:
Such is her sovereign mien.

(lines 1598–1606)

It is significant that Emily's despair is a political rebel to her natural gentleness, exactly as the rising in the North was to that other virgin Queen in the South.

Now "thoroughly forlorn," Emily exchanges stolidity for her previous random wanderings through her native lands, when her grief caused her unhuman passiveness. Loss of control is loss of human power: earlier she roamed "Driven forward like a withered leaf, / Yea like a ship at random blown / To distant places and unknown" (lines 1614–16). But bearing and accepting sorrow result, ironically, in a reciprocal kind of unhumanness—the freezing of the soul:

Her soul doth in itself stand fast,
Sustained by memory of the past
And strength of Reason; held above
The infirmities of mortal love;
Undaunted, lofty, calm, and stable,
And awfully impenetrable.

(lines 1623–28)

Is she the Happy Warrior, or more like that figure in Gray's "Ode to Adversity": "Melancholy, Silent Maid / With leaden eye, that loves the ground"? As if to amplify the previous image of Emily upon a primrose bank, Wordsworth reflashes the picture at us, but with a variation: now, she is sitting "beneath a mouldered tree, / A self-surviving leafless oak / By unregarded age from stroke / Of ravage saved" (lines 1629–32). No longer a virgin Queen, she is seen in her essential fragility, not her imperial melancholy:

"There did she rest, with head reclined, / Herself most like a stately flower, / . . . whom chance of birth / Hath separated from its kind, / To live and die in a shady bower, / Single on the gladsome earth" (lines 1633–38). Herself the fairest flower, we might hear echoed, along with reminders of another Wordsworthian solitary who lives alone in a shady bower—"a maid whom there were none to praise, / And very few to love."

Whereas Lucy's memory is preserved and cherished by her poet-lover, Emily finds connection with a different kind of attendant. The appearance of, and subsequent relationship with, the Doe are a muted parody of the calm of mute insensate things. When the Doe, recognizing Emily, "Fixes her large full eye" upon her, she establishes a mystical bond comparable to those uniting other Wordsworthian solitaries with their audiences: Cumberland Beggar, discharged soldier, and leech-gatherer, for example. The Doe's purgative effect enables Emily to release her sublimated or repressed emotion in a "flood of tears" and to go with her in a celebration of their joint sustenance. Emily, beatified by suffering, has become the Doe's "sainted mistress"; for her part, the Doe is a history, like the Cumberland Beggar, a "lovely chronicler of things / Long past, delights and sorrowings."

Their relationship is quasi-religious: the earlier Miltonic echo is repeated as Emily is now a soul, "blest / With a soft spring-day of holy, / Mild, and grateful, Melancholy" (lines 1756–58). It is also quasi-erotic, as the Doe, "unwooed, yet unforbidden," follows her mistress into deeper recesses of the forest, where she intuitively understands, with "a power like human reason," every look, gesture, word, and wish of Emily: when to approach, when to retire. They wander in a pastoral, amatory bliss: "How pleased, when down the Straggler sank / Beside her, on some sunny bank! / How soothed, when in thick bower enclosed, / They, like a nested pair, reposed" (lines 1734–37). Tears to human suffering *are* due, as Wordsworth reminds us in

"Laodamia," but at the end of *The White Doe* the still sad music of humanity, which chastens and subdues, is replaced by Emily's tears, not for family or estate, but for her one remaining faithful partner: "A few tears down her cheek descend / For this her last and living Friend" (lines 1795–96).

Precisely this replacement, or sublimation, of human attachment assures Emily's final "re-ascent in sanctity." She becomes the saint of Rylstone as she disentangles herself from it. The climax is a paradox, but we have become used to such strangeness. When we hear of Emily as a pilgrim, moved by sorrow toward God, "Uplifted to the purest sky / Of undisturbed mortality" (lines 1852–53), we may wince, but the ascent is possible only as she asserts her mortal nature. Ironically, it is the release of stoic fortitude, through her attachment to the doe, that ensures her beatification. In relationship she is most undisturbed and single; in mortality, she becomes "thus faintly, faintly tied / To earth, she was set free, and died" (lines 1864–65). Her soul rises, her mortal frame is buried: the Doe is the unhuman agency that stimulates liberation. As her father found sainthood in military martyrdom, and her brother in the submission to filial duty, Emily finds her saintly vocation in a paradoxical detachment, through attachment to her animal.

Ultimately, the Doe itself assumes Emily's role as genius loci, haunting Bolton Priory and churchyard, gliding silently, like a ghost (line 1883; on its first appearance it is "soft and silent as a dream," line 57). There is the suggestion of metempsychosis—as the Doe attends not the grave of Emily at Rylstone, but that of Francis at Bolton Priory; that is, her attachment is not to Emily herself, but to the experiences they have shared and the customs they have developed (another reminder of Seneca's habitualism). Visiting the old haunts, the Doe is both a grieving widow, finding solace in an attempted repetition of the past, and Emily's heir and surrogate—a motif suggested by Dr. Whi-

taker's note (which Wordsworth, curiously, in his many remarks about the poem, does not mention):

> This incident awakens the fancy. Shall we say that the soul of
> one of the Nortons had taken up its abode in that animal, and
> was condemned to do penance, for his transgressions against
> "the lords' deere," among their ashes? But for such a spirit the
> wild stag would have been a fitter vehicle. Was it not, then,
> some fair and injured female, whose name and history are for-
> gotten?[15]

Moreover, the Doe's final apotheosis distinctly resembles Emily's: with "a mind / Raised far above the law of
kind," she realizes the Stoic ideal as much as any of the
people in the poem:

> There doth the gentle Creature lie
> With those adversities unmoved;
> Calm spectacle, by earth and sky
> In their benignity approved!
> And aye, methinks, this hoary Pile,
> Subdued by outrage and decay,
> Looks down upon her with a smile,
> A gracious smile, that seems to say—
> "Thou, thou art not a Child of Time,
> But Daughter of the Eternal Prime."
>   (lines 1901–10)

The ending reminds us of the more than casual resemblances among the central figures in the poem. The overall
consonance of the poem's parts and of its form reveals a
powerful rage for organization equivalent to the ordered
comparisons and contrasts among the four similarly heroic
characters.[16]

The poem's basic structure is quasi-Aristotelian: a tragedy with a carefully plotted rising and falling action, in
which falling is ironically related to the conquest of the
soul over outward sense, and to martyrdom through either
action or patience. But this balanced symmetry is modified
in certain ways. For one, the harmony of circularity makes
the poem a Romantic nature lyric, according to the conven-

tional formula posited by M. H. Abrams.[17] It deliberately
rounds to a close where it began—with the Doe alone, an
emblem of solitude and patience, of superhuman or unhuman calm. For another, the poem plumbs the matter of
origins or beginnings as if to demonstrate the difficulty of
learning how or when something starts. "The nature of infinity" thus applies to action as well as to suffering. Richard Norton, thinking of Emily's reformed faith, speaks
pointedly of this problem. It was his wife, long dead, who
first "in reason's dawn beguiled / Her docile, unsuspecting
Child: / Far back, far back my mind must go / To reach the
well-spring of this woe!" (lines 885–88).

The question of origins is, of course, best exemplified in
the poem by the mystery of the Doe's identity, which is not
explained until the end. We see the Doe after the events in
the first canto, where it teases the imaginations of its be-
holders.[18] For a moment in canto 2 Francis points to it, to
include it (wrongly, as it turns out) in his list of what will
disappear from Rylstone; in canto 4 the Doe is an agency of
recollection, allowing Emily to remember her sainted
mother. But the Doe, like Emily, does not assume prominence until the end—the poem returns circuitously to it,
and only in an almost parenthetical remark do we learn
that it was brought home years before by the youngest
Norton brother, and, after many years of roaming free, it
has returned to its adopted home. In its end is its beginning.

The origin of, for example, an animal with a seemingly
inexplicable attachment to a place, or of the changed faith
of two of ten children, or of memory itself—all illustrate a
problem at the heart of Wordsworth's need to assert independence (which may verge on solipsism) in the face of his
knowledge of interdependence (which may verge on an
undifferentiated loss of identity).[19] In *The White Doe*, the
problem is related to the question of genre. The circular
construction of a Romantic lyric, the clear depiction of public action as an Aristotelian tragedy, are both colored by the

self-consciously "Romance" frame and mood of the poem. Wordsworth varies the theme of variation itself, of Ovidian metamorphosis; just as other poems suggest "the internalization of quest romance," or of more capacious epic forms, so *The White Doe* calls into question the imaginative basis of metamorphosis.[20] There is a natural connection between imagination and metamorphosis; as Wordsworth put it, "Objects (the Banner, for instance) derive their influence not from properties inherent in themselves . . . but from such as are *bestowed* upon them by the minds of those who are conversant with or affected by those objects" (*PW* 3: 547).[21]

The tension beneath the seeming calm, assurance, and dignity of the poem's tone permits us glimpses into Wordsworth's nervous need to include contraries—Christian and Stoic ethics; the alternating dangers of impetuousness turning to willfulness, and resolution turning to paralysis; Catholicism and Protestantism—and yet to blur them (all the Nortons, rising and falling, are types of the same Warrior). For this reason, the poem's seemingly irrelevant beginning, in the distant aftermath of the events of the Rebellion, is crucial. Wordsworth deliberately delays the presentation of his narrative in order to provoke his audience to ask the simple questions: Why is this so? What is this Doe? At the beginning of this naturalized and updated Ovidian myth or fable, instead of explaining how the crow became black, Battus a touchstone, or Syrinx a reed, Wordsworth forces us, with his *faux-naif* narratorial stance, to ask, Why is this Doe sitting in this churchyard?

The strategy of confronting first the natural scene, or aftermath of an event, is a centrally Wordsworthian one. In *The Ruined Cottage*, we face the desolation of the cottage and then are schooled in tragic suffering by the Wanderer's story; in "Michael," there is the bleak and treacherous landscape, which we might pass over inattentively as we might the Doe, until the poet opens our eyes to and through his story. Even in "The Thorn," where there is a developed fiction about the narrator himself, the narrative tactic raises doubts and questions and then attends to their resolution.

As oppositions yield to resemblances, *The White Doe* permits the explanation of mysteries and the discovery of origins. The first canto invites the reader to test his imagination against those of the other spectators in the Priory Churchyard. The narrator is amazed at the Doe:

> 'Tis a work for sabbath hours
> If I with this bright Creature go:
> Whether she be of forest bowers,
> From the bowers of earth below;
> Or a Spirit for one day given,
> A pledge of grace from purest heaven.
>   (lines 73–78)

And he is equally uncertain: "Comes she with a votary's task, / Rite to perform, or boon to ask?" (Lines 108–25 pose a long series of such questions.) Watched by the crowd, the Doe assumes an identity determined by the imaginative needs of each witness. An old man sees in her the founder of the Priory; a haughty dame staring down at the grisly chapel vault infers some vile intent; an Oxford scholar with "his own conceit" sees her as a Romantic fairy who attended a shepherd Lord. All are confined by perplexity, delusion, or "idle fear." Only the inspired narrator-minstrel, aided by a spirit's hand, which touches his harp at the canto's end, will speak for "sober truth," undeluded by fancy, projection, or myopia.

The questions of genre, of Ovidian metamorphosis, and of the role of imagination in interpreting physical or (for a reader) narrative data are ultimately related to the larger question of the poem's style, which is Wordsworthian mainly in its clear diction. At the heart of the poem's peculiar brilliance are three stylistic features: the variety in versification and rhyme, the use of paradox, and the allied tropes of redundancy and repetition. The first is a freely acknowledged debt to "Christabel," while the latter two move us toward an affective stylistics, an educative tool for the reader as Wordsworth realized in his remark about the mind's conferring qualities upon perceived objects. Paradox, especially the vocabulary of rising and falling that rings throughout the poem, is one way for contraries to meet and mate; repetition is the stylistic gesture that encourages us to consider growth, origins, and the unfolding of reality at the heart of metamorphosis.[22] True, repetition is also a hallmark of Romantic balladry, but Wordsworth's use of the trope exceeds a simple imitation of the old naive style.

We may examine Wordsworth's technique in the tantalizing deployment of words and syllables initially introducing the Doe. Between dusky trees, down a path, through a green, a gateway, beneath an arch, to the churchyard—the prepositional phrases trace and station the movement while at the same time constricting and confining it:

> Comes gliding in with lovely gleam,
> Comes gliding in serene and slow,
> Soft and silent as a dream,
> A solitary Doe!
>
> (lines 55–58)

The heavily repeated internal rhymes and sounds, and the series of sibilant adjectives ambiguously equivalent to adverbs suggest not only the Doe's movement but also the readjustment of the spectator's point of view. Further on, in a similar section the repeated words define equally the movement of the subject and the focus of the speaker-viewer:

> the enamoured sunny light
> *Brightens her* that was so *bright;*
> Now doth a delicate shadow *fall,*
> *Falls* upon *her* like a breath,
> From *some* lofty arch or wall,
> As *she* passes underneath:
> Now *some* gloomy nook partakes
> Of the glory that *she* makes,—

High-ribbed vault of *stone*, or *cell*,
With perfect cunning framed as well
Of *stone*, and ivy, and the spread
Of the elder's bushy head;
Some jealous and forbidding *cell*,
That doth the living stars repel,
And where no flower hath leave to dwell.
                    (lines 85–99, emphasis mine)

The peculiar pun in the last line, from a poet not particularly playful with language, reflects a fancifulness at odds with both the Virgilian public scenes and the *lacrimae rerum* of Emily's despair. Thus, in one important way, Geoffrey Hartman is right in labeling *The White Doe* a lyrical ballad: repetition, as a stylistic habit, is conventional in ballads, both in the older native style and in those modernized poems of 1798 like "The Idiot Boy" and "The Thorn." Either straightforwardly or chiasmically, Wordsworth laces his narrative with grace notes of balladry:

he had grasped unknowingly, / Had blindly grasped (lines 436–37)

she had tried and tried in vain (line 1014)

with mild looks and language mild (line 1036)

how proud and happy, / . . . how pleased and proud (lines 1180–81)

O Pair / Beloved of Heaven, Heaven's chosen care (lines 1665–66)

white as whitest cloud on high (line 1741)

faintly, faintly tied / To earth (lines 1864–65).

The repeated echo of *Il Penseroso* is matched by a double echo of the opening rhyme of the *The Hind and the Panther* (lines 79–80, 1119–20).

The reductive, some might say childlike, repetitiveness in the poem, indicative of Wordsworth's obvious desire to write something like a traditional ballad, allows us to see his ambivalence about his enterprise, the genre of romance, and more fully, his own relationship with his audience. Like Keats, who thought that "Lamia" would give people a sensation of sorts, but who also considered the piece the most strenuous and difficult he had written, Wordsworth felt understandably proud and awkward with his strange work. According to his sister, he would rather have left all his poetry unpublished until his death, and consented to publication only to make money (*MY* 1: 236). Yet his high opinion enabled him to send *The White Doe* into the world in quarto. Ballads, equivalent in Wordsworth's mind to romance, are the object of his scorn in a letter to Francis Wrangham (June 5, 1808) because they indelicately foster superstition. But he goes on to confess:

> I have many a time wished that I had talents to produce songs, poems, and little histories, that might circulate among other good things in this way. . . . Indeed some of the Poems which I have published were composed not without a hope that at some time or other they might answer this purpose.
>
> (*MY* 1: 248)

Responses to romance, the "food" for "our dumb yearnings" and "hidden appetites" (*The Prelude* V, 530), are the subject of Wordsworth's dedication of *The White Doe* to his wife, written in 1815 to accompany its publication. Their reading of *The Faerie Queene* gave them stock delight in the "pleasing smart" of Una and her milk-white Lamb. It was easy to shed tears, an indulgence in *Schadenfreude*. But after their loss, first of Wordsworth's brother, then of two children, "the stream of fiction" ceased to flow until, at last, winter gave way to spring, and they discovered new, unconventional pleasures in reading romance, able now to share compassionately *in* Una's sorrows.[23] In his story, Wordsworth now asserts, there is not just "pleasure light and fugitive" or "sorrow's thrilling dart," but an exemplum, "amid life's ordinary woes" in which "this moral strain" may impart solace. Anguish is tempered and allayed by—in the very imagery of his poem—"sympathies / Aloft ascending and descending deep." Just as our "crav-

ings for the marvellous" give way in adulthood to "sober
truth, experience, sympathy" (*The Prelude* V, 564–67),
Wordsworth can attest to the effect of *The Faerie Queene*
upon him, before and after tragedy. "Our divine Spenser,"
with his "moral and imaginative genius," is a model of a
poet, like himself, committed to teaching as well as to the
"grand elementary principle of pleasure" which he relishes
in the Preface to *Lyrical Ballads* (*PrW* 1: 140).

Adhering to both the *dulce* and *utile* of traditional aes-
thetics, Wordsworth blurs the line between the two in *The
White Doe* exactly as he does those between opposing
forces, characters, and themes. Not only has the "marvellous" given way to the steady sympathy of Emily and her
Doe but, more important, as a "forger" of a daring tale (*The
Prelude* V, 548) he has brought his readers and his characters into a world that shares the infinity of the northern au-
roras: "Here, nowhere, there, and everywhere at once"
(*The Prelude* V, 557). The world of romance, shimmering in
realms of spirit and action, and of an origin and destina-
tion not readily discernible, is a dream and a deep reality;
it makes "our wish our power, our thought a deed" (line
552). Its elements, like those of the great apocalypse in *The
Prelude*, are "the types and symbols of Eternity, / Of first,
and last, and midst, and without end" (VI, 571–72).

7

The Excursion

If *The Excursion* "will never do," in Francis Jeffrey's infamous evaluation, in what way won't it do, and why? The longest poem that Wordsworth published, which Lamb called "a day in heaven" and Keats thought one of the three great things in his age to cheer about, has fallen into the slough of neglect to which Matthew Arnold would happily have consigned it. The poem remains dismissed although unread, scorned but unfathomed. Yet by looking steadily at our subject, we can see the excellences that remain in the poem and understand why Wordsworth, although withholding *The Prelude* from publication, thought well enough of his other long poem to bring it into the world.

The worst, as Geoffrey Hartman allows, has already been said. From the time of Jeffrey and Hazlitt, who made fun of the phony ruralism in the Pedlar's speech and manner, boredom, outrage, hostility, and sarcasm have been the commonest responses. Byron labeled it "a drowsy, frowsy poem called *The Excursion,* / Writ in a manner that is my aversion." Arnold put it down haughtily: "a tissue of elevated but abstract verbiage, alien to the very nature of poetry." Even Hartman condescends: "those famous misreaders of Wordsworth who say he advocates rural nature as a panacea should be condemned to read *The Excursion* once a day. It might not raise their estimate of the poem, but it would certainly be fit punishment."[1] Everyone has acknowledged the poem's *longueurs,* its tedious and often redundant moralizing, its reversion to eighteenth-century abstraction and periphrasis, its lack of sufficient discriminations or engagements among characters, its failure to show whether the Solitary can be cured of his malingering despondency—a failure to resolve what seems to be the poem's only major theme.

But readers have been too cavalier in their easy jibes at the excesses, divagations, and unconscious self-parodyings of a poem that took almost twenty years to finish, and of which Wordsworth said simply: "It is serious, and has been written with great labour" (*MY* 2: 144). In this case the poet understood his achievement as well as his intention. He makes no claims for the poem that it does not bear out: "And, as it is in some places a little abstruse, and in all, serious, without any of the modern attractions of glittering style, or incident to provoke curiosity, it cannot be expected to make its way without difficulty" (*MY* 2: 211). *Caviare* to the general, in other words, from the man who, following Milton, hopes for a fit, if not plentiful, audience, in the preface to the unfinished *The Recluse*, which stands at the head of the poem. But, at the same time: "One of my principal aims in *The Excursion* has been to put the commonplace truths, of the human affections especially, in an interesting point of view; and rather to remind men of their knowledge, as it lurks inoperative and unvalued in their own minds, than to attempt to convey recondite or refined truths" (*MY* 2: 238).

On the one hand, "abstruse," "serious," and "difficult," and, on the other, "commonplace truths" and an attempt to force upon the reader a self-discovery through poetry, similar to Keats's description of the "wording of one's highest thoughts . . . almost a Remembrance."[2] Small wonder that readers have been irked and bored, offended and provoked: reading *The Excursion* engages us in a pursuit of those thoughts that do often lie too deep for discovery, Platonic reminiscences that are all we can ever know, and which, if retrieved from our inner depths, may be seen in their essential, often redundant, simplicity. *De nobis fabula narratur*.

The plan is the exact opposite of that of *The Prelude*, where Wordsworth reasons analogically from his own exemplary life outward ("What one is / Why may not many be?" XII, 91–92); here, through various screens and masks, the ventriloquism of the four voices through which he speaks, and a score of characters, living and dead, the poet asks us to uncover the denominator uniting us, to prove his earlier and most important article of faith, not that love of nature leads to love of man but that "we have all of us one human heart."[3]

At the paradoxical intersection of multeity and singularity the poem finds its organizing principle and its highest, most energetically creative moments. Redundancy and repetition, although risking prolixity, are essential; multiple human experiences and a large cast of characters effect variations on a theme: how suffering, imagination, and thought itself possess heroic possibilities. The paradoxes continue. Although Wordsworth's heroes are his rural characters, here his democratic instincts, adumbrated in the Preface to *Lyrical Ballads*, are complicated by his use of the recondite as the vehicle for the commonplace. His acceptance of inevitable hierarchies conflicts with his egalitarian inclinations and results in an intellectual and social ordering of the characters. The same paradoxicality appears in the poem's philosophical core, reached in the Wanderer's "eloquent harangue" (IV, 1276) to cure the Solitary of his despondency. The acceptance of necessity as true freedom, whether we take it as a sign of Wordsworth's growing orthodoxy or as a reflection of his quasi-Roman stoicism, is central to his moral and educational schemes. Just as passivity, first in sensory experience and a sensitivity to nature's graces, then in reading, marks the beginning of an active development of the soul's excursive power, so does the moral refining and tempering of the conscience enliven the active, imaginative intelligence.

For Wordsworth as for Stevens, the true hero is "he that

is of repetition most master." Since we can learn only what we already know, according to Wordsworth's stated aims for his poem, tautology, too easily mistaken for simple-mindedness, gives one key to the poem's length. Repetition educates, and although didactic poetry has been disparaged by Keats ("We hate poetry that has a palpable design upon us") and by Shelley ("Didactic poetry now and always has been my abhorrence"), Wordsworth's poem is a pedagogic effort of the highest sort.[4] Modern readers may go, like Pound, in fear of abstractions, but the poem wishes to instruct us, quite simply, in the arts of living and dying. Paradoxes, variations, and repetition are the essence, it turns out, of uniqueness, just as the amassing of exemplary lives, especially in Books VI and VII, provides the solid facts demanded by the Wanderer and the Solitary as ballast for theory; the population of the rural churchyard affirms commonalty, the one great society, and it also shows us unity in variety. Repeated material, the turns and returns in space, time, and language itself, and the accumulation of a harmony in doctrine and sermon, make tautology and redundancy, which we might take as limitations of rhetorical or psychological freedom, into the paradoxical essence of human strength.[5]

Repetition may yield either accurate resemblances or confused patterns of implied and mistaken sameness: things may rightly or wrongly be thought equivalent to one another. The poem asks us to distinguish and attempts to show us how. The twilight scene that concludes Book IX gives two such examples of repetition-as-unity. Crossing a bridge on their way to the margin of a lake, the characters see

> A twofold image; on a grassy bank
> A snow-white ram, and in the crystal flood
> Another and the same! Most beautiful,
> On the green turf, with his imperial front
> Shaggy and bold, and wreathèd horns superb,

The breathing creature stood; as beautiful,
Beneath him, showed his shadowy counterpart.
Each had his glowing mountains, each his sky,
And each seemed centre of his own fair world:
Antipodes unconscious of each other,
Yet, in partition, with their several spheres,
Blended in perfect stillness, to our sight!

(IX, 440–51)

The fragile unity of the spectacle, evidence of what Words-worth refers to in *The Prelude* as the dark invisible work-manship building a harmonious soul (I, 351–55), reappears as the gathered company watches the sunset from an is-land peak at the moment before the Priest's final oration. The clouds have become "vivid as fire":

clouds separately poised,—
Innumerable multitude of forms
Scattered through half the circle of the sky;
And giving back, and shedding each on each,
With prodigal communion, the bright hues
Which from the unapparent fount of glory
They had imbibed, and ceased not to receive.
That which the heavens displayed, the liquid deep
Repeated; but with unity sublime!

(IX, 600–608)

Such sublimity is parodied and violated by the Solitary's tragic conversion to political radicalism during the French Revolution, when he sees what seems to be a golden pal-ace arise from the wreck of the Bastille:

The potent shock
I felt: the transformation I perceived;
As marvellously seized as in that moment
When, from the blind mist issuing, I beheld
Glory—beyond all glory ever seen,
Confusion infinite of heaven and earth,
Dazzling the soul.

(III, 716–22)

Jacobin excesses, and the Solitary's own subsequent disil-lusion and flight to America, shatter his millenarian hopes for a new covenant, a new heaven and earth. His disappointment has resulted in a life full of "the repetitions wearisome of sense" (IV, 620) from which no outward spiritual movement has, so far, succeeded in transporting him. What is most important here, for the poem's rhythm, is Wordsworth's insistence on doublings, in space or through time, as either a lifeless, mechanical motion or as the outward signs of visionary power. Memory, one kind of repetition, triggers either disappointment or salutary revelation. In resemblance adheres power.[6]

The same may be said for the characters, living and dead, who inhabit the poem. Both as versions of Wordsworth's own life and as impersonations of each other, they develop our sense of the unlikely connections among all of us.[7] The poet creates, and the speakers invoke, them so that we shall learn "to prize the breath we share with human kind; / And look upon the dust of man with awe" (V, 655–56).

The inhabitants of the country churchyard form the neatest picture of our society. Ranging along a social scale from nobility to peasantry (but coming mostly, like Chaucer's Canterbury pilgrims, from the middle classes), and including types of human failing, weakness, deprivation, and endurance, they are a Wordsworthian world in microcosm. While none of the individual portraits (with the exception of the Deaf Man in VII, 395–481) is as moving as the comparable portraits in *The Prelude* or many of the shorter poems, the whole is greater than the sum of its parts. Resemblances accumulate impressively: the various examples of shame and escape (the Prodigal, VI, 275–375; the Hanoverian and the Jacobite, VI, 392–521; Sir Wilfred Armathwaite, VI, 1078–1114) are the foils to the life of the Solitary, which forms the substance of Books II and III; the symbolic use of funerary monuments or natural objects are evidence of something, however weak, that endures (e.g., the Path of Perseverance, VI, 253) or fades (hapless Ellen's path, VI, 818). Above all, the miniature biographies are occasions for sermons and observations by the four main characters and, therefore, touchstones for our understanding of those figures and ourselves. "We see then as we feel" (V, 558), says the Wanderer in the simplest version of a Romantic subjectivism in the poem. But we are also capable of changing our feelings, as the characters' responses indicate. What does Wordsworth hope we shall learn from the Priest's extended tour of the necropolis in these two books?

We may take a cue from the Wanderer's speech, which comprises most of Book IV and readies us for the graveyard disquisitions that follow. Many readers might consider this cure for despondency worse than the disease itself, but it is more than a tissue of Wordsworthian commonplaces. Replacing human conflict with the dialectical agons of thought, the Wanderer's discourse testifies to Wordsworth's tragic sense, despite Lionel Trilling's claim that Wordsworth lacks one.[8] The sermon defines psychological integrity, personal happiness, philosophical maturity, and heroic stature, the very standards by which we can judge the biographies of the characters in the graveyard books.

More important is the way the Wanderer seems to have abstracted dramatic action. His prescription for spiritual success calls for equal doses of stoic resolution, a cleaving to faith and duty (lines 66–238); philosophical understanding, or an ecological sense of the communities and interdependencies in the natural and human worlds, which conduces to love (lines 332–504); and the development of the creative imagination, which, even if based on superstition, will create systems, out of "hopes that overstep the grave" (lines 631–887). These constituents are Wordsworth's *pathema*, *mathema*, and *poiema*, what Kenneth Burke calls the bases of dramatic feeling, knowing, and making.[9] Wordsworth implicitly organizes all these human activities along a path of progressive difficulty. Knowledge, for instance, begins as a passive endeavor that gradually rises to systems building and the religious or imaginative gestures of the creative mind.

Even the Wanderer's language, far from settling into the petrifactions of orthodox rhetoric, demonstrates the subtle richness of human intellection: all objects of creation are spiritual and alive rather than dead. A "Man so bred" (in the proper understanding of the relationship of moral duties to natural holiness), says the Wanderer,

> lives and breathes
> For noble purposes of mind: his heart
> Beats to the heroic song of ancient days;
> His eye distinguishes, his soul creates.
> (IV, 830–33)

The chain of verbs, from the passive "bred" through the intransitive "lives and breathes," stops logically at a trio of active words that are themselves arranged along a line of increasing power: "beats to," "distinguishes," "creates." Full transitive force never comes immediately, either in life or in language; the Wordsworthian chain of being and action is analogically present even in the language that describes it.[10]

The oration eddies between two major points: man's weakness, the tenuousness of his hopes and work; and the power of his soul, the strength of imagination that may falter but will never fully abandon him. (Cf. *The Prelude* XI, 325–27: "So feeling comes in aid / Of feeling, and diversity of strength / Attends us, if but once we have been strong.") Like the reflected unity of the two rams in Book IX, or the dark inscrutable workmanship of *The Prelude* I, the hopes of man are a pillar of dust, destructible by a breath. At the same time, this central statement, in one of the poem's few extended similes, dramatizes the mind's excursive and controlling power:

> Within the soul a faculty abides,
> That with interpositions, which would hide
> And darken, so can deal that they become

Contingencies of pomp; and serve to exalt
Her native brightness. As the ample moon,
In the deep stillness of a summer even
Rising behind a thick and lofty grove,
Burns, like an unconsuming fire of light,
In the green trees; and, kindling on all sides
Their leafy umbrage, turns the dusky veil
Into a substance glorious as her own,
Yea, with her own incorporated, by power
Capacious and serene. Like power abides
In man's celestial spirit; virtue thus
Sets forth and magnifies herself; thus feeds
A calm, a beautiful, and silent fire,
From the encumbrances of mortal life,
From error, disappointment—nay, from guilt;
And sometimes, so relenting justice wills,
From palpable oppressions of despair.
                         (lines 1058–77)[11]

The Wanderer tells the Solitary that he is more saved
than he realizes, and the unhappy recluse may remind us
of another Wordsworthian solitary whose soul was inspired by a shock from the external world. The Solitary is a
later, adult version of the Boy of Winander; he does not
know, claims the hopeful sage, the extent of human dignity:

                         Here you stand,
Adore, and worship, when you know it not;
Pious beyond the intention of your thought;
Devout above the meaning of your will.
—Yes, you have felt, and may not cease to feel.
The estate of man would be indeed forlorn
If false conclusions of the reasoning power
Made the eye blind, and closed the passages
Through which the ear converses with the heart.
Has not the soul, the being of your life,
Received a shock of awful consciousness,
In some calm season, when these lofty rocks
At night's approach bring down the unclouded sky,
To rest upon their circumambient walls.
                         (lines 1147–60)

The Solitary has no chance to answer the question, but the Wanderer goes on, in his final statement of hope (lines 1230–75) with the same logic and imagery. Nature speaks to social reason's inner ear an inarticulate language disseminating love, which forces us to seek kindred objects for that love. Thus, we dissipate hostility and despair; the inevitable end is rhetorically simple and automatic: "he looks round / And seeks for good; and finds the good he seeks" (lines 1223–24).

Equally, the contemplation of forms yields an understanding of the spiritual presences of absent things and, consequently, sense will be subservient to duty as the eye will become servant to the mind's excursive power (line 1263). Freedom and necessity are synonymous: paradox yields to tautology in Wordsworth's rhetoric, and heroic striving becomes a natural inevitability:

> —So build we up the Being that we are;
> Thus deeply drinking-in the soul of things,
> We shall be wise perforce; and, while inspired
> By choice, and conscious that the Will is free,
> Shall move unswerving, even as if impelled
> By strict necessity, along the path
> Of order and of good. Whate'er we see,
> Or feel, shall tend to quicken and refine
> The humblest functions of corporeal sense;
> Shall fix, in calmer seats of moral strength,
> Earthly desires; and raise, to loftier heights
> Of divine love, our intellectual soul.
>   (IV, 1264–75)

Mere "Being" turns out to be the work of a lifetime of "building"; inspiration comes "by choice"; freedom moves metaphorically along the path of strict necessity. Wordsworth maintains his insistence upon action, or upon seeing and feeling as symbolic action, once more by the deployment of his verbs: rather than saying that "our feelings will strengthen our character," he insists forcefully on the mind's "excursive power" by impelling the final sentence through a series of purely verbal emphases: "what we see or feel shall tend to quicken and to refine, shall fix," and at last, after the infinitives and the future tense, the line comes to rest on a simple present verb, with implications of both futurity and infinity. Our feelings "raise" (shall tend to raise, shall raise) our intellectual soul to loftier heights.

Perhaps Wordsworth has enlarged the Wanderer's speech in order to emphasize the central connection that he made passingly in "Tintern Abbey"—that the joint agency of memory and feeling, tipped by the presence or recollection of nature, results in a love that is more than Romantic *Einfühlung*: it comes out in action, "that best portion of a good man's life / His little, nameless, unremembered acts / Of kindness and of love." Memory, in other words, leads not only to its own obliteration but also to another sphere of behavior where particularity, all that is important, is forgotten. Automatic action—unconscious and uncontrollable by will or memory—is paramount, and therefore, in *The Prelude*, Wordsworth emphasized internal action, those spots of time, traumatic as they may be, that prove that the mind is lord and master of outward sense. To write an autobiography is, by definition, to be thwarted from one kind of heroism, since one never remembers the social bonds, words, or gestures, in which love is fully expressed. One can never accurately see or hear oneself.

For this reason, *The Excursion* urges the importance of the dead as reminders, preserved in the recollections of living observers. The churchyard cast is divided equally between actors and sufferers, agents and patients. But can action ever succeed? Wordsworth seems to have it two ways: he stresses both the necessity and the futility of reasoned action. The human endeavors of the now dead seem more pathetic and ill-favored than the outward events of fortune visited upon them. Nevertheless, the insistence upon "meditated action" is the Wanderer's, and the poem's, central tenet.

Even though the Pastor has vowed to pass over stories of crime, degradation, and deformity, the Solitary reminds him that genuine knowledge of heroism or human reality must include the "pestilential swamp" as well as the "pellucid lake" (VI, 595–99). So the Parson agrees to tell tales that will accord only with love, esteem, and admiration, in order to picture clearly "nature's unambitious underwood / And flowers that prosper in the shade." But these flowers were not born to blush unseen. The adulterer, Sir Wilfred Armathwaite (VI, 1079–1114), is beset with guilt and dies of remorse: "pitied among men, absolved by God, / He could not find forgiveness in himself" (lines 1112–13). The gifted woman (VI, 675–777) overcome by thrift, and thrall to maternal love, hoarding everything, becomes an agitated brook whose gentle repose is never seen by the timid and whose mind is "intolerant of lasting peace." The native heroic youth (VII, 695–890), a radical peasant in whom "the spirit of a hero walked our unpretending valley," is roused by patriotism at the threat of war with France, but dies ignominiously from a chill after swimming. Life is incessantly banal. The sordid and trivializing reality of death absconds with what little of heroism is possible, as in the most unfortunate case, the girl who dies of some "viewless obstruction" "raised in the tender passage of the throat" (VII, 684–85). The living wagon-driver (VII, 590–631), a figure from Marvellian pastoral, occasions sermonizing on the inevitable mowing of the mower: "His own appointed hour will come at last; / And, like the haughty Spoilers of the world, / This keen Destroyer, in his turn, must fall" (VII, 629–31).

The Wanderer is able to use all this as fodder for his fixation on mutability. The last epitaph is of a knight, not cast down, merely dead, during an age of violent change and religious and political ferment (VII, 921–75). Only a stone remains of the monument to this Elizabethan knight, Sir Alfred Irthing, and this "faithless memorial" testifies to the restless decay and unceasing generation of human progress. Comparing himself to the knight—both have outlived the usefulness of their social roles—the Wanderer, who we know has one foot in the grave ("Life's autumn past, I stand on Winter's verge; / And daily lose what I desire to keep," IV, 611–12), becomes his surrogate, a voice from and for the dead. The final, partly ironic comparison that he makes unites distant ages and the far ends of the social scale, and attests to a degree of providential connection within the vast commonwealth of society and history itself. As a student, the Wanderer has absorbed the Parson's lessons; Book VII ends with his gratitude for the "pathetic records," which he now judges

> words of heartfelt truth,
> Tending to patience when affliction strikes;
> To hope and love; to confident repose
> In God; and reverence for the dust of Man.
> (VII, 1054–57)

According to the Pastor, who speaks for the classical bent to Wordsworth's didacticism, we must celebrate the good man's purposes and deeds in order to spread virtue and piety (VII, 375). Example fosters imitation, another kind of repetition, which we may associate with Wordsworth's use of memory as a basis for metaphor and of tautology as a rhetorical hammer. Just as the Wanderer's last speech in Book VII indicates a present, even if attenuated, connection with a distant figure, the Poet too has learned the important lessons of repetition from the Pastor's elegies. His meditation at the beginning of Book VII reiterates the educative value of aesthetic response that the entire first book exemplifies. The Pastor's rehearsal of the dead instills in the Poet a feeling for salvation through the internalized means of memory and art. The words of the "historian" and the present scene awaken the Poet's memories of earlier years, in other places, when he listened to other storytellers, poets or bards, dispensing their own solemn tunes. He compares past experiences to a present one, proving that memory not only keeps the dead alive but also revives the dead days within that are no more and yet are eternally present:

> Strains of power
> Were they, to seize and occupy the sense;
> But to a higher mark than song can reach
> Rose this pure eloquence. And, when the stream
> Which overflowed the soul was passed away,
> A consciousness remained that it had left,
> Deposited upon the silent shore
> Of memory, images and precious thoughts,
> That shall not die, and cannot be destroyed.
>
> (VII, 22–30)

Remembering is active toil: "That music in my heart I bore / Long after it was heard no more," remarked the earlier traveler in the Highlands. Even the automatic and unwilled recollection of the joyous daffodils is replaced by an active participation with the flowers: "And then my heart with pleasure fills / And dances with the daffodils." The repetition of the event, far from diminishing the original experience, in fact enhances and strengthens it. Food for thought, the deposits made in memory's bank—those staples within Wordsworth's seemingly trite store of images—are given ample power as they are seen literally, not metaphorically, to redound upon and enrich their owner. And, as so often in his major rhetorical flourishes, Wordsworth concludes the revelation with a tautology (line 30).

Communal recollection commemorates and therefore revives the dead as examples for the living; an aesthetic response, through private memory, maintains its own legacy within and for the individual mind. As the Wanderer remarks in an earlier speech (IV, 109), sight may fail in age as the struggle for salvation replaces rapture, but the memory of visionary power endures. Sensory excitement is to internal vision, recollection, or metaphor (a kind of second sighting), as successful action is to struggle, regardless of outcome. This is why Wordsworth insists upon the need for action, irrespective of result, while simultaneously dooming all action as feckless or, at most, irrelevant to final questions. The action of salvation is visionary: it is a struggle first of all to recall youth's "visionary powers of eye and soul," and then "the most difficult of tasks to *keep* / Heights which the soul is competent to gain" (IV, 138–39). As the Wanderer's counsel to cure the Solitary's despair hinges on the difficulty of transcendence through an arduous path of faith and duty, so too does the Pastor's rehearsal of the dead instill in the Poet a feeling for salvation, now through the wholly internalized means of art and memory.

The ideas that nature imitates art and that the living can use the dead as almost artistic models of excellence may attest to a new aestheticism in Wordsworth's outlook. The poet who nominally recommends love of nature as the base of further spiritual and social development constantly refers in *The Excursion* to forms of aesthetic experience or to literary genres as models for nonartistic ventures. Certainly there has been a marked change from *The Prelude*, in which seeing and living were tantamount, always, to heroic striving. In *The Excursion*, vision and life are more often reduced to self-consciously "artistic" engagements, stripped of the heroic possibility that informed even Wordsworth's "spectatorial" impulses in *The Prelude*.[12] The Pastor, for example, compares himself to a great collector after he has finished his display of specimens from the grave:

> my zeal
> To his might well be likened, who unlocks
> A cabinet stored with gems and pictures—draws
> His treasures forth, soliciting regard
> To this, and this, as worthier than the last,
> Till the spectator, who awhile was pleased
> More than the exhibitor himself, becomes
> Weary and faint, and longs to be released.
> (VIII, 21–28)

Wordsworth understands at least in part the potential tedium of the enthusiastic but prolonged lecture. The Solitary,

even before the tour of the graveyard has begun, construes
it as a library:

> If this mute earth
> Of what it holds could speak, and every grave
> Were as a volume, shut, yet capable
> Of yielding its contents to eye and ear,
> We should recoil, stricken with sorrow and shame.
>
> (V, 250–54)

A bit later the Solitary refers to life for the multitude as
"fashioned like an ill-constructed tale" (V, 432). Appropriately, too, it is the Solitary (depicted as a tragedian in III,
463–68) whom the others see inside the country church in
a rapt, abstracted pose:

> gracefully he stood,
> The semblance bearing of a sculptured form
> That leans upon a monumental urn
> In peace, from morn to night, from year to year.
>
> (V, 214–17)

Memory itself provides the surest store of treasures, as the
Wanderer advises the Solitary to take a tour of his own private museum:

> Yet doth remembrance, like a sovereign prince,
> For you a stately gallery maintain
> Of gay or tragic pictures
> ·
> These hoards of truth you can unlock at will.
>
> (IV, 560–70)

And, midway through the Pastor's tales, it is again the Solitary who adopts a pointedly aesthetic response to these
stories, suggesting that the fictions of myth of any age can
be redesigned, recycled, and updated:

> Fictions in form, but in their substance truths,
> Tremendous truths! familiar to the men
> Of long-past times, nor obsolete in ours.
> Exchange the shepherd's frock of native grey
> For robes with regal purple tinged; convert
> The crook into a sceptre; give the pomp

> Of circumstance; and here the tragic Muse
> Shall find apt subjects for her highest art.
> (VI, 545–52)

The Solitary speaks here from one part of Wordsworth's imagination and for one solution to the epistemological problem at the center of all his major poetry. Before beginning his tale, the Pastor announces that we cannot both object and subject at once: Our nature

> Angels may weigh and fathom: they perceive,
> With undistempered and unclouded spirit,
> The object as it is; but, for ourselves,
> That speculative height *we* may not reach.
> The good and evil are our own; and we
> Are that which we contemplate from far.
> (V, 486–91)

Knowledge is a hard-won prize and never, he goes on to suppose, fully kept; it resembles virtue itself, a goal to be pursued but never achieved. This eternal elusiveness explains both Wordsworth's many-sided didacticism throughout *The Excursion* and much of his difficulty in locating his "self" in *The Prelude*. As human knowledge is a noble aim or a mere effort, like moral perfection, then self-knowledge is, in theory and fact, the most difficult prize to win. For this reason, Wordsworth divides himself into four spokesmen—his equivalent of Blake's four zoas—who together make the one full man. His act of ventriloquism gives him the chance to address his main themes from different positions, even though the diction makes it hard to think of the central figures as fully distinct individuals.[13]

Likewise, Wordsworth cannot survey mankind from China to Peru, because he is of it. The characters within the graveyard population are valuable because they are completed, hence knowable, although they recede in time and space from our best efforts to recall them to, or instill them within, our minds. Using artistic metaphors and the language of aesthetic experience in general compensates for the eternal shifting of the human creature whom the author wishes to identify, observe, and analyze. And the prospective anatomist who wishes to dissect without murdering his specimens chooses ones already dead, distancing and clarifying them through the lenses of art.

These specimens, like the epitaphs Wordsworth discusses in his three essays on the subject, must be typical and individualized. Wordsworth ranges from the theoretical (the *beatus ille* construction in IV, 331–72; V, 37–48; and similar idealizations throughout) to the particular, which, when unsuccessful, most proves his unfortunate aptitude for banality. Individuality often occasions bathos in its presentation; abstract generality offers more power (e.g., IX, 209–28) than the troublesome idiosyncracies of particular lives. The most moving human portraits in the poem's lengthy gallery are those that blend the individual and the type, endowing the subject with distinctiveness and still lifting it into higher realms. And these can be understood by everyone, although more fully appreciated only by literati, aesthetes, the happy few.

A common individual may still suggest heroic stature, like the Stonecutter in Book V, the repository of old, noble English genes:

> In such a man, so gentle and subdued,
> Withal so graceful in his gentleness,
> A race illustrious for heroic deeds,
> Humbled, but not degraded, may expire.
> This pleasing fancy (cherished and upheld
> By sundry recollections of such fall
> From high to low, ascent from low to high,
> As books record, and even the careless mind
> Cannot but notice among men and things)
> Went with me to the place of my repose.
> (V, 790–99)

The perception has a double origin; it is both fanciful, the construct of a sensitive literary mind weaned on books, and natural or automatic, such as even the most careless observer might have. Wordsworth stresses the creative and receptive powers of the perceiving mind, seeing as it feels, but simultaneously feeling what a scene legitimately provokes it to. Natural symbolism, relying on books as well as nature, is an equivalent to natural piety and natural heroism. A naturally didactic imagination construes scenes and characters symbolically, deriving morality from them and injecting meaning into them. Wordsworth methodically accumulates details, which build to a fullness in his presentation. Repetition, of phrase, detail, or situation, creates connection; the mighty commonwealth of *The Excursion* expands along a network of interrelationships.

The evaluation of the Stonecutter is the culmination of a lengthy description of the man and his wife within the frame of both an inserted tale and a defining landscape. As the symbolic setting for action, nature magnifies and illuminates the human beings whose characters it creates and reflects. Organically alive, nature is fixed in its function. By providing the commonest analogue to the human self in the poem, it is the clearest evidence of Wordsworth's typological mind. Margaret's roofless house and decayed garden, to cite the most powerful examples, are the equivalent to, or independent expression of, her psychic disintegration. Human life is a landscape, from such small references as "the tamer ground / Of these our unimaginative days" (II, 23–24) to the larger articulation of the Pastor:

> We safely may affirm that human life
> Is either fair and tempting, a soft scene
> Grateful to sight, refreshing to the soul,
> Or a forbidding tract of cheerless view;
> Even as the same is looked at, or approached.
> (V, 526–30)

At the same time, nature and landscape assume a dramatic character, almost an existence, of their own at those moments when a panorama is inserted to silence, or implicitly to resolve, an argument among the characters. Since we see as we feel, what we see (and what we readers have no choice but to see in a panorama of the page) impiies an answer to what has preceded it. Thus, in VIII, 434ff., after the Solitary condemns those bovine idiocies of rural life that allow no "liberty of mind," the Parson recommends a walk to the parsonage, during which the language of nobility, safety, and enclosure counters the Solitary's earlier mock-heroic image of the country bumpkin. Even more to the point, the Pastor's wife and children present a generic picture of country ease; the children themselves (lines 572–87) trigger the Wanderer's concluding speech about the active principle within the soul that delivers "meditated action" as the essential sustenance and product of the active self (IX, 1–137).

Likewise, the final tableau, when the gathered group prepares for an evening picnic, puts the landscape in the role of a symbolic character, silently participating in the dialogue and having, if not the final, at least the most eloquent, word. Where the Solitary sees in the dying embers of a fire (IX, 555) a symbol of human ingratitude and the evanescence of joy, the "unity sublime" (line 600) of clouds and water procures happiness for those capable of seeing it. The scene looks as if "paradise, the lost abode of man, / Was raised again: and to a happy few, / In its original beauty, here restored" (lines 717–19). Because the Poet emphasizes the power of the sensitive mind to retain the image of the beautiful scene beyond the capacities of mimic art (lines 512–17), he implicitly invites us to consider the effects of other landscapes throughout the poem.

The final unity and repetitions in Book IX recall a similar use of the landscape in Book IV. The Wanderer's lengthy discourse has ended, and the Poet immediately receives it as a bequest:

> The words he uttered shall not pass away
> Dispersed, like music that the wind takes up
> By snatches, and lets fall, to be forgotten;
> No—they sank into me, the bounteous gift
> Of one whom time and nature had made wise.
> (IV, 1284–88)

A listener, like a reader, responds to and therefore inherits a heroic challenge. The subsequent view of the sunset revolves around the same motifs of disappearance and survival, and adduces a natural "bequest" as the appropriate setting for the intellectual one that the Poet has just accepted:

> The Sun, before his place of rest were reached,
> Had yet to travel far, but unto us,
> To us who stood low in that hollow dell,
> He had become invisible,—a pomp
> Leaving behind of yellow radiance spread
> Over the mountain-sides, in contrast bold
> With ample shadows, seemingly, no less
> Than those resplendent lights, his rich bequest;
> A dispensation of his evening power.
>
> (IV, 1299–1307)

At last, as the inevitable climax of human and natural bequeathings, the three travelers arrive at the humble shepherd's cottage where they will spend the night:

> A grateful couch was spread for our repose;
> Where, in the guise of mountaineers, we lay,
> Stretched upon fragrant heath, and lulled by sound
> Of far-off torrents charming the still night,
> And, to tired limbs and over-busy thoughts,
> Inviting sleep and soft forgetfulness.
>
> (IV, 1320–25)

The description of a natural setting and a practical human beneficence follows fast upon the bequest, a form of symbolic action, of the Wanderer to Poet and Solitary. A series of greetings and acceptances expands the human and natural horizons of the poem's world.

There are two Natures, broadly speaking, in the poem: that of the Solitary, and that of the other three figures. The first is "of the dissolute" (III, 808), a Hobbesian view compounded of the cynicism of the viewer and the savagery of human nature. The Solitary's flight to America (III, 835–955) is a desperate attempt to flee from himself, which convinces him that he has merely brought his own curse with him across the seas, since he finds in the New World an image of the Old, the squalor of cities and the base venality of the human archetype. (Cf. the Poet's Horatian remark in V, 20–21: "How vain, I thought, is it by change of place / To seek that comfort which the mind denies.") The lengthy closing simile of Book III (lines 967–91) uses nature to mirror the Solitary's life, his longing for death and his submission to some unfathomable gulf. The stream of his life reflects but inverts natural objects: mimic art appears more apt to lead to labyrinthine confusion and danger than to the sublime repetition in those reflected scenes that the other characters perceive. Precisely because he wants to be a spectator *ab extra*, neither acting nor feeling (III, 891–96) since he thinks that both activities will create bondage or limit freedom, the Solitary can discover no freedom at all.

Having rejected "fostering Nature" (III, 809), the Solitary sees landscape mostly, but not exclusively, as entrapment, threat, or irrelevancy. The Wanderer conceives the scene as evidence of God's artistry, the design of a "power intelligent," but the recluse seems to mock the usual Wordsworthian language of Nature's maternal affections: "How Nature hems you in with friendly arms! / And by her help ye are my prisoners still" (III, 14–15). At the end, balancing the jocular tone of his invitation, the Solitary compares his life to a mountain brook in which one can see the inversion of heavenly objects—mere bubbles that alone betray the living stream which otherwise would be a dead mirror. What at different moments in Wordsworth's poetry might be a symbol of unity, stillness or commonalty, is here a version of a static, deadly existence, quietly passing its spirit and energy into a sunless sea at the end of its journey. The Solitary defines himself by his imagery.

Similarly, a single spot such as the Country Churchyard may assume prominence not just as the scene of the Parson's instructions or the dwelling of the noble and pathetic dead, but also as the lively inspirer of virtue, a cause of growth and pleasure, an antidote to depression. The Parson tells the story (VI, 392ff.) of the quarrelsome Hanoverian and Jacobite lured by the Genius of the Hills to seek concealment there. The two men meet in unhappy but mock-heroic encounters, which gradually produce a bond of affectionate connection between them. While living they are sanctified by the blessedness of the churchyard as their scene of instruction; in death, they add their blessedness to it for the benefit of others, just as a sundial replaces their seat in a yew tree and marks their release from time's subjection.

The divergent views of Nature that invite us to see it as a guide to human behavior (IV, 490) or as mocking sadistic deity (III, 126), as an Eden or a desert, remind us that *The Excursion* is a conversation poem, a working-out of things, a debate. Despite strong Virgilian touches, it is not a genuine georgic because Wordsworth cannot muster sufficient certainty to teach without hesitations and demurs. Even the dialectic is unresolved: not only does the Solitary leave uncured, like Shakespeare's Jaques, at the end, but even the very terms of the debate have shifting grounds and definitions. Every Wordsworthian piety, every cherished value, it seems, has an equal chance of proving a dangerous lure or a beneficence. That good exists seems undeniable, but its nature is less than clear: every virtue may easily become its opposite. As a moralist, Wordsworth has no use for orthodoxy and certainty.

Like its maker, the poem remains forward-looking and memory-laden. Wordsworth balances his feelings of regret for "ancient virtues overthrown" (IX, 252) with his hope for evolutionary progress through education and practical policy (IX, 293–335). His political sentiments come naturally from his ontology. The memory of "visionary powers" (IV, 111) is enough to compensate for the deprivations of age; it is an indestructible force, capable of nourishing whatever comes closest to eternal life in mortals, those "precious thoughts, / That shall not die, and cannot be destroyed" (VII, 29–30). Raised to a communal level, this memory is the prime agent of inculcating moral worth through education. But at the same time, memory is the baneful canker in the Solitary's life. The joint agency of recollection and stoicism, here seen as a weakness, has deadened him: "I remember, and can weep no more" (III, 487). Likewise, reason may be either the legitimate sanction of behavior, "an effort only, and a noble aim" (V, 502), or the desiccating faculty of a haughty presumption. Stoic fortitude and acceptance may be the strong, life-affirming response to hardship, or the denial of life-giving hope, as in the reaction of the Solitary's wife to the deaths of their children: "Calm as a frozen lake when ruthless winds / Blow fiercely, agitating earth and sky" (III, 650–51).

Solitude, whether of an individual or a monastic band, palliates the dreariness of cities, the indifference of men, and the weariness of the self. It is the very heart of contemplation, the beginning of imaginative activity culminating in communion with God. Or is it the escape of a tortured and misanthropic soul, unwilling to delight in either man or nature but, instead, feeding his melancholy with a solipsistic despair?[14] The placidity of rural innocence, love within a "narrow sphere" (IV, 353–72), the ease of country life for the unambitious poor: are they delights or horrors from which the thinking mind recoils? Those who "follow reason's least ambitious course / . . . unperplexed by doubt, / And unincited by a wish to look / Into higher objects farther than they may" (V, 595–98): do they provoke us to envy or contempt? No contention to virtue may lead to no virtue or, worse still, to torpor and sluggish ignorance (VIII, 391–432; IX, 156–82). Is love the product of knowledge (IV, 345), which creates tenderness and reduces aversion (IV, 1207–29), or is it, especially when directed toward a sexual object, likely to produce obsession, thraldom or, in the case of unrequital, "a betraying sickness" that first discolors and then kills (VI, 155–61)?[15]

Though we do not expect philosophic regularity from Wordsworth, it is surprising to find such constant wavering of design and definition in a poem often depicted as the triumph of dull orthodoxy over poetic power. Ideas, morality, abstractions, however, are less than certain in the poem, not because Wordsworth's mind has gone fuzzy but because the dialectic form of the book allows him to use "ideas" in the same way he uses landscape, as an equivalent to, or expression of, a dramatic character. Everything is subservient, in other words, to the human level of the poem; the characters are not merely vehicles for ideas. "All things speak of man" (IV, 1239) and man speaks all things. As a debate, *The Excursion* demonstrates the active excursive power of several minds, or the several minds of one author, and is left deliberately unresolved.[16] The corollaries, then, to the motif of repetition—whether verbal, visual, or didactic—are division, the reduction of the author into four constituents, and multiplication of points of view. The ideas of the four main characters are not so important as the means of presenting them or as the dramatic functions they perform within the text. Taken together, Wanderer, Solitary, Parson, and Poet create Wordsworth's Albion, his one great hero, and their opinions a catalogue of his thoughts.

What Coleridge noticed early on as a characteristic of Wordsworth has long been regarded as a flaw: his "prolixity, repetition, and an eddying, instead of progression of thought."[17] If we are accustomed to, or prefer, the linear working-out of an idea in a clear pattern, Wordsworth will not satisfy. The argument proceeds haltingly with responses *by* the landscape, or of the characters *to* the landscape; in either case, the whole is pitched at a level of generality that reflects not so much a vagueness as a commitment to a now-unfashionable brand of teaching. The characters are themselves deliberately balanced in changing configurations: Solitary and Wanderer are old friends from Scotland; Solitary and Poet are young students of the wisdom and experience of Pastor and Wanderer (metaphorically joined as a pair of trees in V, 455); Parson and Solitary are, or have been, family men and both are defined by their residences, while Wanderer and Poet are alone and mobile.

More important, all are versions of their creator. In the Fenwick note, Wordsworth says that he based both Wanderer and Solitary in part on real models (*PW* 5: 373–74), but clearly the early life and education of the first, and the political disappointment and domestic tragedy of the second, are versions of Wordsworth's autobiography in *The Prelude*. Additionally, he confesses that had money not been available for education, he might have become a pedlar himself. In his married and domestic contentment, as in his doctrinal orthodoxy, the Parson speaks more or less for the paterfamilias Wordsworth had become in 1805.

Self-division of this sort bespeaks a rage for anonymity, a powerful deflection away from the egotistical sublime. The rage extends to the namelessness of the central figures and most of the people whom the Parson invokes in his tour of the dead (hapless Ellen was originally Ellen Dalton in the MS version of Book VI), and to the more generalized urges of the characters for enclosure and confinement.[18] The Solitary, we learn, is "Steeped in a self-indulging spleen, that wants not / Its own voluptuousness" (II, 311–12); the Parson, from an aristocratic family, withdrew to his native hills for solitude at an early age; the Poet, bidding farewell to the Solitary's valley before moving on, thinks of it as "the fixed centre of a troubled world" (V, 16), and theorizes that knowledge should be allowed its anchorites, happy in a retreat: "Sheltered, but not to social duties lost, / Secluded but not buried" (V, 54–55). The distinction between seclusion and death is a major one in this poem, which asks us to distinguish, even as we see the possible resemblances, between suicidal withdrawal and salubrious retreat, between solitude as best society because often shared (as in the mixture of aloneness and conversation of the main characters facing the last vista in Book IX) and the condition of the Solitary who, having lost inner peace, "moral dignity, and strength of mind" (II, 288), can find no "better sanctuary / From doubt and sorrow than the sense-less grave" (III, 223–24).

What the Solitary labels "the universal instinct of re-pose" (III, 397) tests the characters' mettle in *The Excursion*. Variations on the theme of repose and its garlands, which are sometimes fruitful and sometimes wilted, are woven throughout. By dividing the ideas among his characters, as if dissociating them from a fully articulate human voice, Wordsworth bestows upon them an independent existence and covers his own reluctance to acknowledge truths that may still frighten him. The Solitary, for example, talks charitably and convincingly of the Epicurean end of har-monious tranquillity (III, 359–66), and he sounds like the Poet who later on (V, 292–308) defends the *idea* of baptism and Christian perfectability while still admitting human er-ror and sin. Indeed, the temperate, almost modern, rela-tivism with which the Wanderer in Book IV talks about pa-gan mythology as embryonic stirrings of the imagination bespeaks Wordsworth's tolerance of doctrines, in this case those of Lucretius, which he might otherwise condemn. (The Solitary again speaks for Lucretius in VI, 538–47, when he remarks that the fictions of myth are in their form and substance truths.) The misanthropic view exemplified by the Solitary reflects one side of Wordsworth's mind,[19] the presentation of which his dramatic dialogue seeks to clarify simply by admitting.

The project of the poem, in this way, is to cure not only the Solitary, called the "recluse" throughout the poem, but also his author, the eponymous hero of the unfinished epic *The Recluse*. That the Solitary goes away unchanged at the poem's end supports the contention that self-help is tenta-tive—always in need of added doses of homeopathic med-icine—and that Wordsworth's pieties, as late as 1814, were far from secure. We can see in the Solitary not only another version of Peter Bell but the very type of Wordsworthian separation. His delight in nature is fanciful, not imagina-tive, combining an "antiquarian humour" (III, 134) with a superficiality, "pleased to skim along the surfaces of things," which inverts the normal emotional well-being of the other figures. What raises their minds to exalted pitch merely depresses him. He is a "detached spectator," who prefers observation to feeling and acting (III, 901). Depression and shame are his motive forces; he cannot understand how the Prodigal Youth who has ruined himself (VI, 380ff.) can return to his native soil instead of fleeing elsewhere.

Yet his misanthropy (and even the other characters agree with his realistic objections to "savage nature" in VIII, 353 and to the horrors of rural life) is countered by his delight in the happiness of the anonymous and humble (V, 849–61), by his sociable treatment of Poet and Wanderer (II, 635–36), and by the words of comfort that we overhear him deliver to the small child who is mourning the death of an old man. Such is our first introduction to the Solitary (II, 508–11): dignity and strength of mind exist in practice, if not in theory. He is an inadequate skeptic, a Jaques who does not waste tears on stricken deer but has genuine pity and fellow-feeling.

It was Wordsworth's confessed intention to display "the points of community" (Fenwick note, *PW* 5: 375) "in [the] nature" of his characters. Thus, the Poet undergoes a transformation, coming gradually to resemble both Pastor and Wanderer who are schooling him; by the end, he is helping to school us. Initially passive in Book I, listening to the story of Margaret and her ruined cottage, he rises to the level, not of storytelling, but, probably second best, to oratory. The Wanderer's discourse against despondency in Book IV "sinks" into him (lines 1276–1325); having passively received his teachers' various lessons, he comes, by Book V, to make his own moral generalizations. He moves from orphanhood to full membership in a community of anonymous heroes. In fact, Book I presents in miniature the larger pattern of the Poet's development. His initial chance meeting with the Wanderer reminds him of how, as a child, he was singled out by the Pedlar as a colleague, a potential apprentice, much as Coleridge's Wedding Guest is schooled by the Mariner. (Wordsworth originally tried a different tone at the end of "The Ruined Cottage," in which the narrator turns into "a better and a wiser man," *PW* 5: 400.) The fraternal "impotence of grief" (I, 924) with which he blesses Margaret prepares him for his later absorption into a fourfold brotherhood. Becoming more conventional as he goes on, perhaps as a result of Wordsworth's own conventionality, it is the Poet who addresses the Church and State of England (VI, 1–87), who wishes to preserve the old domestic morals (VIII, 231–51), but who also dramatizes the nourishing and reviving effects of memory (VII, 1–30) and speaks for "future labours" as the poem ends.

He becomes, in other words, more like the Wanderer himself, the archetypal Wordsworthian hero who combines passive receptiveness and feeling with active physical and mental life. Although the old man lacks words (one of the strongest unintentional ironies in the poem, however, is his endless torrent of them), he is a natural poet, possessing "the vision and the faculty divine," and therefore a model for his young protégé.

Rich in experience, heroic from the start, this modern Odysseus ("much did he see of men," I, 341) with his active, nervous gait (line 424) is hardly laconic, but the Poet can read "his overflowing spirit . . . in the silence of his face" (II, 40–41). He is a text and an explicator of other texts to his student. His longest speeches, the philosophical core of the poem in Books IV and IX, are statements, not discoveries or explorations, of faith. At the center of his method, as of his argument, lies the proposition that "moral truth" (or, we might say, artistic truth) "is no mechanic structure, built by rule" (V, 562–63). Just as "meditated action" (IX, 21) is the heart of the active principle that, coupled with benignity of spirit, provides the basis for moral and imaginative growth, so active meditation, often indistinguishable from rambling or discursiveness, becomes the rhetorical instrument of advanced instruction. It partakes occasionally of metaphor and metonymy but rarely of irony; for this lack, modern readers may find Wordsworth unappealing. Wordsworth would agree with his primary spokesman that man was born "to obey the law / Of life, and hope, and action" (IX, 127–28)—and, we might add, of discourse itself as symbolic action.[20]

Talk *is* action. Throughout, the poem constantly measures the effects of speech against other speech, natural detail, or symbolic objects. In the culminating and most urgent response, the Pastor's wife echoes the Wanderer's assertion that "faculties, which seem / Extinguished, do not, *therefore*, cease to be" (VII, 519–20) with a metaphor reverberating from other major images of the poem:

> While he is speaking, I have power to see
> Even as he sees; but when his voice hath ceased,
> Then, with a sigh, sometimes I feel, as now,
> That combinations so serene and bright
> Cannot be lasting in a world like ours,
> Whose highest beauty, beautiful as it is,
> Like that reflected in yon quiet pool,
> Seems but a fleeting sunbeam's gift, whose peace
> The sufferance only of a breath of air!
>
> (IX, 465–73)

As a listener, the Wife has not mastered the heroic art of representing absent things—the art that defines the poet, according to the Preface to *Lyrical Ballads*: "a disposition to be affected more than other men by absent things as if they were present" (*PrW* 1: 138). She is sympathetic and responsive while the Wanderer is speaking; she shares in his participation in natural beauty, her soul only slightly less pure than his spirit:

> How pure his spirit! in what vivid hues
> His mind gives back the various forms of things,
> Caught in their fairest, happiest attitude!
>
> (IX, 462–64)

The entire poem thus rounds to its conclusion with a reminder of the ending of the first book. Previously the Wanderer had peopled the air for the Poet, had revived by representing for him the life and story of Margaret and her family. Having been schooled in tragic art and the pathos of ordinary human life, the Poet was readied for the ensuing days of debate and story with his three companions. Here, however, neither tragedy nor any other form of art promotes the Wife's response. The poem has lifted itself, and its audience along with it, to the level of abstract or intellectual discourse. It shows how fragile a thing is human thought, like human life, and how discourse, whether plain or abstruse, can be measured or contemplated in the same way as fleshed-out human stories. The poem has moved away from the pure narrative of the first book, through the autobiography of the Solitary in the third, and the epitaphic reminiscences in the sixth and seventh, away from participation in human action, as it, or its author, seeks progressively more attenuated and visionary schemes of connection for unfolding its meaning to an audience within and a reading audience without.

These connections in the poem, between storyteller and audience, speaker and listener, writer and reader, are all types of bonding, analogous in form and effect to the bonding created by the repeated motifs in rhetoric, description, and teaching, and by those duplications in the characters that pull them together. The network of human figures has produced a fully articulated and populated world, richly and amply grounded in fact and building toward spiritual and philosophical harmonies. From the impotence of grief, which is all that the Poet's fraternal love for Margaret can amount to, the poem ends with a farewell at sunset that promises renewed pleasures and connections the following day. The bond is harmoniously tied to earth's own diurnal balance, as the Solitary leaves with the assurance that "Another sun . . . shall shine upon us, ere we part; / . . . / If time, with free consent, be yours to give, / And season favours" (lines 779–83).

The conditions of this assurance are repeated by those of the Poet to *his* audience in the last paragraph, as he vows to continue the tale of the healing of a wounded spirit and of the solace fetched by faith and imagination, "if delightful hopes, as heretofore, / Inspire the serious song, and gentle Hearts / Cherish, and lofty Minds approve the past" (lines 793–95). His last words betoken more than a conventional leave-taking: the Poet's "future labours" depend vaguely, but deliberately, upon the approval of—*whom?* The Poet's family and friends? his critics? the anonymous reading public? From the simple to the noble, he resurveys, taking in with one sweep, the limits of his human world. Wordsworth's longest poem ends with a formulaic reminder of the scope of his inevitable, natural heroism: the gentle Hearts and lofty Minds which he salutes are those of all of us.

Notes

CHAPTER 1

1. Ralph Waldo Emerson, *Representative Men*, in Edward Waldo Emerson, ed., *The Complete Works of Ralph Waldo Emerson* (Cambridge, Mass.: Riverside Press, 1903) 4: 23. All citations from Emerson are from this edition.

2. Eric Russell Bentley, *A Century of Hero-Worship* (Philadelphia: J. B. Lippincott, 1944), pp. 287–88.

3. Wallace Stevens, "Notes Toward a Supreme Fiction," *The Collected Poems* (New York: Alfred A. Knopf, 1954), p. 388.

4. Walter L. Reed, *Meditations on the Hero* (New Haven: Yale University Press, 1974), p. 18; Bentley, *Century of Hero-Worship*, p. 56. See also Karl Kroeber, *Romantic Narrative Art* (Madison: University of Wisconsin Press, 1960), p. 90: "Wordsworth as he appears in *The Prelude* is the prototype of the contemporary hero: the man who fights against his culture." The separatist view, originally that of Hegel, Byron, and Kierkegaard, may be contrasted to the more inclusive, assimilationist understanding of Wordsworth and Emerson. Frederick Garber, "Self, Society, Value, and the Romantic Hero," *Comparative Literature* 19 (1967): 321–33, traces a wide range of possible relationships, "a rhythm of attraction and repulsion," between the hero and his society.

5. Emerson, "Circles," *Complete Works* 2: 304, 308.

6. Otto Rank, *The Myth of the Birth of the Hero*, ed. Philip Freund, trans. F. Robbins and Smith Ely Jelliffe (New York: Vintage, 1959), p. 72. See also Joseph Campbell, *The Hero with a Thousand Faces*, 2d ed. (Princeton: Princeton University Press, 1968).

7. Charles Rowan Beye, "Greek Lyrics In and Out of Brackets," *Parnassus* 9 (1981): 199–216; for the fullest recent treatment of concepts of the hero in archaic Greek poetry, see Gregory Nagy, *The Best of the Achaeans* (Baltimore: Johns Hopkins University Press, 1979).

8. George E. Dimock, Jr., "The Name of Odysseus," *Hudson Review* 9 (1956): 52–70; this essay has been widely reprinted.

9. José Ortega y Gasset, *Meditations on Quixote*, trans. Evelyn Rugg and Diego Marin (New York: W. W. Norton, 1961), p. 149. See also Michael Cooke, *The Romantic Will* (New Haven: Yale University Press, 1976), pp. 88–93, 103–6, for a discussion of the will in *The Prelude*.

10. C. M. Bowra, *Heroic Poetry* (London: MacMillan, 1962), p. 1.

11. G. W. F. Hegel, *The Philosophy of History*, trans. J. Sibree (New York: Dover, 1956), p. 30.

12. Emerson, "Heroism," *Complete Works* 2: 257.

13. Karl Kroeber, *Romantic Landscape Vision: Constable and Wordsworth* (Madison: University of Wisconsin Press, 1975), p. 38, writes sympathetically of Wordsworth's "poetry of commonplace uninterestingness" and of his aim to "speak for the inarticulate, to be an artist of the inartistic." He becomes the voice of the speechless, whether children, outcasts and vagrants, or senile figures. Donald Wesling, *Wordsworth and the Adequacy of Landscape* (London: Routledge & Kegan Paul, 1970), p. 66, uses similar paradoxical language to describe Wordsworth's achievement: "there is a non-tragic form of heroism in sheer suffering, in states rather than in active sequences of feeling."

14. The seminal estimates are found in Samuel Taylor Coleridge, *Biographia Literaria*, ed. J. Shawcross (London: Oxford University Press, 1907), chaps. 17 and 22; and *Table Talk*, in Thomas M. Raysor, ed., *Coleridge's Miscellaneous Criticism* (Cambridge, Mass.: Harvard University Press, 1936), p. 412: "I think Wordsworth possessed more of the genius of a great philosophic poet than any man I ever knew, or as I believe has existed in England since Milton; but it seems to me that he ought never to have abandoned the contemplative position, which is peculiarly—perhaps I might say exclusively—fitted for him. His proper title is *Spectator ab Extra*." Also, William Hazlitt, "On The Living Poets," in *Lectures on the English Poets; The Spirit of the Age*; and the three-part review of *The Excursion*, which originally appeared in *The Examiner* of 1814: *Complete Works*, ed. P. P. Howe (London: J. M. Dent & Sons, 1930–34), vols. 5, 11, and 19. Hazlitt was the first to pinpoint what he called Wordsworth's "intense intellectual egotism," his mind that "preys upon itself," his "levelling Muse" and his "proud humility." This is the Wordsworth who "sees nothing but himself and the universe" (5: 163).

15. Every Wordsworth scholar owes an incalculable debt to the criticism of Geoffrey Hartman, especially *Wordsworth's Poetry*,

1787–1814 (New Haven: Yale University Press, 1964). Less fashionable nowadays, but exemplary as pieces of humane intelligence and valuable to those who wish to place Wordsworth closer to a center than to a periphery, are the two essays of Lionel Trilling, "The Immortality Ode," in *The Liberal Imagination* (New York: Viking Press, 1950), pp. 129–59; and "Wordsworth and the Rabbis," in *The Opposing Self* (New York: Viking Press, 1955), pp. 118–50.

16. Harold Bloom, *Agon* (New York: Oxford University Press, 1982), p. 287.

17. Elizabeth Bishop, *The Complete Poems* (New York: Farrar, Straus & Giroux, 1969), pp. 94–96. I discuss Bishop's treatments of heroism in "Elizabeth Bishop's 'Natural Heroism,'" *Centennial Review* 22 (1978): 28–44.

18. William Empson, *The Structure of Complex Words* (London: Chatto & Windus, 1951), pp. 294–95, first mentioned the paradox of "the light of sense / Goes out in flashes" (VI, 534–35) in relation to the meanings of *sense* in *The Prelude*.

19. For a concise history of these tropes from Homer through the Renaissance, see Georgia Ronan Crampton, *The Condition of Creatures* (New Haven: Yale University Press, 1974), chap. 1, "*Agere et Pati*: Deed and Pathos," pp. 1–44.

20. The best recent discussion of the conflict in *The Recluse* between an egocentric and a social vision is Kenneth R. Johnston, "Wordsworth's Last Beginning: *The Recluse* in 1808," *ELH* 43 (1976): 316–41.

21. Michael Riffaterre, "Interpretation and Descriptive Poetry: A Reading of Wordsworth's 'Yew-Trees,'" *New Literary History* 4 (1973): 229–56; Geoffrey Hartman, "The Use and Abuse of Structural Analysis: Riffaterre's Interpretation of Wordsworth's 'Yew-Trees,'" *New Literary History* 7 (1975): 165–89.

22. Mary Moorman, *William Wordsworth: The Later Years* (Oxford: Clarendon Press, 1965), p. 273.

23. Hartman, "Use and Abuse," p. 170; both he and Riffaterre address the problems of personification in Romantic poetry; see also M. H. Abrams, *The Mirror and the Lamp* (New York: Oxford University Press, 1953), pp. 55–56, 64–68.

Chapter 2

1. Douglas Bush, *Mythology and the Romantic Tradition in English Literature* (Cambridge, Mass.: Harvard University Press, 1937), pp. 56–70.

2. Harold Bloom, *The Anxiety of Influence* (New York: Oxford

University Press, 1973), p. 93; and *A Map of Misreading* (New York: Oxford University Press, 1975), p. 69.

3. Thomas Carlyle, *Heroes and Hero-Worship* (London: Chapman & Hall, 1897), p. 82; see also Colette, *Journal à Rebours* in Robert Phelps, ed., *The Earthly Paradise* (New York: Farrar, Straus & Giroux, 1966), p. 77: "When one can read, can penetrate the enchanted realm of books, why write?"

4. "Reading," as a principle, rather than an activity, of literary criticism, has received considerable attention during the past decade, from both theorists and "reader-response" critics. Representative texts are: Wolfgang Iser, *The Act of Reading: A Theory of Aesthetic Response* (Baltimore: Johns Hopkins University Press, 1978); Susan Suleiman and Inge Crosman, eds., *The Reader in the Text: Essays on Audience and Interpretation* (Princeton: Princeton University Press, 1980); Jane Tompkins, ed., *Reader-Response Criticism: From Formalism to Post-Structuralism* (Baltimore: Johns Hopkins University Press, 1980). My purposes in this chapter are practical rather than theoretical, and deal with Wordsworth's characteristic uses of reading as a metonymy for perception, growth, and control.

5. For a history of the trope of the *liber naturae*, see E. R. Curtius, *European Literature and the Latin Middle Ages*, trans. Willard R. Trask (New York: Pantheon, 1953), pp. 302–47, especially pp. 319–26, "The Book of Nature."

6. The naturally sacramental cast to Wordsworth's imagination suggests a certain degree of religious orthodoxy even in his early creative maturity, well before his supposed "decline" into doctrinal conservatism.

7. See Bloom, *Map of Misreading*, pp. 42ff. for the distinction between the Greek *logos* and the Hebrew *davhar* as motifs of writing and speaking.

8. John Wesley, *Works*, ed. Thomas Jackson, 3d ed. (1831, rep. London, 1872) 1: 229. See Richard Brantley, *Wordsworth's "Natural Methodism"* (New Haven: Yale University Press, 1975), p. 148: any individual is allowed "to interpret for himself the various spiritual meanings of any natural image and its correspondent object."

9. Michael Ragussis, *The Subterfuge of Art* (Baltimore: Johns Hopkins University Press, 1978), p. 25. See also Frank McConnell, "Romanticism, Language, Waste: A Reflection on Poetics and Disaster," *Bucknell Review* 20 (1972): 132, on the *liber naturae*: "the Book remains readable, but as an *impingement* upon the reader's spirit rather than an expansion of it."

10. M. H. Abrams, *Natural Supernaturalism* (New York: W. W. Norton, 1971), p. 107.

11. For Wordsworth's distinction, see *The Excursion* I, 77–107, and IV, 847–87; the opening of Keats's "The Fall of Hyperion: A Dream" provides a parallel argument.

12. W. G. Stobie, "A Reading of *The Prelude*, Book V," *Modern Language Quarterly* 24 (1963): 373, asks the same question; G. Wilson Knight, *The Starlit Dome: Studies in the Poetry of Vision* (London: Oxford University Press, 1941), p. 9, says simply, "the passage is confusing," and points out similarities with the Simplon Pass passage in Book VI.

13. This is the same problem discussed by William Empson in *The Structure of Complex Words* (London: Chatto & Windus, 1951).

14. Hartman, *Wordsworth's Poetry*, pp. 42–48, 60–69, and Frank McConnell, *The Confessional Imagination* (Baltimore: Johns Hopkins University Press, 1974), pp. 137–38.

15. John Hollander, "Wordsworth and the Music of Sound," in Geoffrey Hartman, ed., *New Perspectives on Coleridge and Wordsworth: Selected Papers from the English Institute* (New York: Columbia University Press, 1972), pp. 41–84, discusses this motif. The importance of sound may have had something to do with Wordsworth's almost debilitating fear of holding pen to paper and his frequent habit of composing orally and out-of-doors. See his 1803 and 1804 letters to Beaumont and De Quincey on the holding of a pen, in *EY*, pp. 407 and 453.

16. Herbert Lindenberger, *On Wordsworth's Prelude* (Princeton: Princeton University Press, 1963), pp. 308–9, summarizes the feeding motif in the poem.

17. See, for example, the "Inscription on the Death of Southey," (*PW* 4: 278): "And ye, lov'd books, no more / Shall Southey feed upon your precious lore." Mary Moorman, *William Wordsworth: The Later Years* (Oxford: Clarendon Press, 1965), p. 571, quotes a remark of Wordsworth to a young American, Miss Harriet Douglas: "Pray do not read books to talk and prattle about them, but to feed upon their contents in stillness."

18. Leslie Brisman, *Milton's Poetry of Choice and Its Romantic Heirs* (Ithaca: Cornell University Press, 1973), p. 283.

19. Quoted in Willard Sperry, *Wordsworth's Anti-Climax* (Cambridge, Mass.: Harvard University Press, 1935), p. 133.

20. Richard J. Onorato, *The Character of the Poet: Wordsworth in "The Prelude"* (Princeton: Princeton University Press, 1971), pp. 373–77.

21. Cf. Preface to *Lyrical Ballads* (*PrW* 1: 124) on modern poets

who "separate themselves from the sympathies of men, and indulge in arbitrary and capricious habits of expression in order to furnish food for fickle tastes and fickle appetites of their own creation."

22. For Wordsworth's ideas about poetic language, see Frances Ferguson, *Wordsworth: Language as Counter-Spirit* (New Haven: Yale University Press, 1977). See also Wordsworth's urging a Professor Hamilton of Dublin to look at things "through the steady light of words [which] to speak a little metaphysically, are not a mere *vehicle*, but they are *powers* either to kill or to animate" (*LY* 1: 437).

23. Wordsworth's note to "The Brothers" (*PW* 2: 467–68) mentions "the tranquility, I might say indifference, with which [mountain-dwellers] think and talk upon the subject of death. Some of the country churchyards, as here described, do not contain a single tombstone, and most of them have a very small number." Even when discussing the universality of death, Wordsworth feels compelled to heighten the poet's role as a commemorator. His words, that is, are the equivalent of the mountain-dwellers' collective memory.

24. One might speculate on the Romantics' concern for human presence-in-absence and the devices they employ to make connections with absent individuals. In Coleridge's "This Lime-Tree Bower My Prison," the landscape effects a coming-together; in Keats's famous letter to his brother and sister-in-law in America, literature is the binding force: "I shall read a passage of Shakespeare every Sunday at ten o'clock—you read one at the same time and we shall be as near each other as blind bodies can be in the same room," in Hyder E. Rollins, ed., *The Letters of John Keats* (Cambridge, Mass.: Harvard University Press, 1958) 2: 5.

25. Jonathan Wordsworth, *The Music of Humanity* (London: Thomas Nelson, 1969), p. 95.

26. A modern version of this is the perverse pedagogy of Robert Frost in "Directive," a poem impossible without the precedent of "Michael." The poet leads us to a secret place, testing us by trying to lose us along the way; if we endure, we shall find ourselves and "be whole again." Nature conspires against the fledgling reader, whom only the poet can redeem by explaining the text.

27. Lindenberger, *Wordsworth's Prelude*, pp. 41–67.

28. I use, for convenience, the final text of *The Excursion*, Book I.

29. Jonathan Wordsworth, *Music of Humanity*, p. 225: "The

Pedlar both drinks in the spectacle and is swallowed up by it, in that he is at once a spectator, and a part, of the natural world." It is interesting to speculate on what, exactly, we mean when we say that a book is "totally absorbing"—that is, it swallows us at the same time that we are feeding on it. Cf. *The Prelude* II, 329ff. on Wordsworth's "drinking" of "visionary power" while listening to "the ghostly language of the ancient earth."

30. For a good discussion of the poem's symbolic landscape, see Reeve Parker, "'Finer Distance': The Narrative Art of Wordsworth's 'The Wanderer,'" *ELH* 39 (1972): 87–111.

31. A similar Aristotelian point is made by James Averill, *Wordsworth and the Poetry of Human Suffering* (Ithaca: Cornell University Press, 1980), pp. 55–83.

32. Walt Whitman, "Democratic Vistas," in *Complete Poetry and Selected Prose and Letters*, ed. Emory Holloway (New York: Random House, 1958), p. 720.

33. Walter Pater, *Appreciations* (London: MacMillan, 1889), pp. 41–42.

CHAPTER 3

1. Philippe Ariès, *Centuries of Childhood*, trans. Robert Baldrick (London: Jonathan Cape, 1962), p. 32: "It is as if, to every period of history, there corresponded a privileged age and a privileged division of human life: 'youth' is the privileged age of the seventeenth century, childhood of the nineteenth, adolescence of the twentieth." A. Charles Babenroth, *English Childhood: Wordsworth's Treatment of Childhood in the Light of English Poetry from Prior to Crabbe* (New York: Columbia University Press, 1922), shows how before the nineteenth century children were occasions for, rather than subjects of, poetry.

Other recent treatments of Wordsworth's children include: Jonathan Ramsey, "Wordsworth and the Childhood of Language," *Criticism* 18 (1976): 243–55, which focuses on "Anecdote for Fathers," "The Idiot Boy," and "We Are Seven" as evidence for the thesis that "Wordsworth's recreations of a linguistic and even pre-verbal past are reminders of the 'possible sublimity' (*The Prelude* II, 318) that poetry might still embrace and resurrect"; Laurence Goldstein, "The Wordsworthian Child," in *Ruins and Empire: The Evolution of a Theme in Augustan and Romantic Literature* (Pittsburgh: University of Pittsburgh Press, 1977), pp. 184–207. Jared R. Curtis, *Wordsworth's Experiments with Tradition* (Ithaca: Cornell University Press, 1971), p. 77, cites Jean Piaget on children's confusion of *outer* and *inner* as the basis for their ignorance of metaphor: "What little Wordsworth says about metaphor and image, and his practice in poetry, suggest that he conceived of the poet's task as the reenactment for the reader, who is urged to follow the poet's lead, of this childlike sense of singleness, the one life in all things, the 'points' we all have 'within our souls, / Where all stand single'" (*The Prelude* III, 186–87). See also Mary Moorman's partly biographical essay, "Wordsworth and His Children," in Jonathan Wordsworth, ed., *Bicentennial Wordsworth Studies* (Ithaca: Cornell University Press, 1970), pp. 111–41.

2. The very image of a chain of "natural piety" probably has an origin in Wordsworth's early memories of the scattering and rejoining of the Wordsworth children. Dorothy wrote in 1793 (*EY*, p. 88): "Neither absence nor Distance nor Time can ever break the chain that links me to my Brothers." Twelve years later, after the death of John Wordsworth, Wordsworth wrote to his elder brother, Richard (*EY*, p. 540): "God keep the rest of us together! the set is now broken." There is a clear relationship in his mind between social or family life and the integrity and growth of the individual.

3. Philip Rieff, *Freud: The Mind of the Moralist*, 3d ed. (Chicago: University of Chicago Press, 1979), p. 91, tries to distinguish Freud's view of childhood from that of Coleridge and Wordsworth, whom he dismisses as Romantic primitivists, praising childhood innocence, which the tough-minded doctor refuses to do. See, also, p. 267: Freud is "far from sharing that sentiment for childhood which unites Christian orthodoxy with modern Romanticism, old faith with new sensibility. Christian and Romantic alike refuse to regard a child-like simplicity of vision simply as a mode of immaturity, holding that children may know something—of morals, of beauty—which adults with their complex and limited experience have forgotten." This is only part of the story; clearly Wordsworth arrived at a complex image of childhood well before Freud. See also Susan Hawk Brisman and Leslie Brisman, "Lies Against Solitude: Symbolic, Imaginary, and Real," in Joseph H. Smith, M.D., ed., *The Literary Freud: Mechanisms of Defense and the Poetic Will (Psychiatry and the Humanities* 4, New Haven: Yale University Press, 1980), pp. 29–65, for a discussion of the competing ideas of childhood as paradise and alienation.

4. Paul Alpers, *The Singer of the Eclogues: A Study of Virgilian Pastoral* (Berkeley and Los Angeles: University of California Press, 1979), p. 178. It is important that Wordsworth uses a citation from one of his own poems about childhood to demonstrate the union of tenderness and imagination (*EY*, p. 316).

5. Originally, Wordsworth struck an even more imperial, neo-Augustan note:

the span
A little longer that metes out the Course
Of man and Empires

(*PW* 2: 174)

6. Harold Bloom, *The Visionary Company*, rev. and enl. ed. (Ithaca: Cornell University Press, 1971), pp. 170–77, gives the most cogent analysis of the Intimations Ode as Wordsworth's view of human life as a move from childhood unity, through a fall, to salvation through imagination.

7. In form, the poem resembles the Romantic nature lyric as M. H. Abrams describes it in "Structure and Style in the Romantic Nature Lyric," in Frederick W. Hilles and Harold Bloom, eds., *From Sensibility to Romanticism* (New York: Oxford University Press, 1965), pp. 527–60.

8. The proper balance between the two views is struck by Paul Fry, *The Poet's Calling in the English Ode* (New Haven: Yale University Press, 1980), p. 154: "Wordsworth is never quite easy about the glad animal movements of his little pagan selves, though it would be an exaggeration to insist that his nativity ode exorcises them; early childhood, for him, is simply inadequate."

9. Cf. Freud, *Civilization and Its Discontents*: the limitless, polymorphous power of the child is "the instinct of destruction," which child and then adult must satisfy, if only upon himself. Against this force is the principle of self-control, the "decisive step of civilization"; "the first requisite of civilization . . . is that of justice." In James Strachey, trans. and ed., *The Standard Edition of the Complete Psychological Works of Sigmund Freud* [hereafter *St. Ed.*] (London: Hogarth Press, 1953–74) 21: 95; see also "Three Essays on Sexuality," 7: 160.

10. Mary Moorman, ed., *The Journals of Dorothy Wordsworth* (London: Oxford University Press, 1971), p. 101, proves that it was Dorothy who put the idea for the poem into her brother's mind and that he made the young girl gentler in the poem than the real girl was in life: "I told him I used to chase them a little but that I was afraid of brushing the dust off their wings, and did not catch them." David Ferry, *The Limits of Mortality* (Middletown, Conn.: Wesleyan University Press, 1959), pp. 17–20, discusses both Butterfly poems with an eye to the distinctions between human and nonhuman worlds.

11. Geoffrey Hartman, *The Fate of Reading* (Chicago: University of Chicago Press, 1975), p. 188, says of the Highland Girl

("Vision as thou art . . . I bless thee with a human heart") that "visionariness and human-heartedness are not easily reconciled. In the curse ballads, as even perhaps in the Lucy poems, the human element ('I had no human fears') is spirited away." This distinction is similar to my earlier one between nature and heroism.

12.   I can think of no other terms to describe this dialectic of encounter. A classic, polite, and humane neutrality cancels the more forbidding, fearful connotations of the words' psychoanalytic meanings. See Erik H. Erikson, *Childhood and Society*, 2d ed. (New York: W. W. Norton, 1963), p. 248, for the standard operating definitions: "Psychoanalysis assumes the early process of differentiation between inside and outside to be the origin of projection and introjection . . . some of our deepest and most dangerous defense mechanisms. In introjection we feel and act as if an outer goodness had become an inner certainty. In projection, we experience an inner harm as an outer one: we endow significant people with the evil which actually is in us." This, of course, describes the boat-stealing scene in *The Prelude* I, 357–441.

13.   Although "the solitary child" of line 4 is living, the peculiar tone of the first stanza, created by the isolated setting, the sense of the child as someone much fabled, and the sighting at the unlikely hour of daybreak, might make a reader think that the vision described here is of an unreal, unliving creature.

14.   Helen Vendler, "Lionel Trilling and the *Immortality Ode*," *Salmagundi* 41 (1978): 66–86.

15.   Florence Marsh, *Wordsworth's Imagery* (New Haven: Yale University Press, 1952), p. 84, suggests that Wordsworth created most of his memorable figures before 1807 and that "in the late poetry the human being has virtually vanished." I think that, rather, the human being has been transformed. An example is what happens to Dora in two sonnets from the *Ecclesiastical Sonnets* (*PW* 3: 385). In the first poem ("I saw the figure of a lovely maid"), Wordsworth has a vision of his daughter; in the second ("Patriotic Sympathies"), the vision, which dissolved during the first sonnet, becomes a surrogate for England, and his "filial love" prompts him to deplore whatever might destroy his country. Thus, father becomes son.

16.   For a discussion of Wordsworth's later style, see Peter Larkin, "Wordsworth's 'After-Sojourn': Revision and Unself-Rivalry in the Later Poetry," *Studies in Romanticism* 20 (1981): 409–36; and Geoffrey Hartman, "Blessing the Torrent: On Wordsworth's Later Style," *PMLA* 93 (1978): 196–204. For Larkin, the later poetry is dominated by Fancy, which Frances Ferguson describes as "an emphasis on sequence or succession which represents a dis-

tancing and deliberation by contrast with the involvement of the affections" (*Wordsworth: Language as Counter-Spirit* [New Haven: Yale University Press, 1977], p. 67). But Fancy and Affection both play a part in the two Ecclesiastical Sonnets mentioned above, as well as in the "Address to My Infant Daughter," with which this chapter began.

17. Freud, *The Future of an Illusion, St. Ed.* 21: 49.

CHAPTER 4

1. Robert Mayo, "The Contemporaneity of the *Lyrical Ballads*," *PMLA* 69 (1954): 486–522.

2. Lewis Carroll, *Through the Looking Glass*, in Martin Gardner, ed., *The Annotated Alice* (New York: Bramhall House, 1960), pp. 307–13. The White Knight's song is a revised and expanded version of an earlier poem by Carroll, "Upon the Lonely Moor," which appeared anonymously, in 1856, in the periodical *The Train*. The opening lines also burlesque Wordsworth's "The Thorn."

3. This is what Karl Kroeber, *Romantic Landscape Vision: Constable and Wordsworth* (Madison: University of Wisconsin Press, 1975), p. 38, means by "the poetry of commonplace uninterestingness."

4. Lionel Trilling, "The Immortality Ode," in *The Liberal Imagination* (New York: Viking Press, 1950).

5. Jared R. Curtis, *Wordsworth's Experiments with Tradition* (Ithaca: Cornell University Press, 1971), pp. 114–15, agrees that "if the poem is about growing up, it must also be about growing old," and that the response to the low ebb at the end of stanza 8 "is an answer willed in the face of frost."

6. See the letter to De Quincey, *EY*, p. 454; also, Mary Moorman, *William Wordsworth: The Early Years* (London: Oxford University Press, 1957), p. 539, on Wordsworth in 1802: "Wordsworth's physical sufferings during the last two or three years—his prostrating headaches, the pain in his chest and side, and above all perhaps his sleeplessness—were arousing in him fears that he would not be able to continue with his poetic vocation. . . . The future may well have looked black, and depression have been a frequent companion. For to Wordsworth poetry was life." It is thus not surprising to us (especially after absorbing Keats's contrast between "easeful death" and the weariness and fever that accompany human life) that Wordsworth welcomed the possibility of the quiet tomb as respite from earth's tortures; see Dorothy's journal of April 29, 1802, describing her brother and herself at John's Grove, both lying in a trench, listening with shut eyes to

birds and waterfalls: "He thought it would be as sweet thus to lie so in the grave, to hear the *peaceful* sounds of the earth and just to know that our dear friends were near" (*Journals of Dorothy Wordsworth*, Mary Moorman, ed. [London: Oxford University Press, 1971], p. 117). The paradox of hearing after death may have influenced Wordsworth's description of the Deaf Man in *The Excursion* (VII, 477–81) and also his lines in the Intimations Ode, which offended Coleridge and which he subsequently omitted, about the child's perception of death as a waking state beneath the ground.

7. David Ferry, *The Limits of Mortality* (Middletown, Conn.: Wesleyan University Press, 1959) and John Jones, *The Egotistical Sublime* (London: Chatto & Windus, 1954) make the best case for Wordsworth's misanthropy.

8. "Poems Referring to the Period of Old Age" are the third celandine poem (1804), and "The Farmer of Tilsbury Vale," "The Old Cumberland Beggar," "The Two Thieves," and "Animal Tranquillity and Decay," all written between 1797 and 1800, that is, by a young man. In 1815, Wordsworth included the 1807 sonnet "Though narrow be that old man's cares and near," but later removed it.

9. Cleanth Brooks, "Wordsworth and Human Suffering: Notes on Two Early Poems," in Frederick W. Hilles and Harold Bloom, eds., *From Sensibility to Romanticism* (New York: Oxford University Press, 1965), pp. 373–87.

10. The late sonnet, "To an Octogenarian" (*PW* 4: 162), poses the same problem: if "affections lose their object," then "love must die." It cannot exist in memory alone, at least according to the poem's octave; the sestet weakly reverses this position by telling the old man *not* to share "this belief," but it offers no alternative to bring fulfillment.

11. Geoffrey Hartman, "Wordsworth, Inscriptions, and Romantic Nature Poetry," in Hilles and Bloom, *From Sensibility to Romanticism*, pp. 389–414.

12. Harold Bloom, *The Visionary Company*, rev. and enl. ed. (Ithaca: Cornell University Press, 1971), pp. 178–82; Edith Batho, *The Later Wordsworth* (Cambridge: Cambridge University Press, 1933), p. 45, writes that even in old age Wordsworth answered his cook when she complained of the ingratitude of beggars: "Go on giving, and some day the right beggar will come."

13. Coleridge, *Biographia Literaria*, ed. J. Shawcross (London: Oxford University Press, 1907) 2: 97–104, on Wordsworth's "inconstancy of style" and his "matter-of-factness."

14. Stanley Edgar Hyman, "A Poem of Resolution," *Centennial Review* 5 (1961): 200–201, calls the leech-gatherer "a night-

mare image" of the self, but also "a suffering savior . . . a homeo-pathic vision of Wordsworth's own possible future of poverty and bleakness."

15. Frank McConnell, *The Confessional Imagination* (Baltimore: Johns Hopkins University Press, 1974), pp. 40–42, uses the leech-gatherer as evidence for the motif of salvation through recount-ing; the same would be true of the discharged soldier and the An-cient Mariner. Paul Sheats, *The Making of Wordsworth's Poetry, 1785–1798* (Cambridge, Mass.: Harvard University Press, 1973), pp. 168–72, discusses redemption through ambush. Interest-ingly, the leech-gatherer was originally meant to appear even *more* dead than he does in the printed version. The manuscript (*PW* 2: 236) has him described as "for coffin meet."

16. Wordsworth's letter to Sarah Hutchinson of June 14, 1802 (*EY*, pp. 366–67) calls the poem a character study, but it studies the speaker as well as the old man.

17. Curtis, *Wordsworth's Experiments with Tradition*, pp. 110–11, helpfully summarizes the highly conflicting readings of this poem. Some critics find the end comforting, others disquieting.

18. Moorman, *Early Years*, p. 53, argues that Reverend Taylor has been too hastily identified as the model for Matthew. Readers like Anne Kostelanetz, "Wordsworth's 'Conversations': A Read-ing of 'The Two April Mornings' and 'The Fountain,'" *ELH* 33 (1966): 43–52, simply assume Taylor was the model without con-sidering the implications.

19. Moorman, *Early Years*, p. 51.

20. Kostelanetz, "Wordsworth's 'Conversations,'" p. 48.

21. G. Wilson Knight, *The Starlit Dome: Studies in the Poetry of Vision* (London: Oxford University Press, 1941), p. 46.

22. A letter of November 16, 1842 (*LY* 3: 1386).

23. Wallace Stevens, "Credences of Summer," in *The Collected Poems* (New York: Alfred A. Knopf, 1954), p. 374.

24. Edward Bostetter, *The Romantic Ventriloquists: Wordsworth, Coleridge, Keats, Shelley, Byron* (Seattle: Univ. of Washington Press, 1956), pp. 66–81, emphasizes the Solitary's role in *The Excursion* as the necessary expression of Wordsworth's own dark fears, but fails to see the curative value of silence in this scene when he says that the Wanderer's inability or refusal to answer the Solitary's questions renders his transports hollow.

25. See Batho, *The Later Wordsworth*, and Moorman, *LY*, for accounts of Wordsworth's old age. Batho (p. 49) quotes Isabella Fenwick (June, 1849) on the poet's last months: "his darker moods are more frequent, though at other times he is as strong and bright as ever. . . . His is a strong but not a happy old age."

"The Matron of Jedborough and Her Husband" (*PW* 3: 85), written between 1803 and 1805 and originally published with the poems referring to old age, shows how pleasure and sorrow work together in age. But in the poems in which Wordsworth speaks *in propria persona*, age seems more a threat than a comfort. Similarly, Wordsworth's early and sometimes jaunty humor rarely centers on himself; see John E. Jordan, "Wordsworth's Humor," *PMLA* 73 (1958): 81–93. However, the phrase "gladness seems a duty," from the 1841 "Musings Near Aquapendente" (about the 1837 trip to Italy; *PW* 3: 205) evokes the automatic benevolence and strength described in *The Prelude* XI, 326–28.

CHAPTER 5

1. Much has been written about *The Prelude* and the epic; see Karl Kroeber, *Romantic Narrative Art* (Madison: University of Wisconsin Press, 1960), pp. 78–112; Abbie Findlay Potts, *Wordsworth's "Prelude": A Study of Its Literary Form* (Ithaca: Cornell University Press, 1953); and the suggestive short comments of Elizabeth Sewell in *The Orphic Voice* (New Haven: Yale University Press, 1960), pp. 302–9. Brian Wilkie, *Romantic Poets and the Epic Tradition* (Madison: University of Wisconsin Press, 1965), pp. 59–111, emphasizes the formation of the hero: "In *The Prelude* the heroic ideal . . . is primarily an end and not a means" (p. 71).

2. M. H. Abrams, *Natural Supernaturalism* (New York: W. W. Norton, 1971), pp. 73–80, 278–92; Harold Bloom, *The Visionary Company*, rev. and enl. ed. (Ithaca: Cornell University Press, 1971), pp. 140–77; Herbert Lindenberger, *On Wordsworth's Prelude* (Princeton: Princeton University Press, 1963), pp. 188–97, on vision, loss, and restoration.

3. Christopher Isherwood, *Christopher and His Kind* (New York: Farrar, Straus & Giroux, 1976).

4. Mary Moorman, *William Wordsworth: The Early Years* (London: Oxford University Press, 1957), p. 114, quotes from an early notebook written during the vacation of 1788 before Wordsworth went up to Cambridge: "Shall I ever have a name?" See also Coleridge's remark that the first edition of *Lyrical Ballads* should be anonymous, because "Wordsworth's name is nothing, and mine stinks" (p. 373).

5. Cf. *Aeneid* 4: 465–73 (Loeb Library translation; emphasis mine):

> In her sleep fierce Aeneas himself hounds her in her frenzy; and ever she seems to be left lonely, ever wending, companionless, an endless way, and seeking her Tyrians in a land forlorn—even as raving Pentheus sees the Furies' band, a double sun and twofold Thebes rise to

view; or as when Agamemnon's son, Orestes, *driven over the stage*, flees from his mother, who is armed with brands and black serpents, while at the doorway crouch the avenging Fiends.

It is important to remember the equation made by John Jones between *acting* and *doing* in Greek tragedy; see *On Aristotle and Greek Tragedy* (New York: Oxford University Press, 1962), p. 68n., and pp. 11–62.

6. I am taking my cue from Richard J. Onorato, *The Character of the Poet: Wordsworth in "The Prelude"* (Princeton: Princeton University Press, 1971), p. vii.

7. Henry James, "The Art of Fiction," in Leon Edel, ed., *The Future of the Novel* (New York: Vintage, 1956), pp. 15–16.

8. Robert M. Adams, *The Roman Stamp* (Berkeley and Los Angeles: University of California Press, 1974), pp. 1–4.

9. Coleridge, *Biographia Literaria*, ed. J. Shawcross (London: Oxford University Press, 1907) 1: 184–85. On the impossibility of object-subject identity, and on self-exploration as a heroic adventure, see Philip Rieff, *Freud: The Mind of the Moralist*, 3d ed. (Chicago: University of Chicago Press, 1979), p. 65: "Psychoanalysis begins with a heroic exception to the rule that the self may not know the self, the subject not be its own object. . . . In the summer of 1897, at the age of forty-one, [Freud] embarked upon an epic exploration of himself."

10. Leslie Brisman, *Romantic Origins* (Ithaca: Cornell University Press, 1978), pp. 276–82, writes persuasively of Wordsworth's obsessive labor and the myth of the revisability of the self as both a refutation of those who wish to see a "simple Wordsworth" and as a faith for moderns.

11. Helen Vendler, "Lionel Trilling and the *Immortality Ode*," *Salmagundi* 41(1978): 66–86.

12. Richard Poirier, *The Peforming Self* (New York: Oxford University Press, 1971), p. xiii, defines performance as "any self-discovering, self-watching, finally self-pleasuring response" to the difficulties of selfhood; additionally, his title essay, pp. 86–111, discussing writers who "are preoccupied with the possible conjunctions of acts of poetic with acts of public, sometimes even political power" (p. 93), suggests paths that Wordsworthians might profitably follow.

13. As I point out in Chapter 3, the children in Wordsworth's later poetry seem substantially tamer than those in the earlier work. Jonathan Wordsworth, *William Wordsworth: The Borders of Vision* (Oxford: Clarendon Press, 1982) discusses what he calls "versions of the fall" in *The Prelude*, but limits his discussion to Book III and following; see pp. 235–59.

14. Onorato, *Character of the Poet*, p. 93.
15. Søren Kierkegaard, *Repetition: An Essay in Experimental Psychology*, trans. Walter Lowrie (Princeton: Princeton University Press, 1941), pp. 3–4. On the importance of the revisions in *The Prelude*, see Leslie Brisman, *Milton's Poetry of Choice and Its Romantic Heirs* (Ithaca: Cornell University Press, 1973), pp. 262–96.
16. John R. Nabholtz, "The Journeys Homeward: Drama and Rhetoric in Book IV of *The Prelude*," *Studies in Romanticism* 10 (1971): 79–93, treats these moments as part of a pattern of the narrator's awareness of humanity via the landscape from which the humans derive; Lindenberger, *Wordsworth's Prelude*, pp. 205–20, discusses Wordsworth's encounters with solitaries as projections of himself.
17. Lindenberger, *Wordsworth's Prelude*, pp. 3–40, analyzes the idealized "older rhetoric" of many of the poem's public portions.
18. Bruno Snell, *The Discovery of the Mind: The Greek Origins of European Thought*, trans. T. G. Rosenmeyer (Cambridge, Mass.: Harvard University Press, 1953), p. 21: "Homeric man has not yet awakened to the fact that he possesses in his own soul the source of his powers, but neither does he attach the forces to his person by means of magical practices; he receives them as a natural and fitting donation from the gods."
19. Thomas Greene, *The Descent from Heaven* (New Haven: Yale University Press, 1963), p. 39.
20. Greene, *Descent from Heaven*, p. 15.
21. The fullest account of the episode, with attention to the manuscript variants, is C. F. Stone III, "Narrative Variation in Wordsworth's Versions of 'The Discharged Soldier,'" *Journal of Narrative Technique* 4 (1974): 32–44.
22. Alan Wilde, *Art and Order: A Study of E. M. Forster* (New York: New York University Press, 1964), pp. 16–71, distinguishes between what he calls "the aesthetic view of life," and "the ideal of active participation" (p. 17). More remains to be said about the connections between Wordsworth and twentieth-century novelists.
23. Onorato, *Character of the Poet*, pp. 319–23, calls him a father figure; Greene, *Descent from Heaven*, p. 15, argues for "names" as the sign of man's middle isthmus: we share them with the gods, just as we share death with the animals.
24. The doublings have been discussed from Coleridge's point of view (in "To William Wordsworth") by Paul Magnuson, *Coleridge's Nightmare Poetry* (Charlottesville: University of Virginia Press, 1974), p. 122, and Reeve Parker, *Coleridge's Meditative Art* (Ithaca: Cornell University Press, 1975), pp. 217–44. John Jones,

The Egotistical Sublime (London: Chatto & Windus, 1954), p. 122, calls the Miltonic echo "almost certainly an accident," but it almost certainly is not.

25. Lindenberger, *Wordsworth's Prelude*, p. 305, summarizes the trope of panegyric, the decorum of elegy and public speech, in contrast to the specificity of private sentiment; see also E. R. Curtius, *European Literature and the Latin Middle Ages*, trans. Willard R. Trask (New York: Pantheon, 1953), pp. 165–66, and 178–79.

26. Coleridge, *Table Talk*, in Thomas M. Raysor, ed., *Coleridge's Miscellaneous Criticism* (Cambridge, Mass.: Harvard University Press, 1936), p. 430. Abbie Findlay Potts, *The Elegiac Mode* (Ithaca: Cornell University Press, 1964) traces elegy as Wordsworth's characteristic major form, with reference to his classical antecedents and to the centrality of *anagnorisis* to the mode; James Averill, *Wordsworth and the Poetry of Human Suffering* (Ithaca: Cornell University Press, 1980), p. 207, says that elegy is "suspended between narrative and lyric." For a different treatment, see Paul Fry, "The Absent Dead: Wordsworth, Byron, and the Epitaph," *Studies in Romanticism* 17 (1978): 413–33: "the urge to express burial . . . is at bottom always the urge to bury expression" (p. 413). This rather strong statement means simply that the epitaph is the mode farthest from sublimity, the least adventurous discourse, preferring metonymy to metaphor, and represents "the gravesite of the sublime" (p. 433).

27. Freud, *The Ego and the Id*, St. Ed. 19:37.

28. Onorato, *Character of the Poet*, p. 245.

29. Averill, *Poetry of Human Suffering*, pp. 238–40, asserts that sympathy with man leads to love of nature; Frances Ferguson, *Wordsworth: Language as Counter-Spirit* (New Haven: Yale University Press, 1977), p. 146, says essentially the same thing.

30. On the Romantic will, see Michael Cooke, *The Romantic Will* (New Haven: Yale University Press, 1976); on the motif of grace that has been granted, although the bequest may remain unknown, see Richard Brantley, *Wordsworth's "Natural Methodism"* (New Haven: Yale University Press, 1975), pp. 80–110, and Frank McConnell, *The Confessional Imagination* (Baltimore: Johns Hopkins University Press, 1974), pp. 127–45, and 160–64.

31. Ferguson, *Language as Counter-Spirit*, p. 42 and passim, discusses the nature of shared identity; for example, pp. 150–51, on the addresses to Dorothy, Mary, and Coleridge: "His assertion of and his quest for self-love have yielded a self which can only be charted through the illusion of stability and wholeness which is the recurrent product of the affections. . . . Love [for Dorothy, Mary, Coleridge] has involved him in that complicated process of

the self's projection of itself upon others and the projections from other selves upon it."

32. Adam is formed for valor and contemplation (*Paradise Lost* 4: 297), just as the Wordsworthian hero strives for the perfect balance between active life and imaginative or meditative wholeness. In these lines, Wordsworth attempts to differentiate between articulate speech and something deeper, more elemental.

33. E. J. Morley, ed., *Henry Crabb Robinson on Books and Their Writers* (London: J. M. Dent & Sons, 1938) 2: 535.

34. See Geoffrey Hartman, *Wordsworth's Poetry, 1787–1814* (New Haven: Yale University Press, 1964), pp. 65–67.

35. Kenneth R. Johnston, "The Idiom of Vision," in Geoffrey Hartman, ed., *New Perspectives on Coleridge and Wordsworth: Selected Papers from the English Institute* (New York: Columbia University Press, 1972), pp. 1–39, gives a persuasive reading of "A Night-Piece" as a visionary encounter; Frederick Garber, *Wordsworth and the Poetry of Encounter* (Urbana: University of Illinois Press, 1971), pp. 146–86, discusses the balance between particularity and unity in the Snowdon episode, "I Wandered Lonely as a Cloud," and "Resolution and Independence." Although Wordsworth frequently uses, as in the first two poems, a theatrical metaphor, rarely does he go in search of the spectacle; rather, the show seems to come to him.

36. For example, Jonathan Wordsworth, M. H. Abrams, and Stephen Gill, eds., *The Prelude* (New York: W. W. Norton, 1979), p. 464n. mistakenly say that the "highest bliss" is "self-awareness."

37. Cedric Whitman, *Homer and the Heroic Tradition* (Cambridge, Mass.: Harvard University Press, 1958), p. 214.

CHAPTER 6

1. The poem was written in 1807–8 and withheld for seven years. Wordsworth's comments are taken from *PW* 3: 535–56, unless otherwise noted.

2. For an important study of Wordsworthian oppositions, see L. J. Swingle, "Wordsworth's Contrarieties: A Prelude to Wordsworthian Complexity," *ELH* 44 (1977): 337–54.

3. Including even the double source of the poem: the ballad "The Rising of the North" in Percy's *Reliques* for the public parts, and Thomas Whitaker's *History of the Deanery of Craven* for the scenery and the story of the Doe.

4. Herbert Lindenberger, *On Wordsworth's Prelude* (Princeton: Princeton University Press, 1963), pp. 24–29.

5. The major criticism focuses on grace and salvation through faith and imagination. See Alice Patee Comparetti, *"The*

White Doe of Rylstone" by William Wordsworth (Ithaca: Cornell University Press, 1940); John F. Danby, *The Simple Wordsworth* (London: Routledge & Kegan Paul, 1960), pp. 131–40; Barbara Gates, "Wordsworth's Symbolic Doe: 'The Power of History in the Mind,'" *Criticism* 17 (1975): 234–45; Geoffrey Hartman, *Wordsworth's Poetry, 1787–1814* (New Haven: Yale University Press, 1964), pp. 324–30; John Jones, *The Egotistical Sublime* (London: Chatto & Windus, 1954), pp. 144–57; and Martin Price, "Imagination in *The White Doe of Rylstone,*" *Philological Quarterly* 33 (1954): 89–99.

6. Wordsworth thought very well of his poem; Edith Batho, *The Later Wordsworth* (Cambridge: Cambridge University Press, 1933), p. 83, quotes from Tom Moore's diary, which mentions Wordsworth's high estimate.

7. Donald Davie, *Purity of Diction in English Verse* (London: Routledge & Kegan Paul, 1967), pp. 111–21, argues that this is the only one of Wordsworth's major poems in which diction really matters.

8. Allen Tate, *The Man of Letters in the Modern World* (New York: Meriden, 1955), p. 197.

9. James A. Heffernan, *Wordsworth's Theory of Poetry: The Transforming Imagination* (Ithaca: Cornell University Press, 1969), p. 200, says that Emily's acceptance of the "final truth" is like Aeneas's burial of Caieta (*Aeneid* 7: 1–7) in that both actions sever the last ties with the past. For another discussion of Virgilian influence on Wordsworth, see my essay "Wordsworth's *Aeneid,*" *Comparative Literature* 26 (1974): 97–109.

10. "We have been Trojans; Troy has been, and the great glory of the Trojans; harsh Jupiter has taken all away to Argos"; "the only salvation for the vanquished is to have no hope." We may regard these lines as the obverse of Wordsworth's positive formulations of hope and aspiration, such as the famous lines after the crossing of the Alps:

> Our destiny, our nature, and our home,
> Is with infinitude—and only there;
> With hope it is, hope that can never die,
> Effort, and expectation, and desire,
> And something evermore about to be.
> (*The Prelude* VI, 538–42)

11. Originally, the sonnet "Weak is the Will of Man" was used as an epigraph to praise imagination's power to elevate suffering. The new lines from *The Borderers* superseded the sonnet, and Wordsworth removed it.

12. Wordsworth quotes Aristotle's synopsis of the virtues

and vices in a letter to Sir George Beaumont, March 12, 1805, after John Wordsworth's death: "It is the property of fortitude not to be easily terrified by the dread of things pertaining to death: to possess good confidence in things terrible, and presence of mind in dangers; rather to prefer to be put to death worthily, than to be preserved basely; and to be the cause of victory. Moreover, it is the property of fortitude to labour and endure, and to make valorous exertion an object of choice; Further, presence of mind, a well disposed soul, confidence, and boldness are the attendants on fortitude: and, besides these, industry and patience" (*EY*, pp. 557–58).

13. *PW* 2: 519. Wordsworth's three endings for the poem, in 1815, 1827, and 1845, show his difficulty in judging, or even labeling, mortal weakness.

14. Gates, "Wordsworth's Symbolic Doe," p. 243. There is ample proof of Wordsworth's broad-mindedness toward Catholicism; see, especially, the *Ecclesiastical Sonnets* II, 2 and 9, for the Church's service to art and order during the Middle Ages.

15. Thomas Dunham Whitaker, *The History and Antiquities of the Deanery of Craven*, ed. Alfred W. Morant (London: Cassell Petter & Galpin, 3d ed., 1878), p. 525.

16. Wordsworth's care reminds me of a remark by Hugo von Hofmannsthal to Richard Strauss: "I build on contrasts to discover, above those contrasts, the harmony of the whole"; *A Working Friendship: The Correspondence Between Richard Strauss and Hugo von Hofmannsthal*, trans. Hanns Hammelmann and Ewald Osers (New York: William Collins Sons, 1961), p. 90; cf. Wordsworth's remark in the Preface to *Lyrical Ballads* about "the pleasure which the mind derives from the perception of similitude in dissimilitude" (*PrW* 1:149).

17. M. H. Abrams, "Structure and Style in the Greater Romantic Lyric," in Frederick W. Hilles and Harold Bloom, eds., *From Sensibility to Romanticism* (New York: Oxford University Press, 1965), pp. 527–60.

18. Heffernan, *Wordsworth's Theory of Poetry*, pp. 210–25, treats the whole poem as an explanation of the opening scene through "a gradual ascent to its mystery in which the spirituality of the doe is imaginatively *earned.*"

19. On the larger problem of the ego's need for self-origination, see Thomas Weiskel, *The Romantic Sublime: Studies in the Structure and Psychology of Transcendence* (Baltimore: Johns Hopkins University Press, 1976), pp. 167–204 ("Wordsworth and the Defile of the Word"). Cf. Wordsworth's remark that it is a "Hard task to analyse a soul, in which / . . . each most obvious and particular thought / . . . Hath no beginning" (*The Prelude* II, 232–37).

20. On the "internalization of quest romance," see Harold Bloom, *The Ringers in the Tower* (Chicago: University of Chicago Press, 1971), pp. 13–35. For a discussion of the problem of genre and Wordsworth's ambivalence toward narrative, see Andrew Griffin, "Wordsworth and the Problem of Imaginative Story: The Case of 'Simon Lee,'" *PMLA* 92 (1977): 392–409.

21. Cf. Preface to *Lyrical Ballads* (*PrW* 1: 129): what distinguishes these poems, claims the author, is "that the feeling therein developed gives importance to the action and situation, and not the action and the situation to the feeling."

22. On repetition and tautology as significant forms of poetic expression, see Frances Ferguson, *Wordsworth: Language as Counter-Spirit* (New Haven: Yale University Press, 1977), pp. 1–34.

23. Wordsworth makes a similar distinction between conventional melancholy and sublime, tragic disappointment in *The Prelude* VI, 375–79:

> 'Twas sweet at such a time, with such delights
> On every side, in prime of youthful strength,
> To feed a Poet's tender melancholy
> And fond conceit of sadness, to the noise
> And gentle undulation which [the trees] made.

Lines 477–87 describe other forms of "dejection taken up for pleasure's sake" right before "how different a sadness" issues from the experience of the Simplon Pass.

CHAPTER 7

1. Geoffrey Hartman, *Wordsworth's Poetry, 1787–1814* (New Haven: Yale University Press, 1964), p. 320. Interest in *The Excursion* has revived somewhat during the past decade. Previously, the only major analysis was Judson Stanley Lyon, *The Excursion: A Study* (New Haven: Yale University Press, 1950). His first chapter, "The Reputation of *The Excursion*" (pp. 1–6), surveys the responses of major nineteenth-century literary figures to the poem, including those mentioned here; additionally, Appendix A (pp. 141–42) lists the contemporary reviews of the poem.

2. *The Letters of John Keats*, Hyder E. Rollins, ed. (Cambridge, Mass.: Harvard University Press, 1958) 1: 238.

3. I use the word "ventriloquism" in the way proposed by Edward Bostetter, *The Romantic Ventriloquists: Wordsworth, Coleridge, Keats, Shelley, Byron* (Seattle: University of Washington Press, 1963), p. 4: "the poet became in reality the divine ventriloquist projecting his own voice as the voice of ultimate truth." This reverses, of course, the usual arrangement in which the poet is,

like the Aeolian harp melodized by the wind, played upon by the spirit of God or of the One. The major difference is that a genuine human modesty prevents Wordsworth from sounding unguardedly oracular for very long. The origin of the term is in Coleridge: "I regard truth as a divine ventriloquist" (*Biographia Literaria*, ed. J. Shawcross [London: Oxford University Press, 1907] 1: 105). Interestingly, Coleridge attacked *The Excursion* for the very thing others find praiseworthy: "Can dialogues in verse be defended? I cannot but think that a great philosophical poet ought always to teach the reader himself as from himself. . . . I have no admiration for the practice of ventriloquizing through another man's mouth," *Table Talk*, in Thomas M. Raysor, ed., *Coleridge's Miscellaneous Criticism* (Cambridge, Mass.: Harvard University Press, 1936), p. 411. Recent criticism has picked up the motif of Wordsworth's self-division. Thus, Kenneth R. Johnston, "Wordsworth's Reckless Recluse: The Solitary," *The Wordsworth Circle* 9 (1978): 132, says "in 1809, he was an author in search of a character other than himself."

4. Although the dialectic structure and the unresolved argument make the poem an incomplete georgic, Annabel Patterson is correct in saying that *The Excursion* "is *about* teaching, metadidactic"; "Wordsworth's Georgic: Genre and Structure in *The Excursion*," *The Wordsworth Circle* 9 (1978): 145–54. Cf. Wordsworth's remark to Sir George Beaumont (*MY* 1: 195): "I have not written down to the level of superficial observers and unthinking minds. ——————Every great Poet is a Teacher: I wish either to be considered as a Teacher, or as nothing."

5. Hartman, *Wordsworth's Poetry*, p. 314: "though repetitious and verbose, the Wanderer's harangue is also affecting because of that."

6. Wordsworth's note to "The Thorn" (*PW* 2: 513) distinguishes between repetition and tautology, but both are important to his brand of teaching. In a letter to Beaumont, he calls redundancy his one incurable fault, which "lies too deep, and is in the first conception" (*EY*, pp. 586–87).

7. Lyon, *The Excursion*, p. 120, puts primary emphasis on characterization: "*The Excursion* is a dramatic presentation of philosophical ideas. The plot and characters are of first importance; the ideas which are developed apply primarily to the particular problems raised in the dramatic development and should not be considered without reference to the plot."

8. Lionel Trilling, "Wordsworth and the Rabbis," in *The Opposing Self* (New York: Viking Press, 1955), pp. 118–50.

9. Kenneth Burke, *A Grammar of Motives* (New York: Prentice-

Hall, 1945), pp. 38–41 ("Dialectic of Tragedy"), on passion, perception, and purpose.

10.   See Wordsworth's distinction between fancy and imagination (*PrW* 3: 30–31): "Imagination . . . has no reference to images that are merely a faithful copy, existing in the mind, of absent external objects; but is a word of higher import, denoting operations of the mind upon those objects." There is a path of increasing activity along which the mental faculties extend themselves; this is the major subject of the 1815 preface (*PrW* 3: 26–39).

11.   Lyon, *The Excursion*, pp. 133–34, lists all the longer similes in the poem. The major ones are few: III, 967–91; IV, 1062–70, 1132–47; V, 531–37; IX, 56–91. There are twenty-five of three lines or longer.

12.   Again, what Alan Wilde calls an "aesthetic view of life" permits a more specific, and more modern, application of Coleridge's "spectatorial" charge; *Art and Order: A Study of E. M. Forster* (New York: New York University Press, 1964).

13.   I take this as a constructive interpretation of Hazlitt's evidence of Wordsworth's intense egocentricity: "Even the dialogues introduced in the present volume are soliloquies of the same character, taking different views of the subject. The recluse, the pastor, and the pedlar are three persons in one poet"; *The Complete Works of William Hazlitt*, P. P. Howe, ed. (London: J. P. Dent & Sons, 1930) 4: 113.

14.   To Beaumont in 1804, Wordsworth wrote that he thought "absolute solitude and seclusion from the world . . . a great evil" (*EY*, p. 499). So much for the opinions of a man living in utter retirement.

15.   Wordsworth's antisexualism has been noted for a long time, beginning perhaps with Shelley's parody in "Peter Bell the Third." Its least hostile recent explicators have been Trilling and F. R. Leavis, *Revaluation* (London: Chatto & Windus, 1936), pp. 164–70. The connections with Lucretius, another strongly antisexual poet, remain insufficiently explored.

16.   Frances Ferguson, *Wordsworth: Language as Counter-Spirit* (New Haven: Yale University Press, 1977), p. 198, recognizes the fluidity of the poem: "The poem thus creates characters who could sometimes be speaking another character's lines; individual characters seem to have no fixed boundaries, so that the speakers tend to merge into one another." This is the antithesis of Lyon's argument. Ferguson's chapter, "Wordsworth's *Excursion*," pp. 195–241, deserves special attention.

17.   Coleridge, *Biographia Literaria* 2: 109; cf. the use of "eddying" in "Dejection: An Ode."

18. Lyon, *The Excursion*, p. 68, puts the matter of anonymity timidly: "Possibly it is significant of Wordsworth's purpose in the character-portrayal of *The Excursion* that none of the characters has a name." Mary Moorman, *William Wordsworth: The Later Years* (Oxford: Clarendon Press, 1965), p. 576, describes guests who descended upon the famous poet at Rydal Mount in his old age (500 of them annually, according to Harriet Martineau). Always polite to people he did not know, "he never inquired names."

19. This is the side argued most persuasively by David Ferry, *The Limits of Mortality* (Middletown, Conn.: Wesleyan University Press, 1959), and John Jones, *The Egotistical Sublime* (London: Chatto & Windus, 1954).

20. Kenneth Burke, *The Philosophy of Literary Form* (Baton Rouge: Louisiana State University Press, 1941), makes the strongest equation, in literary criticism, between verbal acts and symbolic action.

Index

Abrams, M. H., 231*n*7, 236*n*2; on the "prepared mind," 26; on Romantic nature lyrics, 4, 183, 231*n*7, 242*n*17

Action: in childhood, 59–60, 61–62, 69–70, 71, 89, 102, 128; by imagination, 71; mediated, 200, 218; talk as, 219; vs. passivity in character development, 192. *See also* Heroic action

Action vs. contemplation: ambivalent attitudes toward, 16–18, 20–21, 169–71; in autobiographical epic heroism, 114, 118, 119–20, 124–25, 136, 141, 157, 158; in education, 42; in heroism, 218–19; in reading, 30, 31–33, 40. *See also* Heroism in Wordsworth's poetry

Adams, Henry, 114

Adams, Robert M., 119

"Address to My Infant Daughter, Dora," 52–56, 58, 61, 233*n*; influence of Virgil on, 52–53, 55

Aeschylus, 118

"After-Thought," 81

"Alice Fell," 68

Allison, Joseph, 31

Alpers, Paul, 52, 230*n*4

"Anecdote for Fathers," 56, 68

"Animal Tranquility and Decay," 94–95, 234*n*8

Antisexualism, 245*n*15

Ariès, Philippe, 229*n*1

Ariosto, 141

Aristotle, 241*n*12

Arnold, Matthew, 33, 49; on *The Excursion*, 190

Art, 46–49; educative and elegiac, 49; redemption through, 47–48

Auden, W. H., 31

Audience of poetry, 37–38; in *The Excursion*, 220–21; ideal, 153–54; and shift from commonality to privacy, 39–40; in *The White Doe of Rylstone*, 187–88

Autobiographical heroism, 112–65, 215; and abstraction of human nature, 124–27; genesis of, 127–30; "higher minds" in, 157–58; and participation in public life, 116, 130, 138–47 passim

Autobiography, 17, 23, 33; and epic heroism in *The Prelude*, 112–65; and the Wanderer in *The Excursion*, 41. *See also* Egocentrism

Averill, James, 229*n*31; on response to suffering, 149, 239*n*29

Babenroth, A. Charles, 229*n*1

Bacon, Francis, 169

Ballads, Wordsworth's attitudes toward, 188

Batho, Edith, 241*n*6

Beaumont, George, 113, 242*n*12

Beaupuy, Michel, 3, 113; role of, in *The Prelude*, 114, 121, 139–41, 144, 148

Beckett, Samuel, 83

Bentley, Eric, on heroism, 8–9, 10

Bible, 42; and reading of nature, 24–25

Bishop, Elizabeth, 15

Blake, William, 41, 50, 72, 150; *The Book of Thel*, 72; four zoas of, 206

"Blind Highland Boy, The," 73–76

Bloom, Harold, 13, 243*n*20; on the Intimations Ode, 231*n*6; on "The Old Cumberland Beggar," 93; on reading, 23, 26–27, 38

Bonaparte, Napoleon, 76

Books: compared with nature, 23, 37, 41–42; perishable aspect of, 32

Borderers, The, 1; excerpts in *The White Doe of Rylstone*, 166, 172; Oswald in, 166, 174

Bostetter, Edward, 235*n*24, 243*n*3

Bowra, C. M., 11

Boy of Winander, 33, 46, 66; compared to the Solitary in *The Excursion*, 198; death of, 32; education of, 31–32; immortality of, 37

"Boy of Winander," compared with "Characteristics of a Child Three Years Old," 62–63

Brisman, Leslie, 237*n*10, 238*n*15

Brooks, Cleanth, 91, 234*n*9; on "The Old Cumberland Beggar," 92, 93

"Brothers, The," 4, 25, 228*n*23

Burke, Kenneth, 196, 244*n*9, 246*n*20

Byron, George Gordon, Lord, 9, 223*n*4; on *The Excursion*, 190; on heroism, 127; on parody, 84

Calvert, Raisley, 114, 161

Cambridge, Wordsworth at, 121–22, 130

Carlyle, Thomas, 8, 9; on poetry and reading, 23–24

Carroll, Lewis, *Through the Looking Glass*, 84–85, 233*n*2

Catharsis of tragedy, 47, 229*n*31

Character; defined by Wordsworth, 3, 118–19; formation of, 148, 151, 154, 162–63, 192

"Characteristics of a Child Three Years Old," 61–63, 66

"Character of the Happy Warrior," 2–6; compared with "Resolution and Independence," 5–6, 174; compared with *The White Doe of Rylstone*, 5, 173–74, 179; concept of happiness in, 2–4; heroism in, 4–6

Characters in Wordsworth's poetry: completed by death, 36; personal identities of, 73; in *The Prelude*, 114, 118, 126; unnamed, 114

Character types, 1, 2; connection to literary style, 2–3; in *The Excursion*, 12, 192, 195–96, 206–7, 214, 215–16; in *Lyrical Ballads*, 83; vs. symbolic abstractions of human nature, 126

Chaucer, 195; and figure of Troilus, 102; "Prioress' Tale," 71–72

Childhood in Wordsworth's poetry, 50–82; as beginning of potential criminality, 59–60, 128, 231*n*9; compared with old age, 85, 88, 89; and growth into maturity, 57–58, 71; nostalgia epitomized by, 50, 59, 60, 63, 65, 68, 70–71, 81; prophecy epitomized by, 50, 51, 56, 72; relative to politics, 77, 78, 81; role in the human life cycle, 56, 60, 73, 231*n*6; saintliness of, 71–76; symbolized in "River Duddon" sonnets, 70–82

Children in Wordsworth's poetry, 2, 50–82; and adult consciousness, 54–56, 70–71; as gifts, 56; as heroic figures, 51–52, 53, 81–82; as objects of lyric description, 60–67; teaching by, 67–68

Christianity, 52, 216; vs. Stoic ethics, 177, 184

Coleridge, Hartley, 56–58

Coleridge, Samuel Taylor, 90, 106, 112; on action and self-spirit, 119, 237*n*9; on childhood, 230*n*3; "Christabel," 168, 185; compared with Wordsworth, 13; "Dejection: An Ode," 152,

21, 114, 118, 119–20, 124–25, 136, 141, 157, 158, 218–19

Heroism: Bentley on, 8–9; Emerson on, 7–8, 10; and individual identity, 11; natural, 14–15, 201; "separatist" view of, 10, 223n4; Stevens on, 6, 9–10, 192–93; traditional definitions of, 11–12

Heroism in Wordsworth's poetry: ambivalence of, 14–16; and anonymous heroes, 12; and "Central Man," 12–13; and children as heroic figures, 51–52, 53, 81–82; classical basis of, 52 (*see also* Epic heroism); defined, 12, 192–93, 218; distinguished from traditional epics, 113–14, 118, 121, 134; of first-person self, 16, 17–18; ideal models of, 121; martyrdom in, 171, 175, 176; in old age, 84, 85, 86, 96–98; and relationship with the ordinary, 4–6, 10, 53, 66, 125–26, 155–56; and role in reading, 23; and Wordsworth as an epic hero, 112–65

"Home at Grasmere," 104, 146; on heroism, 17–18; on reading, 17

Homer, 24; and epic heroism in *The Prelude*, 132, 133, 149, 151–52, 165; and figure of Achilles, 118, 131, 151, 164; and figure of Odysseus, 11, 153, 218; *Iliad*, 151–52; *Odyssey*, 11

Horace, 79

Human nature, Wordsworth's view of, 9, 34, 93, 192

Hutchinson, Mary, 114, 148, 150, 154

Hutchinson, Sarah, 235n16

Hyman, Stanley Edgar, on the leech-gatherer, 234n14

"Idiot Boy, The," 4, 187, 229n1
"Idle Shepherd-Boys, The," 68
"I Know an Aged Man," 91–92
Imagination, 28–29, 36, 122, 123; commonplace ennobled by, 86; heroic possibilities of, 192, 196, 197; and metamorphosis, 184; and self-knowledge, 159–60; union with tenderness, 52, 230n4; in *The White Doe of Rylstone*, 185; and Wordsworthian heroism, 158

Immortality, 45–46, 64; in epitaphs, 37; and power of speech, 17–18; and redemption through art, 47–48; of Wordsworth, 40

"Infant M. M., The," 73

Intimations Ode. *See* "Ode: Intimations of Immortality"

Isherwood, Christopher, 114

"Italian Itinerant, and the Swiss Goatherd, The," 77

"It is a Beauteous Evening," 61; image of Caroline in, 58, 72

"I Wandered Lonely as a Cloud," 38, 157

James, Henry, on character, 118

Jeffrey, Francis, on *The Excursion*, 190

Johnston, Kenneth R., 240n35, 244n3

Jonson, Ben, 50

Keats, John, 25, 103, 111, 112; on didactic poetry, 193; on *The Excursion*, 190; "The Fall of Hyperion: A Dream," 227n11; "Lamia," 168, 188; on self-discovery through poetry, 191; "To Autumn," 110

Kierkegaard, Søren, 129

Knight, G. Wilson, 101

Knowledge, growth of, 196–97, 206. *See also* Self-knowledge

Kostelanetz, Anne, 101, 235n18, 235n20

Kroeber, Karl, 223n4, 224n13, 236n1; on the commonplace in poetry, 233n3

La Bruyère, Jean de, 3

Lamb, Charles, 39, 52, 106; and action in dramatic poetry, 168; on

141. *See also* Epic heroism in *The Prelude*; "Ode: Intimations of Immortality"; Simplon Pass
"Primrose of the Rock, The," 107–8
Public life, 116, 130; nobility and courage in, 169, 174–75; participation vs. observational passivity in, 138–47

Quintilian, 167

Ramsey, Jonathan, 229n1
Rank, Otto, 223n6
Readers, 2; exemplary, 35–37, 41–42; as explorers, 40; and interaction and collaboration with writers, 40–41
Reading, 16–17, 23–49; active vs. passive aspects of, 30, 31–32, 33, 40; dangers of, 32–33; education of poets for, 45–49; as heroic act, 23, 27, 33, 38–39, 40; and misinterpretation of nature, 38–39; of nature, 24–25, 26, 28, 31, 33, 35–36, 37; perception and learning linked with, 26–31; self-teaching of, 41, 47; of tragedy, 177
Recluse, The, 155, 191, 216
Redemption through art, 47–48. *See also* Salvation
Reed, Walter L., on heroism, 10
Repetition: in *The Excursion*, 192, 193–94, 202–3, 208, 214; in *The White Doe of Rylstone*, 185–86
"Resolution and Independence," 3–4, 46, 56, 57, 84; compared with "Character of the Happy Warrior," 5–6; manic-depressive state of poem in, 99–100; old age in, 87, 95–98, 105; reading in, 24. *See also* Leech-gatherer
Rieff, Philip, 230n3, 237n9
Riffaterre, Michael, on "Yew-Trees," 19, 225n21
"River Duddon" sonnets, 79–82

Robespierre, François, 143; death of, 144–45
Robinson, Crabb, 106, 154
Romantic nature lyrics, 4, 231n7; *The White Doe of Rylstone* as, 182–83
"Ruined Cottage, The" (also *The Excursion*, Book I), 41, 43, 98, 168, 218; compared to *The White Doe of Rylstone*, 168; structure of, 184

Salvation: in *The Excursion*, 198; in poems on childhood, 73, 74, 75–76; in *The Prelude*, 149–50, 164; in story of the leech-gatherer, 97–98, 235n15; and suffering, 178, 180–81
Scott, Walter, 106, 168
Self-knowledge, 114; action and observation in, 119–20, 124–25; and character development, 118–19; difficulty of, 206; discovered in reading poetry, 191; and imagination, 159–60
Seneca, 181
Sensory deprivation: in old age, 107–8; and salvation, 74–76, 102–3
Shakespeare, William, 83, 212; and figure of Macbeth, 108, 142; and figure of Othello, 18
Shaw, G. B., 8
Sheats, Paul, 235n15
Shelley, Percy Bysshe: "Defense of Poetry," 29, 150; on didactic poetry, 193; "The Triumph of Life," 93
Simplon Pass, in *The Prelude*, 30, 74, 115, 123, 136; ambivalence of heroism in, 15–16; effects of, 137, 243n23; Wordsworth's disappointment in, 116–17, 131
Snell, Bruno, 238n18
Soldier, in *The Prelude*, 83, 95, 121, 131; compared with the leech-gatherer, 96–97, 134; as divine messenger, 134–35; interaction with poet, 135–37

Yeats, William Butler, 10; "Among
School Children," 73; golden
Byzantine bird in poems of, 91;
on old age, 83; on wisdom, 99
"Yew-Trees," 19–22; humanity and

heroism in, 20–22; personification in, 20, 21
Youth: compared with old age, 87–
88, 89, 102; vs. compensations
of old age, 108–9

Compositor:	Wilsted & Taylor
Text:	10/12 Palatino
Display:	Palatino
Printer:	Braun-Brumfield, Inc.
Binder:	Braun-Brumfield, Inc.